New Ideas in Needlepoint Lace

VALERIE GRIMWOOD

New Ideas in Needlepoint Lace

B.T. Batsford Ltd · London

First published 1994

© Valerie Grimwood 1994

Typeset by J&L Composition Ltd, Filey, North Yorkshire
and printed in Great Britain by
The Bath Press, Bath

Published by
B.T. Batsford Ltd
4 Fitzhardinge Street
London W1H 0AH

A catalogue record for this book is available from
the British Library

ISBN 0 7134 7193 X

Contents

Acknowledgements

I would particularly like to thank all my own previous lace tutors and also the following for all their stimulating knowledge and without whom this book could not have been written.

My editor, Tim Auger, who was of such help in guiding me with my previous book as well. Caroline Bingham, Lesley Thomas, Tracey Beresford and Susan Malvern have all assisted at the editorial stage. Winifred Clayton for her excellent tuition of cords and tassels; Ann Mockford who has such lovely ideas with beads; Anita Faithfull who taught me and encouraged and stimulated my pleasure in painting on silk; Heide Jenkins whose beautiful silk fabric insects, featuring wings of wire with needlepoint stitches, I so admire. Also my grateful thanks to Geoffrey Wheeler for the photography in the book; to Tessa Halmann and Vikki Jackman for the cover photography; to Carol Mathews for all her excellent help in typing the manuscript; and to Cathy Barley, who again looked through some of the manuscript for me and to Ros Hills and Pat Gibson for providing the inspiration for the Point de Gaze style Bruxelles couronne ground for the box lid (see *Needlework Stitches: Classic and Contemporary*).

On behalf of all lacemakers, I would also like to express my appreciation of all needlepoint lace teachers who are passing on this beautiful craft so that others may enjoy it.

Introduction

Once you have learnt the basic techniques of needlepoint lace, there is endless scope for you to develop and extend your lacemaking, either in traditional classic styles or in more unusual ways for that 'something a little bit different'.

This book is intended both for those who have just learnt the basics and would like to further their knowledge, and also to help more experienced lacemakers develop their own ideas and designs by extending the methods and techniques possible with this fascinating lace.

Inspiration for work may come from many sources and crafts, you just need to keep an open mind and remember that everything is grist to the mill! You might see other handwork, or look at a scene around you, that does not immediately seem to have any relevance to your lacemaking, but you will absorb something essential from it which may well influence or help to inspire a later design.

New and traditional techniques in this book are used in a variety of projects, each having detailed instructions and other design suggestions. Needlepoint lace is a beautiful and adaptable lace. I do hope this book will provide you with the inspiration to develop your own ideas.

Valerie Grimwood

For my mother, Kingsley and Nicola

PART I

Techniques old and new

Adaptations and innovations in any craft seem to be easier if you have an understanding of the basic techniques already used in that craft. I think that it gives you a base from which to launch out and does not lead to quite so much frustration when you come to execute your ideas. New lacemakers may therefore find helpful the detailed basic instruction course in my previous book *Starting Needlepoint Lace — A Course for Beginners* (Batsford).

Basic stages of needlepoint lace

1 Tacking the covered design onto the calico backing.

Needlepoint lace can be divided into five stages, each of which may vary slightly from worker to worker and country to country.

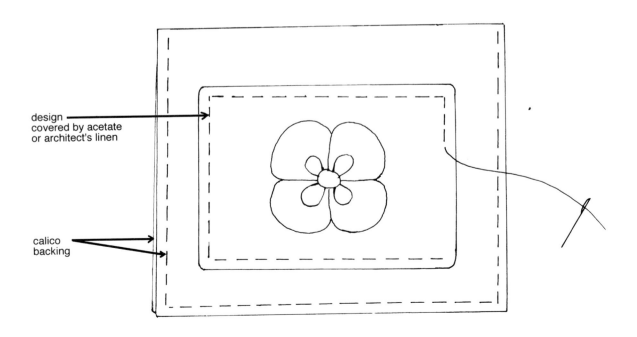

design covered by acetate or architect's linen

calico backing

Stage 1

Preparation of the double layer of backing foundation material, e.g. calico, and the positioning of the design (under adhesive acetate or architect's linen) onto this backing [1].

Stage 2

Couching down the threads along the outlines of the design — often called the 'cordonnet' or 'trace' [2].

I have found that the most adaptable method is to couch down the threads as I go, rather than to make little 'bridges' of couching stitches and then run the outline threads through them. This is mainly because when using wire as the cordonnet in more modern work, you could not easily use the latter technique.

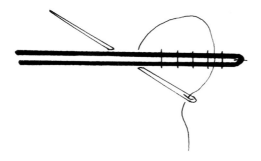

2 Commencing the couching down of the cordonnet. (In the actual lace the cordonnet threads lie closely side by side).

Stage 3

Working the lace filling stitches within the outlines, together with any bars or mesh (reseau) in the piece of lace. In modern lace such things as beads can be incorporated as well. Some further details about stitches are given in the projects in Part II.

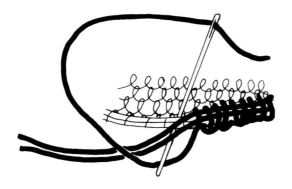

3 The cordonnette — the needle passes under the cordonnet when making each cordonnette buttonhole stitch.

Stage 4

Working buttonhole stitches over the outline cordonnet — this is often called the cordonnette.

Picots and other decorative finishes for the edges can be worked at the same time. Extra threads may also be used to pad out or thicken the outlines [3]. In modern work, rustless wire can be incorporated in the cordonnette to stiffen the edges.

The cordonnette buttonholing can be omitted if a more delicate or natural look is desired.

Stage 5

Removing the finished piece of lace from the backing foundation by cutting the tiny couching stitches (made from the couching down of the cordonnet) **between** the two layers of calico.

Any adaptations and innovations that a laceworker makes to the basic stages may still result in 'classical' needlepoint lace, or they can be extended in many ways to become an exciting piece of modern lace. Many needlepoint lacemakers of today are thus extending and developing this beautiful lace. The projects in the book have been designed to show how the basic stages that we all know can be adapted in a variety of ways.

Basic requirements

1 Ball-pointed sewing needles for the lace filling stitches and cordonnette.
2 Threads. A wide range of threads can be used, dependent upon the design and lace to be worked. Remember that they must be washable if your lace will need to be cleaned.
3 Plain material, such as calico, for the foundation backing.
4 Adhesive acetate or plastic, preferably matt, to cover your design. It is best if it colour-contrasts with the lace so that the stitches show up clearly, as it will be easier on your eyes. Blue or green matt adhesive acetate is the most restful. Architect's linen can also be used.
5 Needlepoint lace pillow. This is optional. Some lacemakers hold their work in their hand, but I find that it helps to give an even tension if both hands are free.
6 Ordinary sharp sewing needles and sewing cottons for the tacking and couching, together with pins, and a thimble if desired.
7 A fine crochet hook is of help when linking the cordonnet threads into each other.

8 Tweezers to pull out couching threads when removing the completed lace from the backing and design.

The same basic equipment is used for most needlepoint lace, together with additional items as needed, such as beads, wire and stiffening agents. Each project will have its own list of special requirements.

Additional items

1 Rustless wire, for example medium and fine fuse wire, brass spangling wire and silver- or gold-plated jewellery wire.
2 Beads, especially small and medium-sized gold-, silver- or bronze-coloured ones.
3 Needle-threader. This may be helpful with some of the metallic-effect threads.
4 Clear adhesive, such as UHU, to seal the ends of some metallic-effect threads.

Adaptations of traditional techniques

The ability to combine traditional forms of lacemaking and new techniques is as important as maintaining those traditional techniques. It is the way that the art of lacemaking develops and it allows us to leave a unique legacy to future generations. The lace you produce, after all, is very much an extension of your personality; it always has something of 'you' in it.

The following adaptations of traditional methods and new techniques show some of the ways in which you can begin to develop your lacemaking. You will find that the projects later in the book use some of these techniques, and I do hope that they will be of help in stimulating and extending your own ideas.

Technique 1
Using wire as the cordonnet outline

This is extremely useful for such things as needlepoint lace jewellery (projects 1 and 8) and the dragonfly wings (project 10).

Method
1 Place your design under the adhesive acetate film and tack it onto the double layer of calico foundation backing in the usual manner.
2 Select your chosen rustless wire — gold-coloured or brass spangling wire looks best with gold or bronze metallic-effect thread, and silver-plated jewellery wire or thin fuse wire with silver-coloured thread. Make sure that there are no kinks in the wire; it must go evenly around the outlines.
3 Use cream thread with 'gold' wire and white thread with 'silver' wire when you tack down the wire cordonnet. First decide upon a suitable starting point for your cordonnet couching or refer to the particular project instructions that you are following. Then bend the starting end of the wire into a tiny hook to stop it pulling through your stitches as you begin to couch [1a]. This hook is cut off when you near the end of the cordonnet.

Useful hints

1 Use smooth, straight rustless wire, without any kinks, so as to go evenly around the design outline.
2 Make a small starting 'hook' to prevent the wire pulling out of the couching. This hook is cut off when you near the end of the cordonnet.
3 Your couching stitches should be about 3mm ($\frac{1}{8}$in) apart and fairly firm, but not so tight that you cannot get your needle under the wire when you work the lace filling stitches.
4 Couch the wire cordonnet towards your left if you are right-handed so that you can hold the wire down with your left-hand thumb as you work. If you are left-handed then work towards the right when couching the wire.
5 Have at **least** a 1cm ($\frac{3}{8}$in) overlap of the starting and finishing ends of the cordonnet so that the outline is secure.

1a *Starting the cordonnet of wire.*

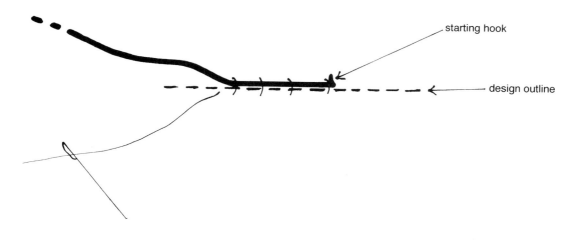

starting hook

design outline

4 Carefully couch down the wire in a **single strand**, making your stitches firm but not too tight and about 3mm ($\frac{1}{8}$in) apart. Complete your couching around the outlines with a continuous strand of wire. It will feel very different to couching down threads — hold the wire down firmly and gently ease it to follow the outline's shape.
5 When you near completion of the couching — about 2cm ($\frac{3}{4}$in) away from your starting point — cut off the starting 'hook', then continue couching down the wire along the remaining cordonnet outline. To

1b *Couching the overlapping ends of the wire cordonnet.*

ensure a secure join, overlap the starting end and the finishing end of the wire by **at least** 1cm ($\frac{3}{8}$in) and couch them down together [1b].

6 Cut off the end of the wire and finish as usual by whipping the two ends together quite closely **on the surface of the design**. Take the thread to the back of the foundation backing material and end it off.

7 Complete the other lace stages (i.e. filling stitches, etc.) in the usual manner. You may decide to omit the cordonnette buttonholing stage to give a delicate effect to your work. In this case, you will have to be very neat in starting and ending the rows of the lace filling stitches.

Technique 2
Working lace directly onto material

Instead of mounting the finished needlepoint lace onto a piece of material, the lace can sometimes be worked in situ directly onto the material (see projects 4, 5 and 9) — although possibly to purists this is verging on embroidery.

Useful hints

1 Keep the material upon which you are working the lace **taut**. In this way the work should not pucker or distort.

2 Have generous seam allowances at the start of the work — they can be trimmed off later where necessary.

3 Remember to be neat when couching down the cordonnet outline, especially where there will not be a buttonholed cordonnette. These couching stitches are permanent and are **not** removed.

4 If the buttonholed cordonnette is omitted then use the **same** thread for the cordonnet outline as the lace filling stitches in that area. Try also to match the couching thread so that it will be as unnoticeable as possible.

5 As you are working directly onto the material you can start and end off threads neatly on the back.

Method

1 Carefully mark out the outlines of the design by lightly using tailor's chalk or trace tacking on the chosen material.
2 If the material is rather flimsy, or small in size, tack it onto a single layer of calico or similar fabric. This gives it 'body' and makes it easier to handle. Do make sure that this extra fabric will not be too bulky or visible when the article is finished.

 You could also iron on a stiffening material such as vilene. Avoid using this for velvet, however, as its use might crush the pile.
3 Couch down the cordonnet outline in the usual manner, but since you are working it directly onto the material you can start and end off the cordonnet and its couching at the back of the material. This keeps a neat outline.
4 Work the lace filling stitches, again starting and ending off on the back of the material.

 You can support the work on a needlepoint lace pillow in the usual way if you wish, or you could use an embroidery frame if it does not mark the material.
5 Work the buttonholing of any cordonnettes required.
6 Make up the material and lace into your chosen article. (The lace is not removed from the material — it is an integral part of it.)

Technique 3
Working lace directly onto adhesive velvet backing

This is a variation of the previous technique and is useful for items such as bookmarks and box lids (see projects 3 and 7). The adhesive velvet-type backing is the kind which is often used by lacemakers to mount lace in a picture or paperweight.

Useful hints

1 Keep the paper backing on the adhesive velvet whilst you work the lace.
2 Your design can be drawn onto this paper backing instead of the velvet front if desired. (The paper backing is later removed.)
3 Keep the cordonnet outlines to the minimum for ease when removing the paper backing.

Method

1 Select your velvet-type adhesive backing upon which to work — there are various colours available. White, gold or silver lace look striking on plain black velvet.

    You can either cut it to the size required or trim it down later.

2 Mark your design onto the velvet backing. If the design is simple, it is best to draw it onto the paper backing rather than the velvet itself.

3 Couch down the cordonnet outlines; again these can be in the same thread as the lace filling stitches. Use a fairly strong matching cotton or polyester thread for the actual couching stitches — the thread needs to be quite strong, since the stitches should hold firmly and not break when the paper backing is later peeled off.

    Normally, I would couch by making a tiny 'ladder' type stitch from side to side, so making two adjacent holes. I find this helps to hold the cordonnet threads parallel. However, because the paper backing is removed at a later stage, I find the best method in this technique is to try to go up and down into the same hole [3a]. This helps the paper backing to peel away more easily. Again, remember that these couching stitches remain in the work.

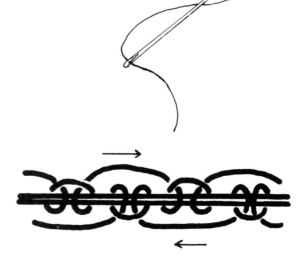

3a *Going up and down into the same hole.*

3b *Ardenza stitch as a decorative cordonnette.*

4 Work the lace filling stitches on the surface of the velvet, together with any cordonnettes desired. A decorative cordonnette stitch such as Ardenza [3b] is very effective with this technique. This stitch is used for the box lid in project 7, around the inside and outside edge.

5 Gently peel away the paper backing from behind the velvet, so that you have the adhesive surface showing, and apply this to the required surface (box lid, picture insert, etc.). Some contact backings are specially made so that they can be moved about slightly before pressing down; but make sure that the article's surface is suitable.

Technique 4
Omitting a cordonnette

This technique was sometimes used in old needlepoint lace such as Venetian Point Plat.

Method
The lace is worked in the normal manner, but do not work a buttonholed cordonnette over the outlines (and remember to keep the ends of rows fanatically neat!). It is especially effective when a 'natural' look is desired, as in flowers where the petals and sepals need to curl.

Technique 5
Working a twisted buttonhole cordonnette

This gives an attractive edge to your lace. It looks quite complicated but is extremely simple to work. Projects 1 and 2 use this decorative finish. It is a technique that modern lacemakers use to great advantage. Further ideas can be seen in *Needlelace Stitches, Classic and Contemporary* by Ros Hills and Pat Gibson (Batsford).

Useful hint
Always count the number of stitches between each 'twist' **as you work them** so as to keep the spirals even. It is the 'knots' (or 'caught' loops) that form the spiral ridge.

Method

1 Couch the cordonnet and work the lace filling stitches as usual.

2 Begin your cordonnette buttonholing in the normal way, working over two or more laid threads depending on the thickness of cordonnette desired. Decide upon the distance you want to have between the 'twists' — this will depend on the number of buttonhole stitches worked between each twist; ten or twelve stitches are generally adequate.

3 Work 12 (or whatever number chosen) cordonnette buttonhole stitches — the 'knots' will be on the outside edge of the work as usual. Take the needle **down** and out behind the cordonnette edge [5a], including the original cordonnet, and gently pull so that the 12

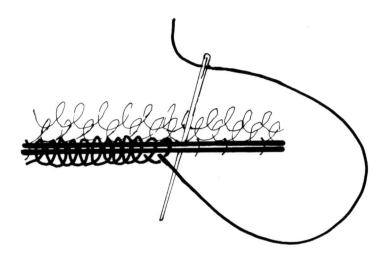

5a *Taking the needle down behind the cordonnet.*

buttonhole stitches you have worked begin to spiral as you pull the thread downwards [5b]. The thread will now be at the bottom edge of the work, and you are ready to go on with the buttonholing of the next spiral.

4 Again work 12 cordonnette buttonhole stitches and form the spiral by taking the needle down and out behind the edge as you did before, so pulling these 12 stitches into another spiral [5c].

As you continue the cordonnette, you will probably find that you work the stitches upwards yourself to help the spiral shape, as well as passing the needle behind the edge to form the twist.

5 Since the beauty of this cordonnette lies in its evenness, count the stitches carefully and when you reach the end of the cordonnette try to make sure that the beginning and end of it match to make a complete spiral.

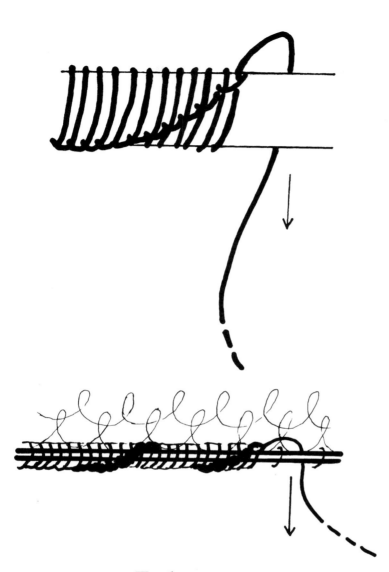

Technique 6
Using a cord as the cordonnette

This is a quick way of producing the finished effect of a cordonnette. You can either make your own cord (see *Other useful techniques*) or use a suitable bought cord.

It looks very effective if you make your own cord using the same thread in which you worked the lace itself. The necklace in project 8 has a handmade gold and silver cord edge and the bag in project 9 uses a handmade cord.

Useful hints

1 Stitch the cord down with identical or closely matching thread so that the stitches do not show (unless of course you wish to have a contrast, for example, bronze stitches over a gold-coloured cord).
2 Make the join at the beginning and end as inconspicuous as possible.

Method

1 Couch the cordonnet and work the lace filling stitches as usual.
2 Instead of working buttonhole stitches over laid threads for the cordonnette, choose, or preferably make, a suitable cord to be couched down.
3 Start at a suitable (or inconspicuous) place such as a corner when stitching down the cord.

    If the cord is a handmade one, then start with the nicely 'looped' end of it instead of the knotted finishing end, and couch it down using the same thread from which the cord was made.

    Make the couching stitches lie in the grooves of the cord [6]; in this way they can be almost invisible. The cord should lie exactly on top of the cordonnet so as to give the finished appearance of a cordonnette.

6 *Couching stitches laying in the grooves of the cord.*

Technique 7
Attaching net, or other transparent material, at the same time as the cordonnette

This is a simple way to mount lace onto net, as, for example, for a needlepoint lace fan where you do not wish to make the net, or for a lace insert on fine transparent material which does not fray easily. The method has been used very effectively by modern lacemakers for such things as handkerchiefs and garments where they do not just want to appliqué on their lace.

Note: This method is only suitable for net or material which would not fray easily or pull away from the cordonnette. If in doubt then mount the **completed** lace onto the net or material in the usual manner, or work a handmade net to your lace as you are making it.

Method

1 Couch the cordonnet and work the lace filling stitches as usual, but do not work the cordonnette. Do **not** remove the lace from the acetate and foundation backing yet.
2 Lay the net or transparent material over the lace and tack it down right through the calico backing so that it lays flat. A good way to work is to tack from the centre **outwards**, and then around the edges [7a].
3 Working over the net, buttonhole the cordonnette around the outlines as usual so that the net is incorporated into the stitches. This has the dual purpose of stitching the cordonnette and attaching the net or material.
4 **Very carefully** cut away the net from over the lace areas where you do not wish it to be, so that the net remains only between the lace motifs

7a *Tacking on the net.*

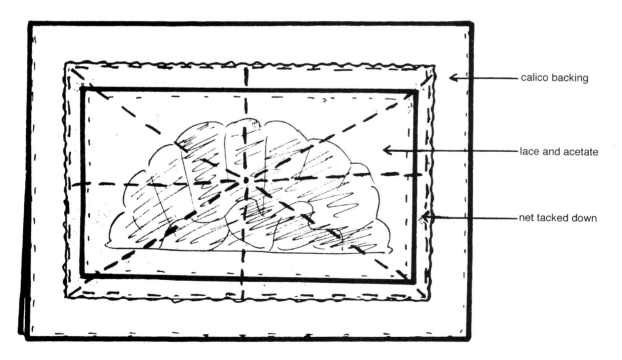

- calico backing

- lace and acetate

- net tacked down

and does not cover them. (Carrackmacross lace scissors could be of use here.) Take care not to cut so close to the cordonnette that the material or net could pull away, and that you do not cut the lace itself.

5 Remove the work from the acetate and backing calico.

Technique 8
Using a stiffening agent

There are several 'stiffening agents' on the market, in addition to starch, which can be used on ribbons, fabric and lace. Their use has greatly extended the ways in which present-day laceworkers, both bobbin and needle, can develop and further their ideas. This technique is used in project 6.

Method

1 Choose a suitable stiffening agent for your lace. Some give a porcelain look as well as stiffening the fabric.
2 Follow the instructions given on the stiffening agent. Make sure that the stiffener is evenly distributed on the lace and does not look clogged.
3 Carefully shape the lace into position (petals of flowers, for example, can be naturally 'curled').
4 Leave the lace to dry according to the instructions on the product.

Other useful techniques

Making a handmade cord

This is best done by two people, although you can manage by making use of a hook on a door.

Method

1 Decide upon the length and thickness of the desired cord and the choice of threads to be used in it. You can make a multicoloured cord which would incorporate the colours of the lace and its backing, or you could just use the same thread – these are doubled over when you start your cord.

2 The finished length of the cord needs to be measured accurately so that enough thread is used. You will need a number of strands of thread, all approximately five times the desired cord length – these are doubled over when you start your card.

   For example, if the finished cord length is to be 20cm (8in) long, then you would need several strands of thread each at least 100cm (40in) long [1a]. The thickness of the cord will obviously depend upon the number of strands you decide to use.

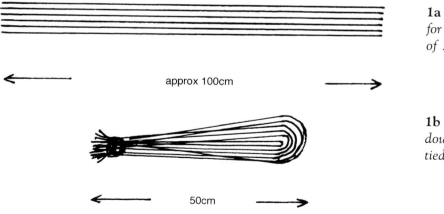

approx 100cm

1a *Starting threads for a finished cord of 20cm length.*

50cm

1b *Threads doubled over and tied.*

3 Double these strands over on themselves and tie a knot with the ends [1b].
4 Working with another person, put a pencil into the centre of the thread bundle at each end [1c]. One person should face the right and one the left so that you are looking in opposite directions, but not back to back, one holding pencil A and the other pencil B [1d].
5 Holding the threads gently, **both** people rotate each pencil in a clockwise direction away from themselves [1e], so twisting the threads. Continue to twist the threads until they are quite tight. Keep the pencils in place.
6 **Keeping the twisted threads taut**, bring together the looped ends B and A, holding it carefully in the middle as you do this so as to prevent it twisting up on itself [1f]. The person at A should now hold both pencils whilst the person at B keeps hold of the middle.

1c *Inserting two pencils.*

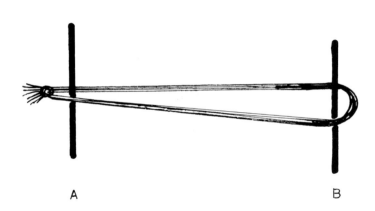

A   B

1d *Face in opposite directions.*

A   B

26

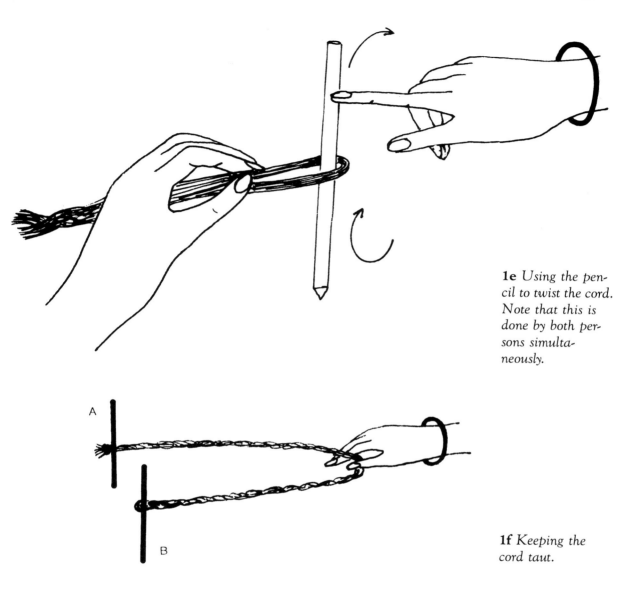

1e *Using the pencil to twist the cord. Note that this is done by both persons simultaneously.*

1f *Keeping the cord taut.*

7 Person B now holds the cord about 3cm (1¼in) away from the folded middle with one hand (1) and using the other (2) carefully 'strokes' this end down so that it makes neat twists [1g].

8 **Keep hand 1 in place** and using hand 2, pinch the cords together about 10cm (4in) from hand 1 [1h].

9 **Now keep hand 2 in place** and with hand 1 stroke the cord downwards from 2 to where it was held by **hand 1** [1i]. (You will probably feel that you should be stroking down with the top hand but **don't** — it is this way that gives such a beautiful evenness to the cord).

1g,h,i *Making neat twists to your cord.*

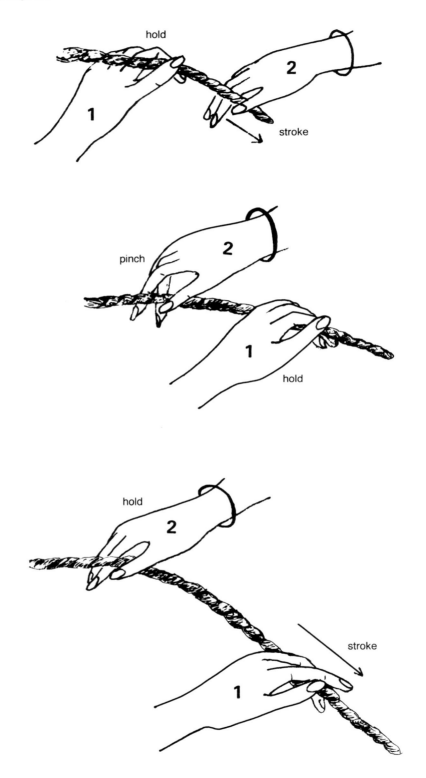

10 Keeping hand 2 in place, now use hand 1 to pinch the cords together about 10cm (4in) above hand 2. Repeat the downward stroking process with hand 2.

Continue in this manner until the whole twisted cord is formed and then knot the ends which were at A together, so preventing the twists from undoing.

Using beads

Used with careful consideration, beads can be incorporated into modern lace to greatly enhance the work. The jewellery pendant and necklace in projects 1 and 8 use beads as a fundamental part of the design.

Beads may be added in a variety of ways, preferably as you are making your lace. They can be added to cordonnette edges or to the lace fillings themselves.

My favourite 'lattice-type' open corded double Bruxelles (Brussels) stitch is extremely pretty when beads are added randomly as it is worked. The following method is the one that I find the most successful as it allows the beads to 'sit' properly and not distort the stitches.

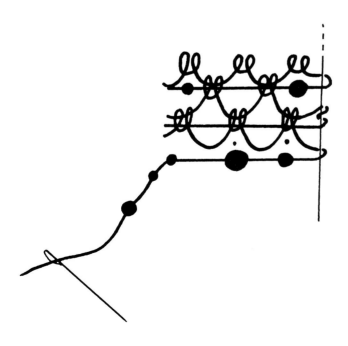

1a *Using beads with lattice-type filling.*

1b *Adding beads into non-corded lace stitches.*

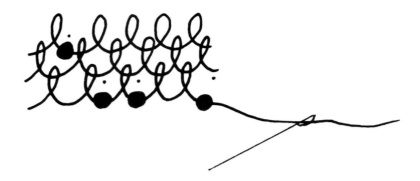

Method (using lattice-type filling)

1 Couch the cordonnet.

2 Work out where you wish beads to be used and prick a small hole into the acetate to mark the 'position' of each bead.

3 Add the beads to the **cord** rows when you are working the lace filling stitch. You do this by threading up the beads as you come to the place where they are required (you might need to adjust their positions slightly so that they do come in a cord row). Thread the required number onto the cord before you lay it across.

4 Work the stitch row below so that the beads sit in the gaps between one pair of stitches and the next [1a]. You do not need to add beads to every corded row as it would look too crowded.

   When working non-corded stitches you obviously have to thread each bead onto the needle as required [1b].

Strings of beads

Beads can be added into tassels after you make them (see *Making a tassel* on page 33), or they can be made up into a bead tassel.

Method 1

1 Attach the thread to that part of the lace where the bead string is required.

2 Thread a bead onto the string in the following manner — take the thread down through the bead and then back down again [1a], positioning the bead on the thread where you want it. Tighten up the thread to hold the bead.

   Some threads may be a little slippery. If so, take the thread down through the bead once more. This results in two threads around each bead [1b].

3 Continue to add beads to the 'string' as required — irregular spacing of the beads gives the best effect.

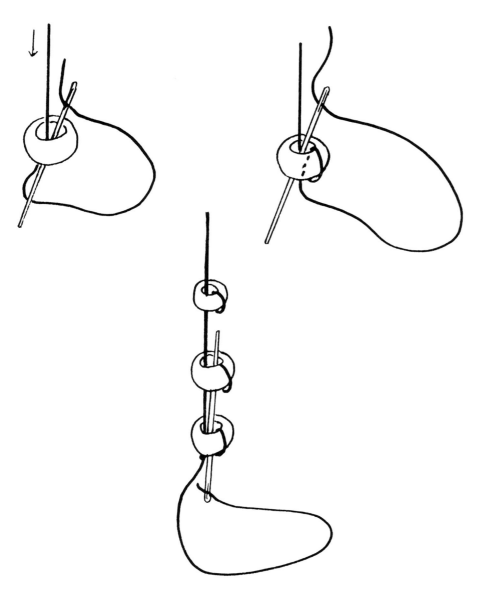

1a Threading on a bead.

1b Passing the thread twice around the bead if necessary.

1c Returning the needle to the top of the 'string' of beads.

4 When you have secured the last bead on the string, make a knot with one or two buttonhole stitches into the threads around the base of the last bead. Then take the needle and thread straight up to the top of the string, passing through all the beads [1c]. Secure the thread at the top.

Method 2

1 Using a **double** thread (with the cut ends threaded into the needle and the loop at the far end) thread up a bead so that it is in position near

*2a Bead near loop
end of doubled
thread.*

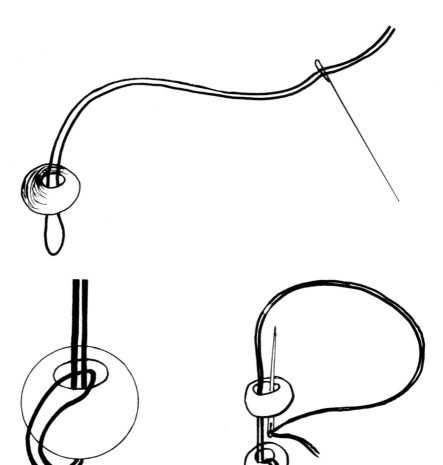

*2b The end bead
secured on the
double thread.*

*2c Adding the sec-
ond bead.*

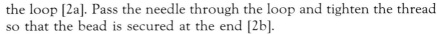

the loop [2a]. Pass the needle through the loop and tighten the thread
so that the bead is secured at the end [2b].

2 Thread the needle through a second bead and then back around this
new bead and up through it again [2c], tightening the thread as before
to hold the bead in position.

This method enables you to ease the bead to its desired position.

3 Continue adding beads as you work to make the required length. The
beads look best if they are not too regularly spaced.

Tassel of bead strings

If you are making a complete tassel of bead strings, work as many strings
as required and drop them from one large bead [1a]. This bead is
attached to the lace.

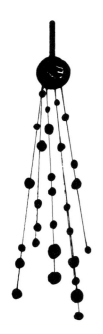

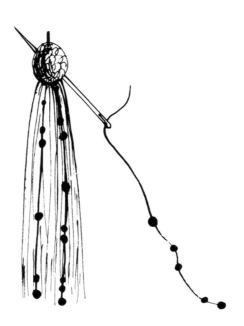

1a Tassel of bead strings.

1b Adding a string of beads into the tassel.

Tassel with added bead strings (see project 1)
The bead strings could be added as you make your tassel, but I find that the easiest way is to stitch in 'strings' of beads after the tassel has been made [1a and b].

Just stitch in as many bead strings as you require by attaching them, unnoticeably, into the head of the tassel so they swing freely with the rest of the tassel's threads.

Making a tassel

There are various methods of making a tassel but the following is one of the simplest:

Method
1 Decide upon the required length of the tassel — a common fault is to make the tassel look too short. Remember, you can always trim it later! Wind the chosen thread around your fingers, bearing in mind the length you eventually want it to be [1a]. If you are making more than one tassel, then wind the thread around a carefully measured piece of card, counting the number of winds.
2 When you have wound enough thread to make a generous tassel, cut

1a Winding the
tassel thread
around your fingers.

1b Tie and knot
one of the looped
ends together.

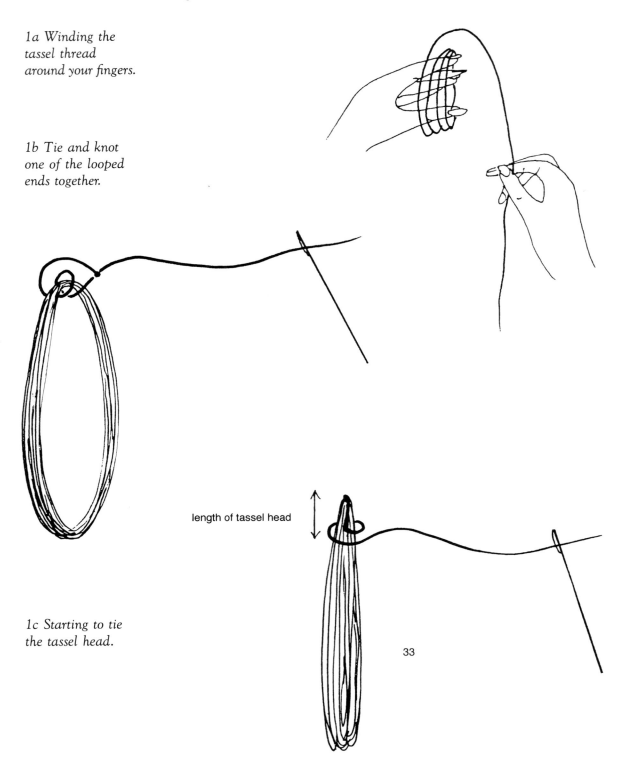

length of tassel head

1c Starting to tie
the tassel head.

33

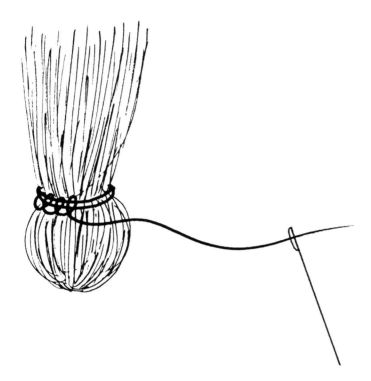

the end off from the skein or ball. **Don't** cut the tassel loops yet, and keep the threads on your hand or on the card.

3   Using either a matching or contrasting colour thread (to give a different-colour head to the tassel), cut and thread up a fairly long length of new thread. Knot the end and use this thread to tie one of the looped ends together [1b]. Knot this firmly so that it does not undo.

4   Decide upon the length of tassel head and bring the tying thread down to that point, taking it twice tightly around [1c]. Secure the thread firmly with a buttonhole stitch. These two wrapping threads will be used to start the buttonholing of the tassel head.

5   Turn the tassel upside-down and begin the buttonholing stitches of the tassel head, working into the two wrapping threads to start with — just as you would do with a cordonnet [1d].

The simplest and most effective stitch to use is a plain single Bruxelles, worked fairly closely. This results in a spiral effect as you work continuously around and around going into the loops of the rows above. You could even add beads into the stitches, or work alternating rows in different colours.

With needlepoint lace jewellery a combination of gold and silver is very effective — for example, the tassel itself in gold and the head in silver.

6 Complete the buttonholing of the tassel head, drawing the stitches up together at the end. Finish off securely, but don't cut off the thread — you use this thread to attach the tassel to your work.

7 Cut through the far loops of the tassel and trim them to the required length.

8 Attach the tassel to your lace where desired by taking two stitches into the lace. Use the thread left from the buttonholing. Leave a very slight gap between the tassel and the lace so that the tassel swings properly. Secure and end off the thread.

PART II

Projects and designs

Each of the projects has a star-rating system of one to three stars, which is used to denote ease of working. One star ★ is the simplest.

Further design ideas and suggestions are provided at the end of each project so that you can try out other ideas and experiment yourself, using your own lacemaking skills and some of the techniques in the book. Refer back to Part I when necessary.

Project 1 Needlepoint lace pendant ★★

The pendant is a development of the Christmas tree sampler in my first book, *Starting Needlepoint Lace* (Batsford).

Materials required
- 22cm (8¾in) gold-plated jewellery wire or rustless brass spangling wire
- Gold metallic-effect thread (medium thickness). The pendant pictured used DMC Fil Or Clair.
- Small gold and silver beads
- Gold or gold-plated chain
- Usual folded foundation calico backing
- Adhesive acetate film
- Cream sewing thread for couching and tacking

Method
1 Trace the design [1a] onto paper and place it under the adhesive acetate or architect's linen. Tack this onto the double layer of calico foundation backing in the usual manner.
2 Couch down the single strand of wire for the cordonnet, using cream sewing cotton with gold-coloured thread. Start at 1 (with a small hook in the wire as suggested in technique 1 in part I).
3 The pendant's hanging loop is formed as you go from 1 to 2 and 3, and then down towards 4 [1b]. Continue round until you reach 1, then cut off the starting hook. Continue couching down the wire until

Useful hints (see also technique 1)

1 Draw the design onto graph paper if you find difficulty in keeping the rows straight.
2 A needle-threader is useful when threading up metallic-effect threads.
3 The ends of metallic-effect threads may sometimes separate out. To help overcome this I use a **tiny** dab of clear adhesive, each as UHU, on the end immediately I cut it off the spool of thread. This dries very quickly.

1a Pendant design pattern.

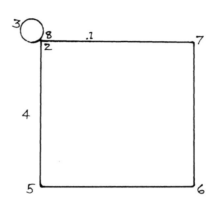

1b Forming the hanging loop.

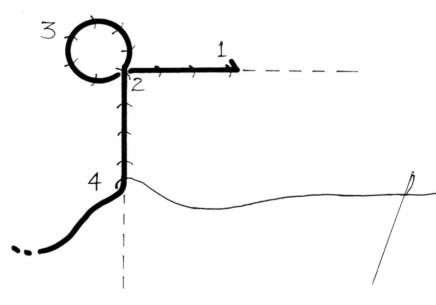

1d 'Lattice-type' filling stitch. (i) Ends of rows. (ii) Stitch detail.

1c Couching down the overlapping end of wire.

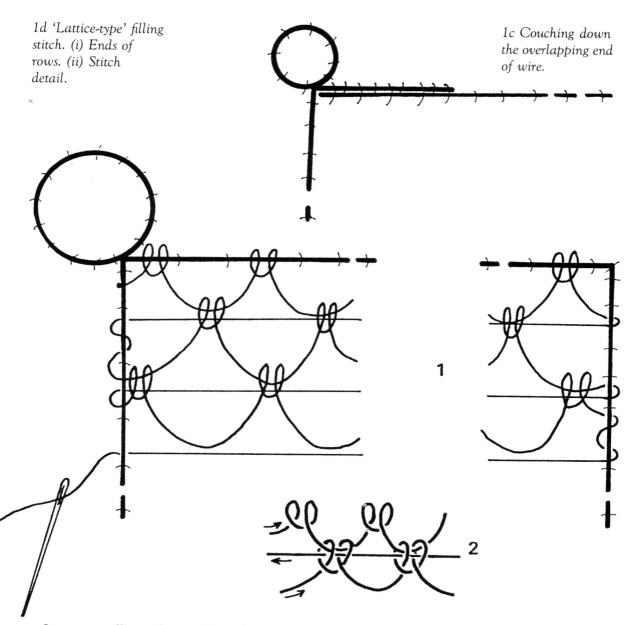

8 — you will now be couching down two strands of wire so that the ends are safely overlapped [1c]. Finish off as usual by whipping the wire ends on the surface and cutting off the wire.

4 Work 'lattice-type' open-corded double Bruxelles filling stitches within the area inside the square [1d], adding beads where desired.

In the pendant illustrated, small gold and medium-sized silver beads were added into some of the cord rows (see also *Other useful techniques* — Using beads).

1e Starting the cordonnette at 6.

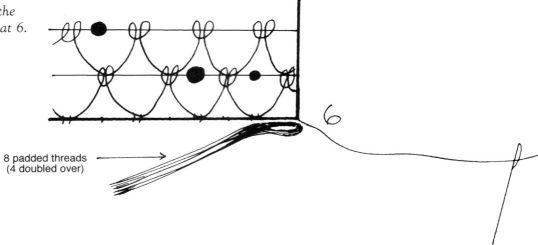

8 padded threads
(4 doubled over)

1f Ending off the old thread (working towards left).

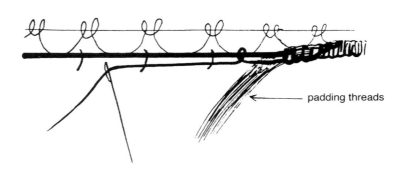

padding threads

1g Laying in the new cordonnette buttonholing thread.

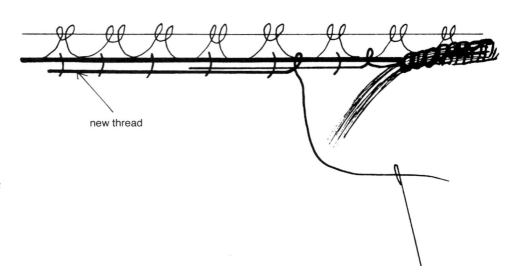

new thread

Whip the last stitch row down onto the wire cordonnet in the usual way.

5 Starting at 6 — the lower right-hand corner — work a twisted buttonholed cordonnette (see technique 5) around the edge up to the hanging loop.

In the pendant pictured, the cordonnette stitches were worked over eight strands of Fil Or as a padding. They were added as four doubled-over strands [1e] and the twisted spirals were each formed by working 12 buttonhole stitches before taking the needle down behind the edge to make the twist.

If you need to start a new thread for the buttonholing, it is best to end off just after forming a spiral — i.e. after the second or third buttonhole stitch. End the old thread by lifting up the eight laid threads and working a fastening-off buttonhole stitch on the original cordonnet, then run the thread under three or four couching stitches and cut it off [1f].

Start in the new thread by running that one under four or five couching stitches and then working one buttonhole stitch into the cordonnet edge [1g]. In this way there is less of a bump formed by keeping one end longer than the other.

Continue the spiral buttonhole cordonnette stitches but link in the new thread by taking it into the 'knot' of your last stitch before you go on with your cordonnette [1h]. Also, count the stitches to keep the spirals even.

6 When you reach the hanging loop, do not work the spiral cordonnette over the eight threads around the loop.

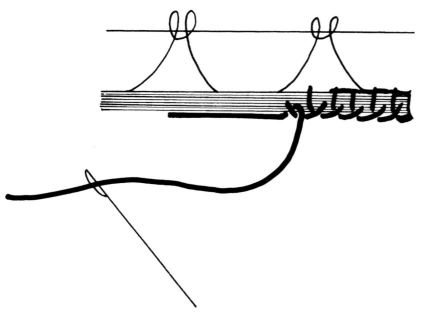

1h Linking in the new cordonnette buttonholing thread.

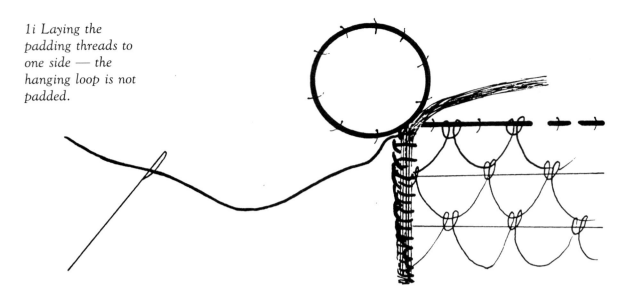

1i Laying the padding threads to one side — the hanging loop is not padded.

Holding the eight padding threads to one side [1i], just work ordinary buttonhole stitches over the wire of the hanging loop to cover it neatly — the 'knots' will be on the outside.

7 When you have worked around the hanging loop, continue with the twisted buttonholed cordonnette over the eight threads. Lay the eight padding threads back in position and continue the spirals, making sure that they have continued evenly. End off neatly when the cordonnette is completed.

8 Remove the lace pendant from its foundation by undoing the tacking stitches around the design and calico. Then part the two layers of calico and cut the small couching stitches carefully as usual. So that you do not distort the wire shape, lift the pendant, **still on** the design, and use tweezers to remove any couching threads attached under the design. **Then** lift the pendant off the design and carefully remove any further threads.

So that the pendant hangs correctly on a chain, turn the hanging loop around 90 degrees so that it is at right angles to the pendant which will now hang down in a diamond shape.

9 Make a tassel (see page 33), using the same gold-coloured thread in which the pendant was worked. It is important that you make it **long** enough to get the visual proportions of the whole pendant right. The tassel will need to be about 10cm (4in) in length — twice the length of the actual motif.

Add in bead strings if required. The pendant tassel pictured had five strings, with a mixture of small gold and medium-sized silver beads threaded with a single strand of thread taken from a length of the three-stranded Fil Or.

10 Attach the tassel to the lower corner of the pendant so that it is not too tight and will swing nicely, and then thread a gold chain through the hanging loop.

Project 1: Further design ideas

The pendant worked in project 1 can be used as a basis to stimulate further design ideas of your own.

The drawings here show some possible designs together with other-sized design patterns.

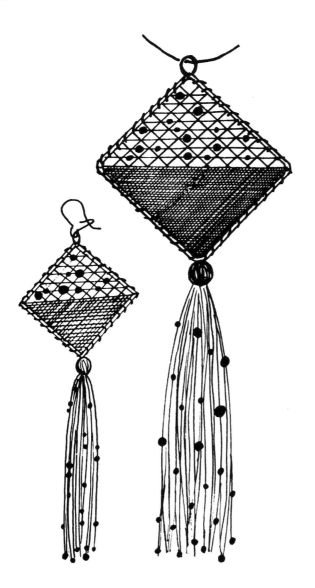

Other design ideas — *Pendant.*

Matching earrings.

Double pendant.

Halving the design to make a triangular pendant.

Pendant — changing the shape completely.

Other pattern sizes.

Earring design pattern.

Project 2 Bracelet ★

This bracelet will match the pendant in project 1 if you use the same thread, since it too has a twisted buttonhole effect.

Materials required
- Gold metallic-effect thread (medium thickness). The bracelet pictured used DMC Fil Or Clair.
- Thin plastic bracelet.

Useful hint

Keep the thread on the spool, don't cut a length off. You can hold the spool in your hand (instead of the needle) to make the buttonhole stitches around the plastic bracelet — it saves joining on!

2a Buttonholing over the bracelet — stitches far apart for clarity.

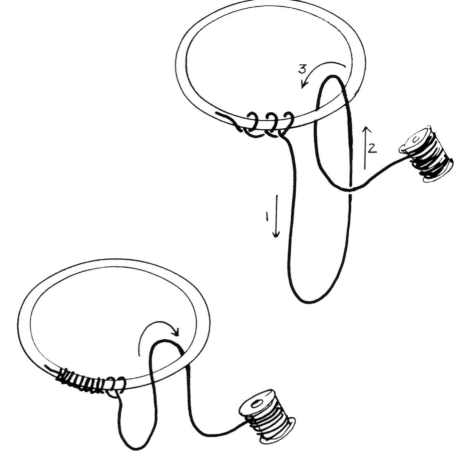

2b Forming the first spiral twist.

2c Continuing the next spiral — the first buttonhole stitch.

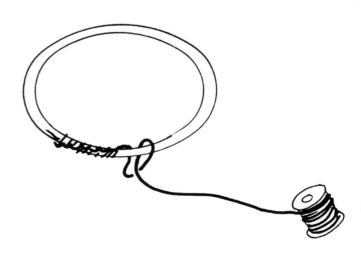

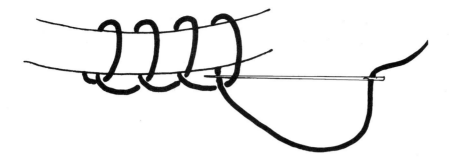

2d The finishing knot.

Method

1 If you are right-handed, hold the plastic bracelet in your left hand and use your right hand to hold the spool of thread and make the buttonhole stitches. (If you are left-handed, work vice-versa.)

    Secure the starting end of the thread on the bracelet with a dab of clear adhesive and begin to form buttonhole stitches over the bracelet [2a]. Do this by passing the spool of thread down through the bracelet, and through the loop of thread formed. This makes the 'knots' lie towards the outside edge.

    Work 12 buttonhole stitches, keeping them firm and close together. (You are working towards the right if you are right-handed.)

2 Form the first spiral twist. Take the spool and thread away from you into the centre of the bracelet. Gently pull downwards [2b] so that the stitches you have made are pulled into a spiral the 'knots' (or 'caught' loops) forming a diagonal ridge.

3 The thread is now at the base and you are ready to continue the buttonhole stitches [2c], making spirals as before. Form 12 stitches before passing the spool into the centre of the bracelet as in number 2 above.

4 Continue the buttonhole spirals until you reach your starting point — you need to cover the glued-down thread end. Make sure you have matched the starting and finishing spirals so that any join will be unnoticeable. (Push the stitches along a bit if necessary!)

5 Cut off the thread from the spool, **leaving about 10cm (4in)** so that you can thread this onto a needle to make the secure finishing knot; do this by making a buttonhole stitch as usual but pass the needle through it once again as you tighten it up [2d]. Run the needle and thread under one of the spirals or through the 'ridge' of knots for about 1cm ($\frac{3}{8}$in) and cut off the thread.

Project 2: Further design ideas

You could do things with the basic project such as using the thread on a needle and adding beads into the spiral's ridges [2e], or working spirals in alternating colours — for example, gold and silver, or black and bronze. You would do this by starting with two spools of thread (one of each colour) and working alternating spirals, laying the unwanted colour along the bracelet under the spiral being worked in the other colour [2f]. Then reverse the process for the next spiral — bring out the hidden colour for working and lay the old one against the bracelet so that this thread is covered as you work the spiral.

2e Using beads on the bracelet.

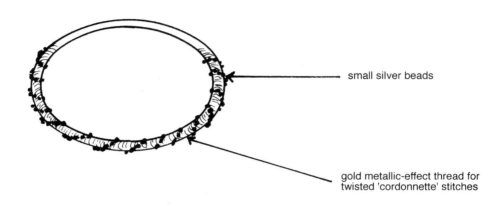

small silver beads

gold metallic-effect thread for twisted 'cordonnette' stitches

2f Starting the bracelet with two different coloured threads.

ends secured onto bracelet

Project 3 Bookmark sampler ★

The sampler can either be worked directly onto a piece of material, such as a heavy silk (see technique 2), or onto adhesive velvet-type backing (see technique 3).

The sampler is mounted in a long three-folded 'presentation card' which is shaped like a bookmark. Its aperture can have rounded or square ends and there are several colours available.

The bookmark in this project was made in gold thread on adhesive black velvet-type backing and mounted in a black presentation card.

Materials required

- Thread for the lace stitches. Gold DMC Fil Or Clair was used for the card bookmark pictured
- Piece of adhesive velvet backing, **just** smaller than the folded card
- 'Presentation card' bookmark mount (supplied with envelope) with cut aperture

---

Useful hints

1 Match the mount and backing colours so that they are the same, or a pleasant contrast.
2 Keep the paper over the adhesive velvet-type backing — only remove it when you use the adhesive surface to stick the sampler into the card.

Method

1 Carefully measure the aperture under which the sampler is to show. You will need to make your sampler area a **little** bigger so that the couched cordonnet edges do not show when it is made up.

   The card's aperture in the photograph measured 3cm ($1\frac{1}{4}$in) across and 12.75cm ($5\frac{1}{8}$in) long and so I made the cordonnet outline almost 4cm ($1\frac{1}{2}$in) across and 13.5cm ($5\frac{1}{4}$in) long.
2 Mark out the cordonnet outline and couch it down (as in technique 3). You can either use the same thread as your lace stitches for the couched threads, or just a number 40 or 60 crochet cotton since the cordonnet will not show, but use a fairly strong thread for the couching stitches [3a].
3 Plan out the sampler areas. You do not need to have a cordonnet

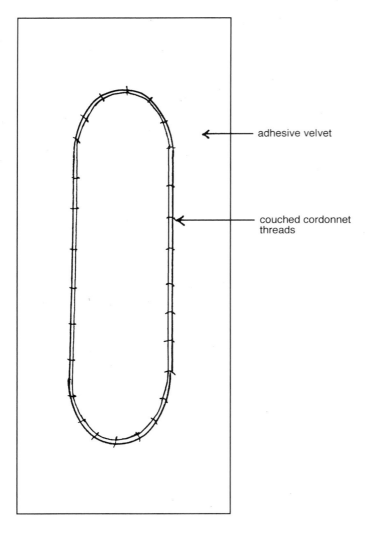

adhesive velvet

couched cordonnet
threads

*3a Couching the
cordonnet onto the
adhesive velvet-type
backing.*

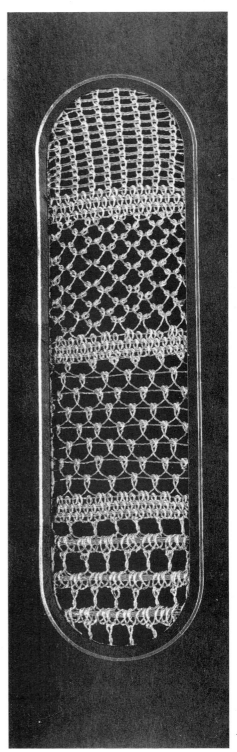

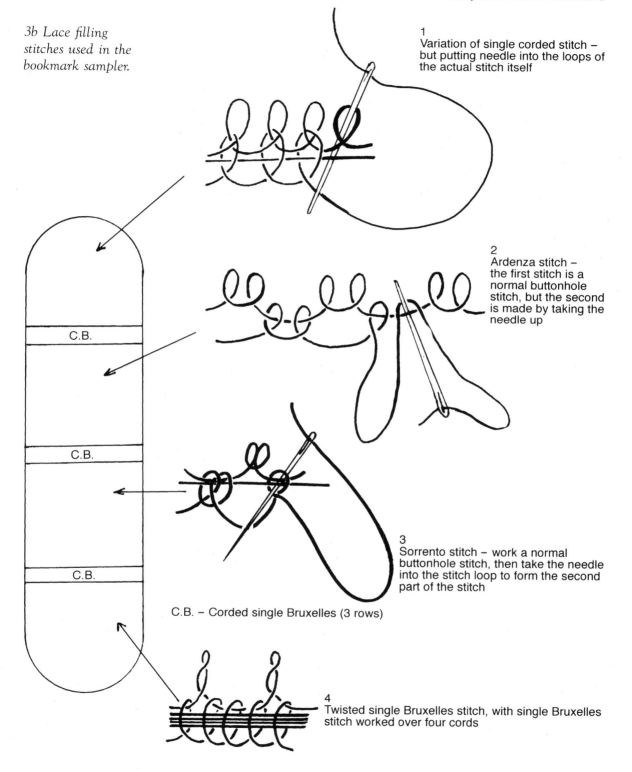

3b Lace filling stitches used in the bookmark sampler.

1
Variation of single corded stitch – but putting needle into the loops of the actual stitch itself

2
Ardenza stitch – the first stitch is a normal buttonhole stitch, but the second is made by taking the needle up

3
Sorrento stitch – work a normal buttonhole stitch, then take the needle into the stitch loop to form the second part of the stitch

C.B. – Corded single Bruxelles (3 rows)

C.B.

C.B.

C.B.

4
Twisted single Bruxelles stitch, with single Bruxelles stitch worked over four cords

53

going across to divide them — simply work the first area of lace filling stitches and then change to working the new lace filling stitches in the next area.

I found that the sampler looked best with three rows of single-corded Bruxelles stitch between each area — it gave the work more stability and improved the overall balance. A cord was laid before working the first corded Bruxelles stitch row.

4   Work the lace filling stitches in the desired areas. The diagram [3b] shows the stitches used in this project. There are many lovely stitches that can be worked. You may like to choose ones that you have never tried before — refer to the excellent needlepoint lace books available.

5   When the sampler area is completed it can be attached to the bookmark card under the aperture.

Simply peel off the paper backing and press the sampler adhesive-side down onto the card which folds under the aperture.

Make sure that the card opens on the right, this means that the sampler is attached to the **underside** of section 3 [3c].

6   Carefully stick this third side down at the edges to section 2 which forms the front of your bookmark [3d]. Finally, stick section 1 to the back of section 3 if desired.

7   A message, greeting, etc. may be written on what was section 1. Gold and silver pens are available and can give a professional effect.

3c Triple folded presentation card used for the bookmark.

3d Opening on the right when folded.

Project 3: Further design ideas
Use a variety of thicknesses and types of thread, but keep to one colour, such as white or silver.

You can obviously vary the dimensions of the areas within the cordonnet outline as well, but make sure you achieve a balanced effect.

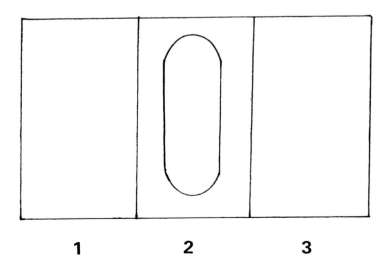

1   2   3

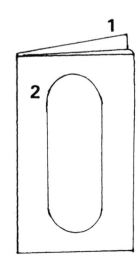

Project 4 Small greetings card H

This card is similar to project 3 in some ways but is worked onto a small piece of velvet material using technique 2.

Materials required

- Small three-folded card mount. The blue one used in the greetings card illustrated was 5.5cm × 9cm (2in × 3½in) with an aperture
- Material. This needs to be bigger than the card for ease of working (blue velvet was used here)
- Small amount of threads. The card pictured used three silver threads in varying thicknesses, with medium-fine gold thread for the sun
- 9 small beads (silver beads used in the original card)

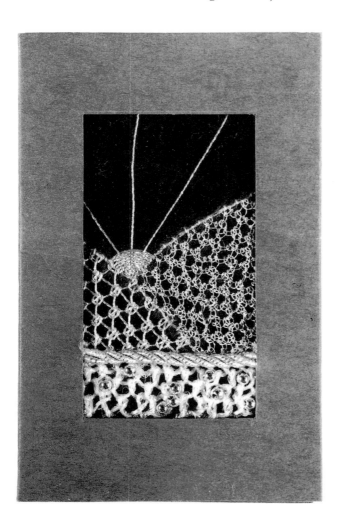

4a Cordonnet outline (1–8) for the card illustrated.

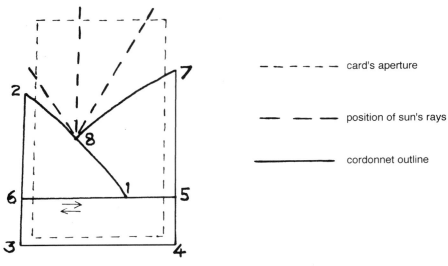

- - - - - - card's aperture

- — - — position of sun's rays

———— cordonnet outline

4b Lace filling stitches used in the actual card.

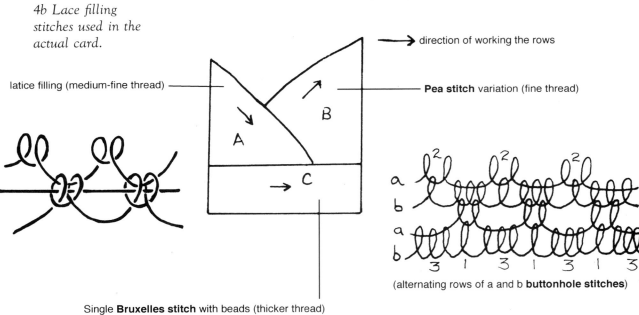

→ direction of working the rows

latice filling (medium-fine thread)

Pea stitch variation (fine thread)

(alternating rows of a and b **buttonhole stitches**)

Single **Bruxelles stitch** with beads (thicker thread)

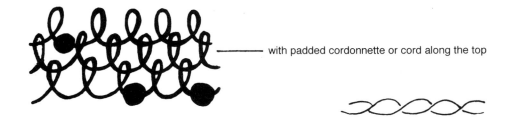

with padded cordonnette or cord along the top

56

Useful hints

1 Don't trim the velvet down until it goes into the card; this prevents too much fray and makes it easier to work on.
2 Pin the material onto your lace pillow for ease when working the lace filling stitches.

Method

1 Carefully mark out the design outline for the cordonnet [4a], the edges of which should go just beyond the aperture so that they will not show.
2 As **invisibly** as you can, couch down a thin cordonnet outline using theads that will match your lace stitches. (The pile of the velvet will help it to merge.)
3 Work the lace filling stitches. Choose a different stitch for each of the

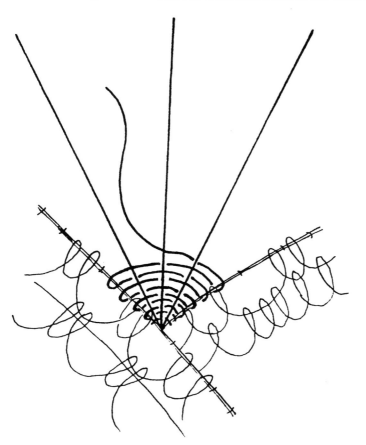

4c Weaving the
sun.

areas (A, B and C,) keeping the finest thread for area B so that it makes it recede visually. The diagram shows the three stitches chosen for the card illustrated [4b]. Silver beads were added to area C. In the card here the areas were worked as in diagram 4b but you can obviously select your own.

4 Using the gold thread, make three long stitches for the sun's rays, taking care that the work does not pucker. They radiate out from the junction at 8, as shown in the design outline. Work a 'woven' segment to represent the sun [4c].

5 Work a cordonnette along the top of area C. This and the beads give more definition to the 'foreground'.

   You may prefer to couch down a short length of silver cord as the cordonnette instead (see technique 6), as in the card illustrated.

6 Trim the velvet to your card (it should not show at the edges).

7 Using double-sided sellotape, or suitable clear adhesive, attach the velvet to the card so that it lies under the aperture, with the opening on the right (keep any adhesive clear of the work within the aperture).

Project 4: Further design ideas

Tiny gift tags could be made in a similar way, or the whole design could be enlarged and elaborated to frame up into a picture.

Project 5 Simple brooch ★

This makes a simple attractive gift which is quick to work. It is also a useful sampler for a new or favourite stitch as it is worked directly onto fabric (see technique 2). The brooch illustrated was worked in Lattice filling using gold DMC Fil Or Clair on bronze-brown shot taffeta, within a gold-coloured oblong mount.

Materials required
- 1 brooch mount (various types available)
- Small piece of fabric, e.g. taffeta, which does not fray easily
- Small quantity of thread. (e.g. metallic-effect thread) to match the colour of the mount
- Drawing or cartridge paper

Useful hint

Use a material which does not fray easily, as it is later trimmed down to avoid bulk when it is fitted into the mount.

Method
1 Mark out the size of the area to be worked by placing the brooch mount's backing, or the piece or card which goes into the mount, onto the piece of fabric. This fabric should be larger than the mount. Allow at least 2mm ($\frac{1}{12}$in) extra around the outline for your cordonnet outline so that it does not show later.
2 Couch down the outline cordonnet through the material.
3 Tack the fabric onto a small piece of stiff drawing or cartridge paper — this acts as a support whilst working the lace stitches onto the surface of the fabric [5a].

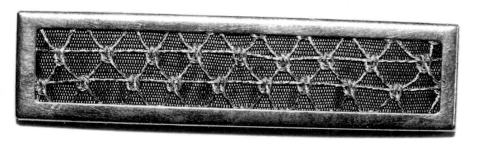

5a Fabric tacked onto supporting cartridge paper.

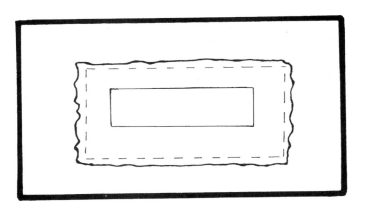

5b Mounting the material.

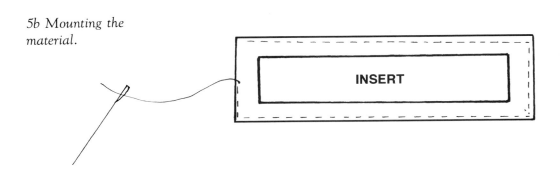

4 Work the lace filling stitches on the surface of the fabric within the outline — do **not** go through the supporting paper. You can either hold the work in your hand, or pin the paper support onto your needlepoint lace pillow.

5 Remove the completed 'sampler' from the backing paper. (You do not need to work any cordonnette.)

6 Trim down and mount the lace by attaching the material (with the lace on the front) to the cardboard insert, either by 'lacing' or by using gathering stitches [5b].

7 Place the mounted lace into the brooch frame and secure the back onto the brooch.

Note: Most brooch mounts have a piece of clear acetate which covers and protects the work within. However, I think that this simple brooch looks best **without** it.

Project 5: Further design ideas

Incorporate beads into the lace filling stitches. Work them onto a **strongly** contrasting piece of material, but tone the beads' colours with the backing.

The same method of working could be used to make an oval or round pendant — these can be obtained from many craft shops. An attractive lace filling could be worked using a wheel filling [5c], perhaps with alternating buttonholed wheels with simple picots [5d].

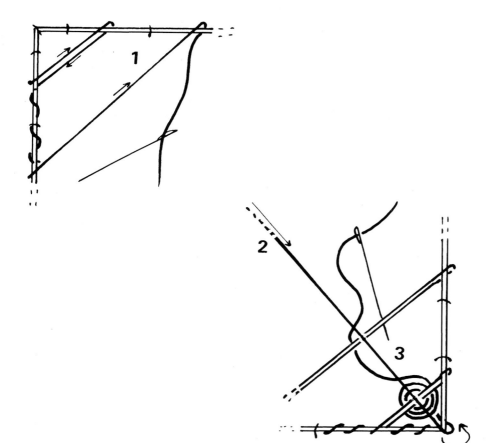

5c Stages in the wheel filling.

1 Laying double diagonal threads.

2 Laying a single thread down at right angles.

3 Returning, weaving in a small wheel.

Repeat 2 and 3 for each line of wheels.

5d *Oval pendant
with wheel fillings
and picots.*

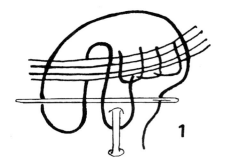

1

2

3

Project 6 Stiffened lace 'bowl' ★

Some of the beautiful antique bead purses that you see today were made on a beading mould, sometimes called a thimble mould. This idea can be adapted slightly by using a plastic bottle upon which to work your lace shape. If you choose the bottle carefully, the shape of the base can vary from a plain round to a square. The lace can then be stiffened (see technique 8) so that it results in quite a firm object. Starch could possibly be used as an altenative.

Materials required

- Clean plastic bottle (e.g. 1 litre water bottle)
- Thread — coton perlé 5 was used for the bowl illustrated
- Stiffening agent
- Coloured spray lacquer

Useful hints

1 Work the rows of lace stitches around the plastic bottle in the direction that suits you, i.e. clockwise or anti-clockwise.
2 As the work is gathered in around the base, avoid using 'corded' lace stitches.
3 Make sure the finished lace absorbs the stiffener but does not look clogged.

6a Working the row of twisted single Bruxelles stitches.

Method

1 Wrap a long thread twice, fairly tightly, around the plastic bottle and knot it firmly. **Do not cut off the thread.**
2 With the same thread, work one row of single twisted Bruxelles

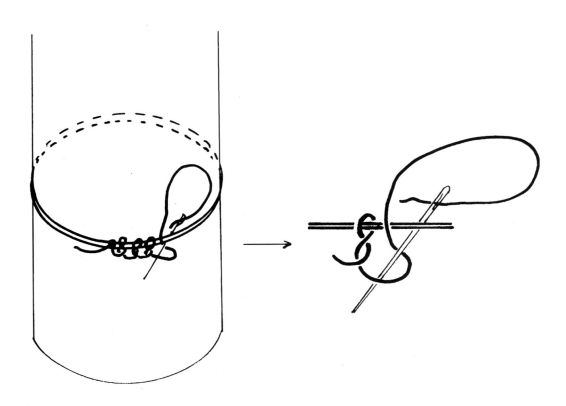

6b Starting the rows of triple Bruxelles stitches.

6c Continuing the rows of triple Bruxelles around the bottle.

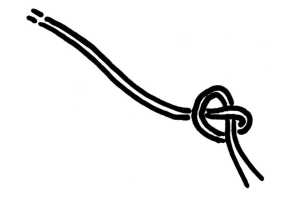

6d Knotting the ends to start a new thread.

6e Working the one row of single Bruxelles stitches.

stitches using the two wrapping threads as a cordonnet [6a]. The stitches need to be about 0.5cm ($\frac{1}{4}$in) apart and the original starting end will be worked over as you go.

3 Work a row of triple Bruxelles stitches into alternate loops of the twisted Bruxelles row above [6b].

4 Continue working down the bottle with the triple Bruxelles stitches as usual, going into every long loop [6c]. Fourteen rows of triple Bruxelles were worked for the round bowl, but this can be changed as desired.

When you need to start a new thread, just knot the ends [6d]. Try to make the knot come in the treble stitch groups if possible so as to be less obvious.

5 Draw in the work by bringing the lace downwards to the end of the bottle (so that the stitches can be worked slightly tighter and drawn up a little as you work this row). Work a row of single Bruxelles with one stitch going into each long loop [6e].

6 Turn the bottle upside-down (it seems easier to work this way) and gather up the lace over the end of the bottle by whipping into each loop between the single Bruxelles stitches [6f], pulling them up as you go.

Pull the thread up tightly, securely knot it and cut it off. The lace has now been completely gathered up [6g].

7 Still with the bottle upside-down, join on a thread at the original top edge and work a row of close buttonhole stitches around the edge [6h] like a cordonnette. You should work about four stitches between each twisted Bruxelles stitch.

8 Stiffen the lace — I did this by brushing the stiffener onto the lace whilst it was still on the bottle and letting it dry slightly (but not so that it sticks immovably!). I speeded up the process with a hair dryer and then removed the lace, washed and dried the plastic bottle and then eased the lace back into position on the bottle, leaving it to dry overnight.

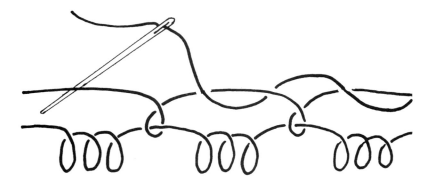

6f *Whipping into each loop (bottle now upside-down).*

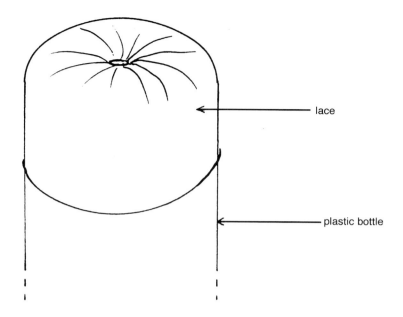

6g The lace gathered up over the end of the bottle.

lace

plastic bottle

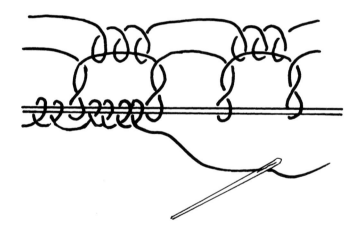

6h Buttonholing the 'cordonnette' edge.

When it was removed from the bottle it was quite stiff and nicely shaped and it was then sprayed with gold lacquer.

Project 6: Further design ideas

Make a handle for your bowl shape to turn it into a basket. Do this by working your lace handle in the usual manner [6i] on acetate and calico foundation backing. It would need to be joined to the lace bowl before any stiffening.

6i *Making the
basket handle.*

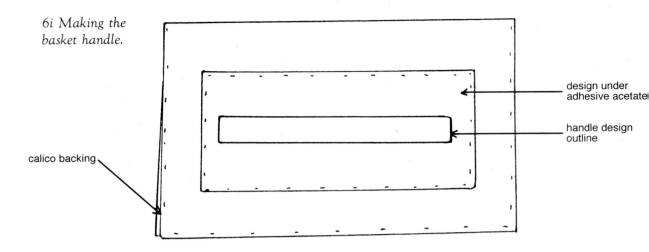

calico backing

design under
adhesive acetate

handle design
outline

A little more ambitious perhaps, but a brim could be made for a hat shape (purchased). Do this by working the lace for the brim shape in the usual traditional manner, and removing it from the calico backing as normal. Then stiffen and shape the brim after joining it to the hat crown. Use ribbon to cover the join and, perhaps, add lace flowers.

Project 7 Covered box ★★

A suitable small cardboard box, such as an earring box, can be covered with adhesive velvet backing upon which you have worked a small piece of needlepoint lace.

The lace is first worked directly onto the velvet backing and then stuck over the box lid, having removed the backing paper. Refer back to technique 3 as necessary.

Materials required

- 1 small box (with drop-on overlapping lid)
- Adhesive velvet-type backing (black was used for the box illustrated)
- Small quantity of thread for the cordonnet, lace fillings and cordonnette, e.g. white 60 or 80 crochet cotton. Note that a very small box (less than 5cms square) will require a finer-thread
- Small quantity narrow gold braid as added trimming (optional)
- White sewing thread for the cordonnet couching

Useful Hint

Keep the cordonnet outline simple by only couching down the actual **outside** lines of the square — all other threads are kept on the surface of the velvet.

7a Adhesive velvet-backing shape for a box top (the actual size will depend upon the box which is used).

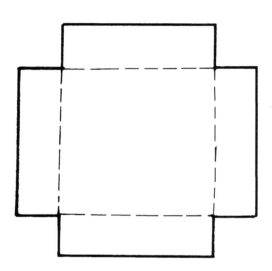

7b Starting the grid within the couched cordonnet.

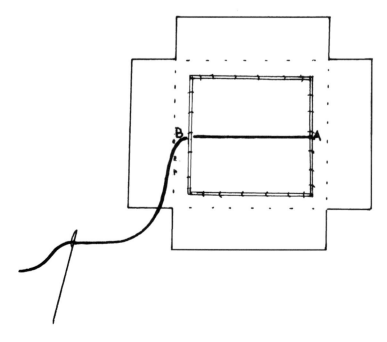

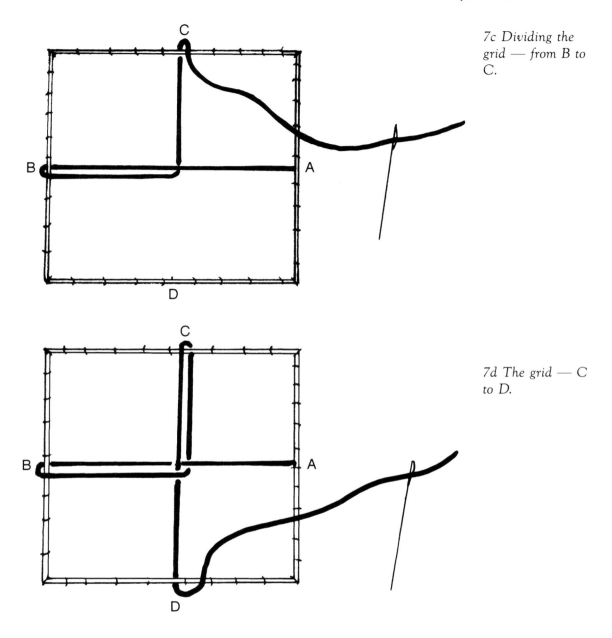

7c Dividing the grid — from B to C.

7d The grid — C to D.

Method

1 Measure out and cut the piece of adhesive velvet contact backing so that it will cover the top and sides of your box lid [7a].

   Although the top area must be measured accurately, the sides could be 'generously' cut and trimmed later if preferred.

2 Couch down the outer crochet-cotton cordonnet of your chosen design (here it was a simple square). Remember to try and make each

couching stitch here go up and down in the same hole (see technique 3), right through the paper-backed velvet.

3 You can obviously experiment with any stitches, either in a grid or filling the entire area. The following instructions are for the grid for the Point de Gaze style wheel fillings.

Divide the square cordonnet area into four sections — this is done completely **on the surface** of the velvet. To start this grid, you just join on a new single thread of crochet cotton halfway down one of the

7e Laying the diagonal threads in one direction.

7f The X in each square (the pairs of threads would lie close to each other).

7g The vertical divisions laid.

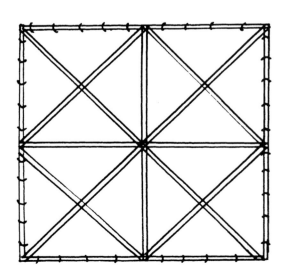

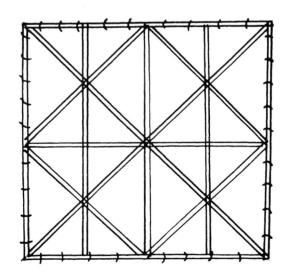

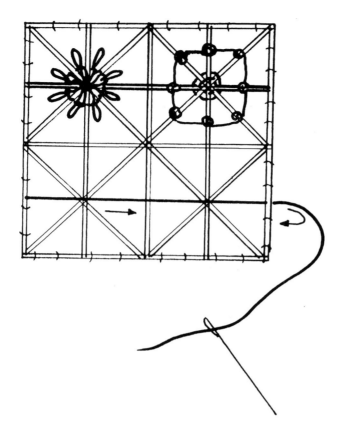

7h Laying the horizontal thread across in one direction before using the returning thread to make the wheel fillings.

cordonnet sides A and take the thread right across and under the cordonnet at B on the opposite side [7b].

Then, almost like a parcel, take it back to the centre and out to C [7c].

Continue in this way to form the grid [7d]. When returning from D, link the thread at the centre and return to the starting point A.

4 Lay the diagonal threads in one direction, taking the thread across and back each time [7e], passing under and over the cordonnet in the usual manner.

5 Lay down the other diagonals in the same manner to give you the X in each square [7f].

6 Now lay the vertical divisions to each square [7g] in the same way.

7 You still have the dividing horizontal threads to lay down, but you **use these to work your lace wheel fillings**. Do this by laying the first thread across from one side of the cordonnet to the other in one direction and then use the **returning** thread to start the wheel filling at the centre of each of the four small squares [7h].

Various wheel fillings can be used. The box illustrated in the

7i Working
between the 'legs'
of the previous
stitches.

7j Ardenza stitch
— the first stitch is
a normal
buttonhole stitch
(one pair of stitches
has already been
worked).

photograph had two buttonholed wheel fillings (with simple loop picots worked in the buttonholing) and two 'woven' wheel fillings.

You can use this box top as a sampler and try out any wheel fillings you may wish. (Details of woven and buttonholed wheels and simple picots are given in diagrams 5c and 5d of the pendant instructions.)

If you run out of thread, just end off and join on at the back of the paper-backed velvet — but remember that you will need to be able to remove the paper backing when you stick the velvet down onto the box lid.

8 Once the wheel fillings are completed, the original centre crossing can then be decoratively buttonholed. This is very simply done by buttonholing along in one direction (leaving small spaces between each stitch), and then returning back working the buttonholing stitches between the 'legs' of the previous stitches [7i].

This is a simple yet effective cordonnette finish, but do not pull the stitches too tightly.

9 The outside couched cordonnet edge is worked last. In the box illustrated, Ardenza stitch was worked around the edge.

I always prefer working this stitch towards the left and also towards me. The first of the pair of stitches is worked as an ordinary detached buttonhole stitch [7j], the second is worked upwards [7k], so that its loop goes in the reverse direction to its partner when gently tightened. Work around the outer cordonnet, then back along its inside edge [7l] to complete this decorative cordonnette.

10 Apply the velvet to the box lid. Peel off the paper backing which covers the adhesive back of the velvet, easing it off **carefully** around any stitches.

Making sure that it is exactly where you want it, press the velvet (adhesive-side down) onto the box lid's top and then onto the sides. Ensure that these are butted exactly at the corners and that no gaps show. Trim off any excess.

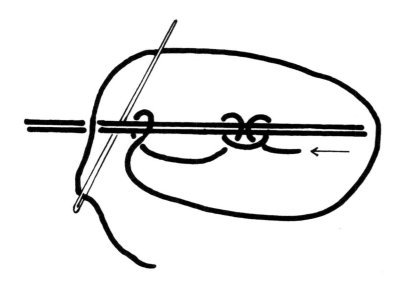

7k Ardenza stitch — the second stitch of the pair, the needle taken upwards.

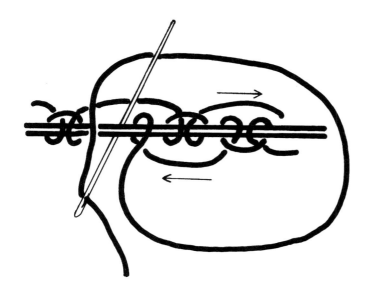

7l Completing the decorative Ardenza stitch cordonnette.

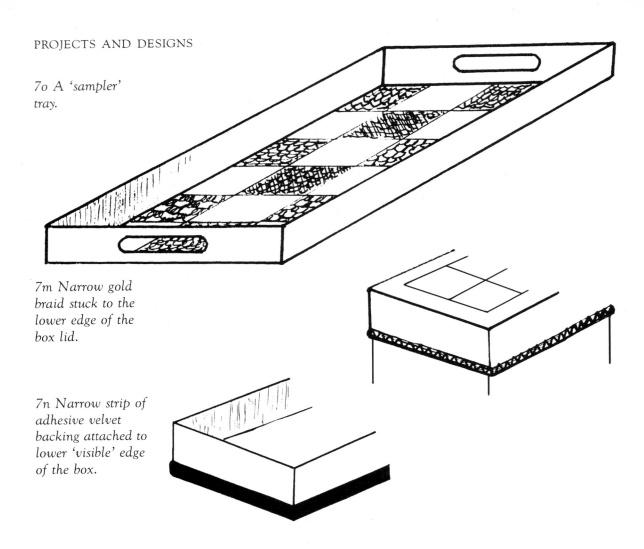

7o A 'sampler' tray.

7m Narrow gold braid stuck to the lower edge of the box lid.

7n Narrow strip of adhesive velvet backing attached to lower 'visible' edge of the box.

11 A narrow gold braid can be added as a trim at the lower edge [7m]. Attach this carefully with a suitable glue.

12 In the box illustrated, a thin strip of the black velvet backing was also stuck onto the lower visible part of the box itself [7n] so that the lid sat properly and the whole box appeared covered.

Project 7: Further design ideas

A very pretty insert for articles such as a handbag mirror, or powderbowl top, could be made using a silver or gold metal thread to match the silver or gilt frame. Suitable mirror and bowl mounts can be purchased from suppliers of lace mounts.

A larger piece of adhesive velvet worked with sampler squares [7o] could be mounted under glass as a picture or a tray — but not for carrying hot things! This is an adaptation of the cushion sampler in *Starting Needlepoint Lace*.

Project 8 Gold and silver necklace ★★★

Needlepoint lace jewellery looks particularly effective if worked in metallic-look theads. The necklace illustrated was worked in silver and gold threads with the addition of groups of tiny, smooth gold beads and medium-sized, ridged silver beads. These were worked in with the lace fillings (see *Using beads* in Part I).

The left-hand, plainer side of the necklace was worked entirely in silver, in a close single corded Bruxelles stitch (with added beads). The 'cord' edge was also worked in silver.

The right-hand side of the necklace was worked in alternating bands of single corded Bruxelles (with a few beads) and 'lattice-type' stitch areas without beads. This was worked entirely in gold thread, as was the cord edge.

To keep the shape, a fine silver wire was used as the cordonnet (see technique 1).

The cordonnette was made from a handmade cord (see technique 6) which was whipped onto the edge and also formed the fastening cord of the necklace.

Materials required
- Gold metallic-effect thread, medium thickness. DMC Fil Or Clair was used in the necklace illustrated
- Silver metallic-effect thread, medium thickness. DMC Fil Argent was used
- Length of thin silver wire to lay as the cordonnet
- Small, smooth gold beads (33 were used)
- Medium sized, ridged silver beads (15 were used)
- White or cream sewing thread for couching down the wire cordonnet
- Folded foundation calico backing
- Blue or green adhesive acetate film for covering the design

Method
1 Trace the design [8a] onto drawing paper, place it under blue or green (preferably matt) acetate film and tack it onto the double layer of calico foundation backing in the usual manner.
2 Couch down the single strand of wire for the cordonnet, using white or cream ordinary sewing cotton (see technique 1).
3 Using the gold thread, start at the **lower** point of the right-hand side of the necklace, and work the first block of close corded single Bruxelles stitch. The design will be worked upside-down as it is easier to decrease stitches than to increase! Add in a few beads as you work

Useful hints

1 A tiny dab of clear adhesive such as UHU will help prevent any possible separation of the ends of metallic-effect threads.
2 A needle-threader is useful when threading up metallic-effect threads.
3 If you find you've missed out any beads where you would have liked them, use a **single** strand of matching thread (pulled out from the twisted thread) to stitch them on invisibly.

8a Necklace pattern.

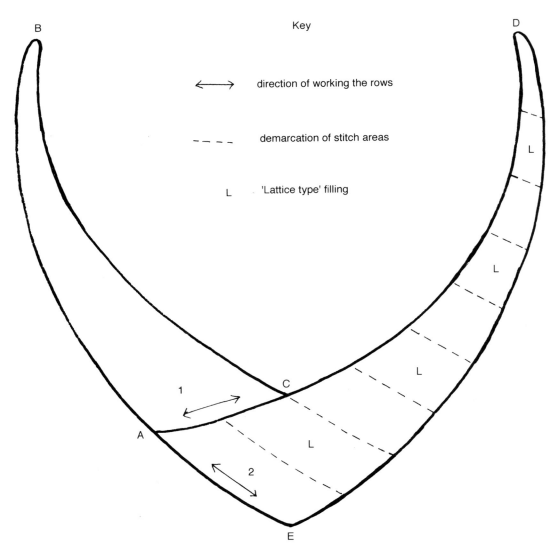

Key

⟵——⟶   direction of working the rows

‒ ‒ ‒ ‒   demarcation of stitch areas

L ⸱   'Lattice type' filling

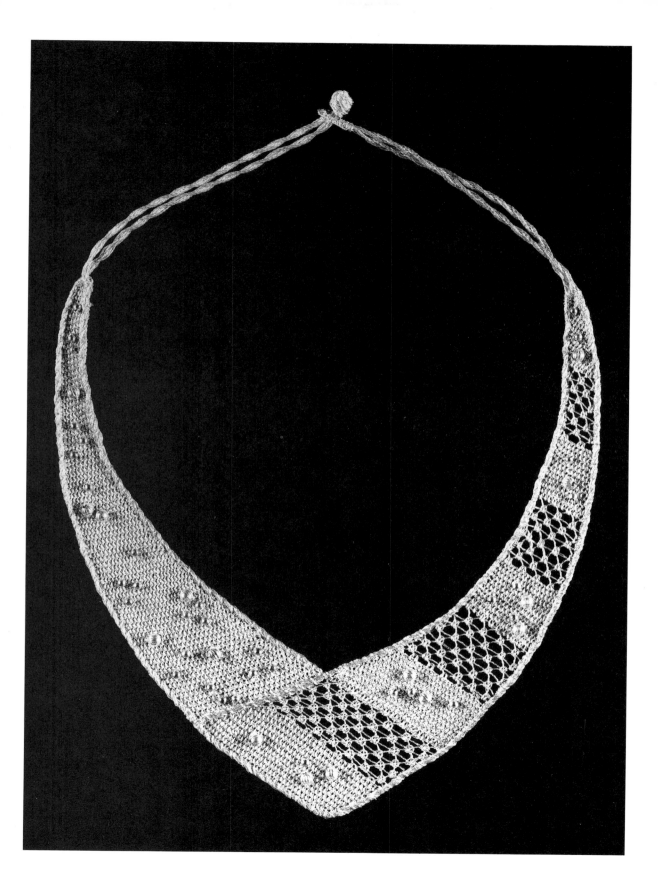

8b Working the first row of 'lattice-type' filling into the last (whipped) row of the corded single Bruxelles area.

8c Changing over from 'lattice-type' filling to the corded single Bruxelles stitch.

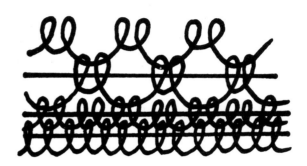

the lace, making 'artistic groups' as you desire. The direction of the rows is shown on the design diagram.

When you reach the first dotted division line, change to the 'lattice-type' filling stitch.

To keep a neat changeover, the last row of corded Bruxelles stitches was whipped (instead of laying the cord across); gently pull up the whipping stitches as you go.

When working the first row of the 'lattice-type' filling, miss two stitches, work two stitches, etc., along the row [8b] leaving the longer loops as usual.

Continue down to the next dotted division line in the 'lattice-type' filling, ending with a cord laid across.

This area does **not** have beads worked into it, as it would otherwise spoil the contrast in texture and stitch.

5 Change to the corded single Bruxelles stitch [8c]. The laid cord ensures a neat changeover. Continue working the alternating bands of corded stitch (with beads) and 'lattice-type' filling (without beads) until this side is complete.

6 Work the left-hand side of the necklace completely in close corded single Bruxelles stitch using the silver thead and adding beads where

desired. Like the other side, this is started at the lower point and the rows worked across in the direction of the arrow on the design. **Do not remove the lace from the backing yet.**

7 The cordonnette cord, which continues into the fastening cords of the necklace, is made next. The silver side of the necklace has a silver cordonnette, and the gold side has gold. These are made using the same metallic-effect threads as were used for the lace fillings.

First make the **finished** cord in silver, about 43–45cm (17$\frac{1}{4}$–18in) long for a fairly close-fitting necklace. If in doubt make it longer as excess can be cut off at the fastening end.

The **finished** gold cord will need to be approximately 53–55cm (21$\frac{1}{4}$–22in) long.

The method of making the cord is detailed in Part I (see **Other useful techniques**). The cord belonging to the necklace illustrated was made using two strands of thread since only a fairly light cord was desired. Too heavy an edge would detract from the lace fillings. The strands were doubled over and knotted [8d].

8 Attach the cord as the cordonnette and fasten the cords – refer back to technique 6 in Part I is necessary.

(a) The silver (left-hand side) cord is attached first [8e]. Beginning at A and using matching silver thread, whip the cord down along the outer edge to B so that it lays immediately over the original cordonnet. Make the couching stitches lie in the grooves of the cord to give a neat finish.

When you reach B, end off the whipping down thread and rejoin it again at C.

Using the **other** end of the silver cord, start from C and whip this down along the edge back to B to meet and catch in the cord from the outer necklace edge. Make sure that the starting ends on both sides are inconspicuous and neat so that the cord has no knots and won't unravel.

(b) The remaining looped length of cord which comes from B is just left free to form the fastening cords of this side.

8d Two strands used to make a cord (knotted ready for twisting).

8e Attaching the
two ends of the
silver cord (working
from A to C).

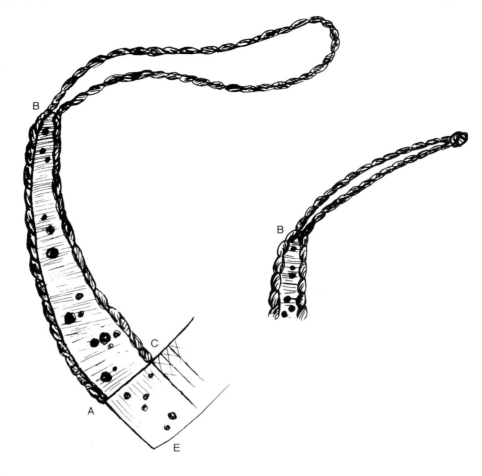

8f The knotted
'bobble' for the
fastening.

8g The gold cord at
D — the long end
looped over to form
the fastening loop.

8h The
buttonholed
fastening loop of
the gold cord
('knots' on the
outside).

Make a knotted 'bobble' at the looped end so that the length is where it is desired for fastening [8f].

(c) The gold cord is then attached to the right-hand side of the necklace.

Commencing at D in diagram 8a (the looped-over end needs to be used for the fastening loop) and starting with an **end** of the cord, whip-stitch the cord down to C and along to A, covering the ends in the silver cord as you go. Continue to E and then back along the outer necklace edge to D. Do **not** cut off the remaining cord.

(d) This remaining gold cord is doubled over [8g]. The looped-over end will form the fastening loop for the silver 'bobble' on the other side so estimate the correct length carefully to match before attaching the final end to D. The join here must be firm but inconspicuous. The looped-over end is then caught together and buttonholed so that a neat loop is formed for the fastening [8h]. The 'knots' of the buttonholing should be around the outside edge of the loop.

Project 8: Further design ideas

A bracelet could be worked, again using a wire cordonnet, to match or complement the necklace, using either gold, or gold and silver metallic-effect threads (and even beads). Make this in a 'strip', and overlap the ends [8i].

Attractive napkin rings [8j] can be made using the same idea on a slightly smaller scale, the ends being joined or butted together.

8i Bracelet — simple strip in needlepoint lace.

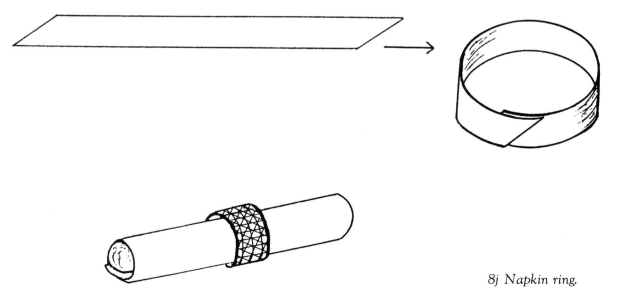

8j Napkin ring.

Project 9 Evening bag/purse ★★★

The small evening bag in the photograph was worked in gold DMC Fil Or Clair (with silver and gold beads) on midnight blue velvet and lined with gold lamé-type material.

The decorative panel of 'lattice-type' stitch was worked directly onto the material before the bag was made up (see technique 2). The hand-made cord was used for both the cordonnette and the thin bag strap.

The 'lattice-type' filling is similar to that used in projects 1 and 8 and so this small bag could be made to match either of these if similar threads and beads were also used.

Materials required

- Fabric for bag (see *Useful hints*). You need about 14 × 42cm (5½ × 16¾in)
- Lining fabric measuring about 14 × 42cm (5½ × 16¾in). Choose a fabric that does not fray too easily, e.g. fine silk or satin
- Interfacing — either iron-on if the bag material is suitable, or soft calico or curtain lining, if velvet is used, again approximately 14 × 42cm (5½ × 16¾in)
- Gold metallic-effect thread, medium thickness (DMC Fil Or Clair was used here)
- Small gold or silver beads
- Medium-sized gold or silver beads
- Tacking cotton
- Sewing cotton to colour-match the bag fabric
- Small amount of fine gold thread to attach handmade cord for the cordonnette. Fine gold (3) Madeira Metalleffektgarn was used here.
- Small piece of card for bag flap stiffening if required
- 1 small press-stud for fastening
- Cartridge paper

Useful hints

1 You might find it easier to work on a heavy silk material rather than velvet, since a velvet pile does tend to 'move around'.
2 Keep the material upon which you work the lace stitches taut so that the stitches do not pucker or distort.
3 Have fairly generous seam allowances at the start of the work. These can be trimmed later as necessary.

Method

1 Draw the bag pattern to the **correct size** [9a] onto cartridge paper, then use this to cut out the bag fabric and the lining fabric. Remember to allow for fairly generous seams.

2 Back the bag fabric with the iron-on interfacing if the material is suitable, or tack an interfacing of soft calico or curtain lining to the back of the velvet if this is being used. The interfacing is cut using the same pattern.

3 On the **underside** (onto the interfacing itself), mark out the area within which the decorative lace stitches are to be worked [9b].

4 With the right side of the fabric uppermost, couch down the cordonnet to the decorative lace area. Make sure that you have it exactly on the lines 1–4 which will not be part of the seams. The other edges are taken 2mm ($\frac{1}{12}$in) into the seam allowances as they will be hidden when the lining is attached to the bag.

The cordonnet outline threads should be the same as those used for the lace stitches. The couching cotton should match the colour of the bag fabric.

If you are using velvet, then make the cordonnet couching stitches slightly closer together, as the cordonnet may otherwise 'move' on the velvet pile.

5 Starting at 6 and working the row towards 1, work the decorative lace filling stitches within the area [9c], using the cordonnet as you would normally do in any piece of lace. You have the added advantage that any starts and joins in the working thread can be made on the calico or interfacing at the back, so as to give a neat appearance.

The stitch used here was the 'lattice-type' filling, with beads added into the cord row where desired (refer back to *Using beads* in Part I if necessary). End the lace filling carefully at any visible edges.

6 Now that the lace area is complete, make the cord using the same thread which was used for the lace stitches. You will need to make a **finished** cord approximately 140cm (56in) long (see *Making a handmade cord* in Part I).

The cord in the bag illustrated was made with four strands of the Fil Or Clair doubled over and knotted prior to being twisted into the cord [9d].

7 Using a fine gold thread for the stitching down of the cord, start at 1 (with the neat loop-end of the twisted cord **not** the knot), carefully attaching the cord as invisibly as possible exactly on the cordonnet almost as far as 4 — about 1cm ($\frac{3}{8}$in) away.

Make sure the stitches are hidden by working them in the same direction along the twist of the cord [9e]. This also stops the cord 'rolling about' on the velvet pile.

Do not cut off the cord here. The lining will be attached next and

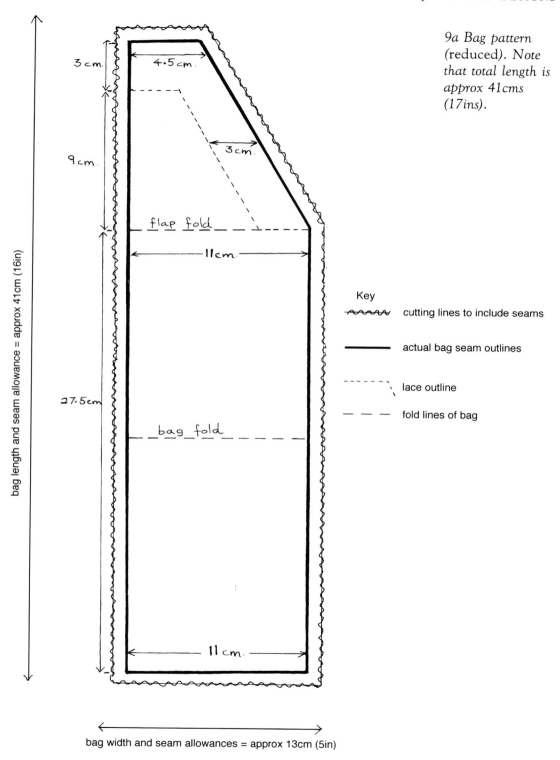

9a Bag pattern (reduced). Note that total length is approx 41cms (17ins).

3 cm.

4·5 cm.

3 cm.

9 cm.

flap fold

11cm.

27·5cm.

bag fold

11 cm.

bag length and seam allowance = approx 41cm (16in)

bag width and seam allowances = approx 13cm (5in)

Key

~~~~~~ cutting lines to include seams

——— actual bag seam outlines

------- lace outline

— — — fold lines of bag

9b Marking out the lacefilling area (on the underside).

Key

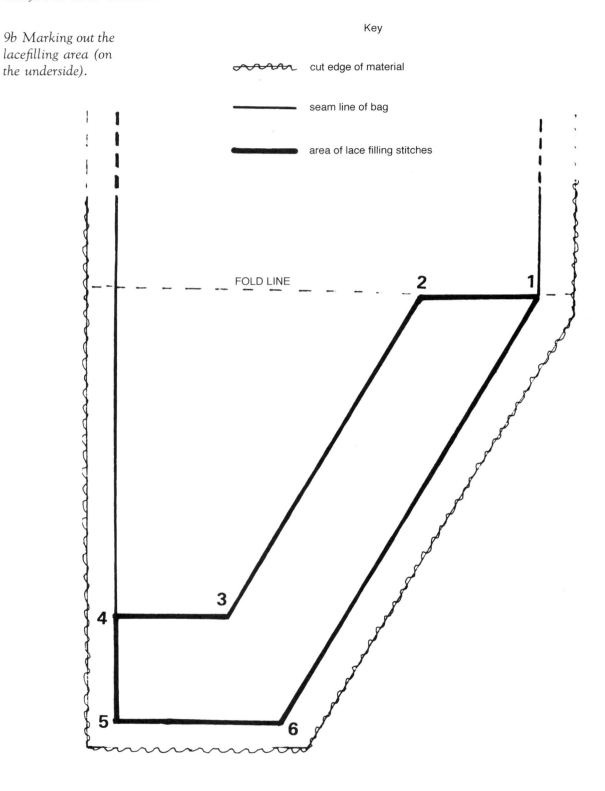

Key

 cordonnet

⟵————⟶ direction of rows

9c Direction of working the lace filling (on the right side of the fabric).

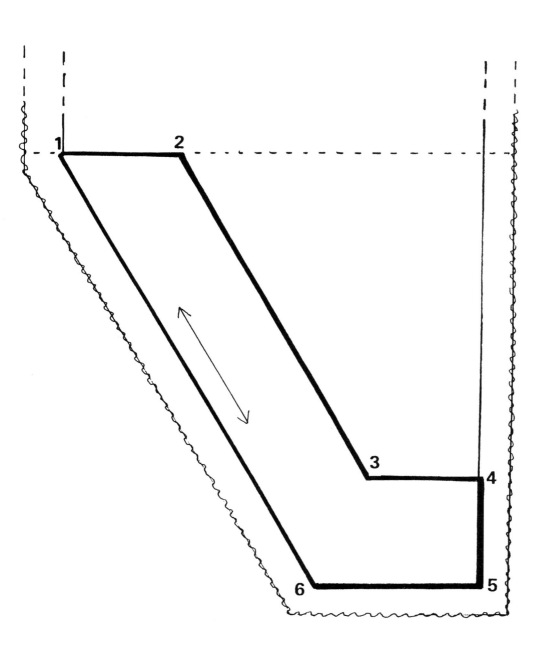

*9d Four doubled-
over strands used to
make the bag cord.*

*9e Stitching down
the cord.*

then the stitching down of the cord will be continued along the finished edge to cover the seam.

8 Using the lining material (cut to the bag pattern) lay this and the bag material **right** sides together. Tack and then machine, or back-stitch, around the outside edge, leaving only the top edge between 7 and 8 open [9f] so that you can turn the bag right-side out. Take care not to catch the cord anywhere in the stitching.

Trim the seams as necessary, but not too close, and turn the bag right-side out. (The remainder of the cord should be left for the moment — **don't** cut it off.)

9 Cut out a piece of light-weight card if added firmness is desired for the bag flap. This will obviously be cut to fit exactly into the flap and not come above the fold-line on the flap.

Carefully push this card down so that it stays exactly in position within the flap. A few invisible catch stitches can be used to keep it in place.

10 Hand-stitch the top seam of the bag (7–8), using a matching thread. If the material is suitable (not velvet) press the bag at this stage by gently ironing it.

Carefully fold the bag into position and then stitch the side seams together [9g]. Use a ladder-type stitch.

11 The remainder of the lace cordonnette is then completed by continuing the stitching-down of the cord along the bag flap edge seam until it meets the start at 1. Anchor the stitching firmly here and end off the thread. **Do not cut off the cord.**

The remainder of the cord forms the bag's strap, with the other end invisibly attached on the opposite side [9h]. Do this by opening a tiny length of the machining, poking through the knot end of the

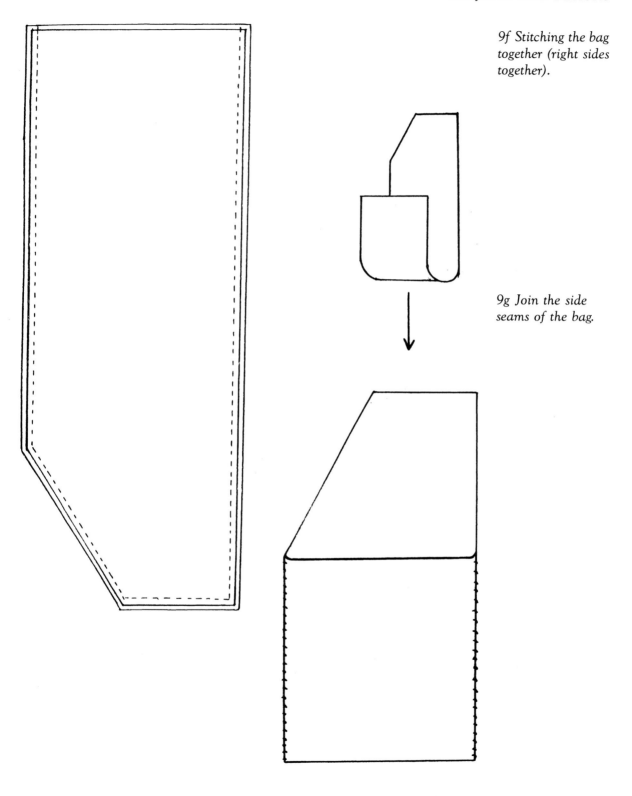

9f Stitching the bag together (right sides together).

9g Join the side seams of the bag.

9h The bag's cord strap continuing from the cordonnette.

9i Needlepoint lace buttons.

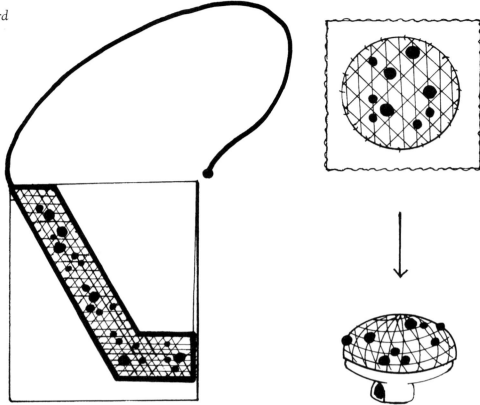

cord and then carefully stitching the seam together again. Make sure that the cord handle is securely fastened.)

12 Finally, attach a small press-stud or fastener to hold the bag's flap closed.

Project 9: Further design ideas

Matching buttons could be made using the same material as the bag. Work 'lattice-type' stitches and beads onto the material before making up the buttons. Many stores stock button shapes which can be easily covered [9i].

A belt could be designed and worked in a similar manner to the bag, repeating the lace pattern if desired.

You could also make a 'patchwork-effect' bag, using a mixture of materials such as velvet, satin, soft suede and leather, etc. Areas could then be worked in lace stitches [9j].

Another possibility could be to hand-dye or silk-paint the fabric for the bag's background material, upon which the area of needlepoint lace could be worked in toning or contrasting silk thread.

9j 'Patchwork-
effect' bag.

Project 10 3-D dragonfly ★★

Sometimes a particular thread sparks off an idea for a piece of lace — that was how this Emperor dragonfly came into being. I saw a beautiful greyish-bluish-greenish thread and immediately thought of dragonfly wings!

The Emperor dragonfly illustrated was worked in soft-coloured blue and black silks. The wings were worked on a fine wire cordonnet. The dragonfly was then mounted on a painted silk background and so formed an attractive picture. (Details of how to make a simple painted background follow the dragonfly working instructions.)

Materials required

Body

- Soft-coloured, blue 100/3 twisted silk thread. Gutermann 100/3 silk thread, number 964 was used here
- Black 100/3 silk thread
- 1 short length of medium pipecleaner and some cotton wool for stuffing
- 2 black beads for eyes
- Short length of stiff black thread for legs and antennae
- Calico backing
- Adhesive acetate, cartridge paper

Wings

- Fairly fine silver wire, about 60cm (24in) long. A medium fuse wire was used here
- Medium-fine irridescent thead. Supertwist number 30, colour 370 was used here
- Short length of fine black silk thread (or cotton) for the black wing tip markings

Method

1 Trace the dragonfly body and wings [10a] onto the paper, and place under contrasting adhesive acetate. Tack onto the calico backing foundation in the usual manner.

2 Couch down the body cordonnet. This is mainly worked in blue silk (later used for the lace), but the head and central abdomen line have a black cordonnet.

Diagram 10b shows a simple way of joining in the central black abdomen line. **Note** – this is also a suitable method of joining any cordonnet thread to an already couched down cordonnet. It is very useful if you find that you have missed out an area of cordonnet!

Useful hints

1 The wire for the wings' outline cordonnet will be fairly soft so make sure that it does not get distorted out of shape as you work the lace or as you put the dragonfly together.

2 Use a contrasting adhesive acetate to help you see the fine stitches more easily.

The body is worked in close corded single Bruxelles stitch, the rows going in the direction of the arrows on the pattern.

The head is worked in black, the thorax in blue with two fine black stripes (these are shown as dotted lines on the design).

The abdomen is worked in blue with fine black stripes or streaks

10a 3-D Dragonfly pattern.

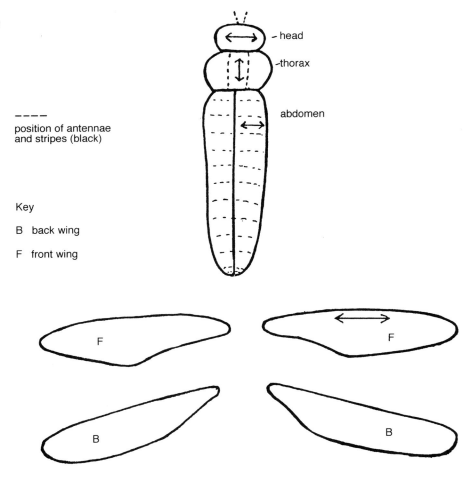

———

position of antennae and stripes (black)

Key

B   back wing

F   front wing

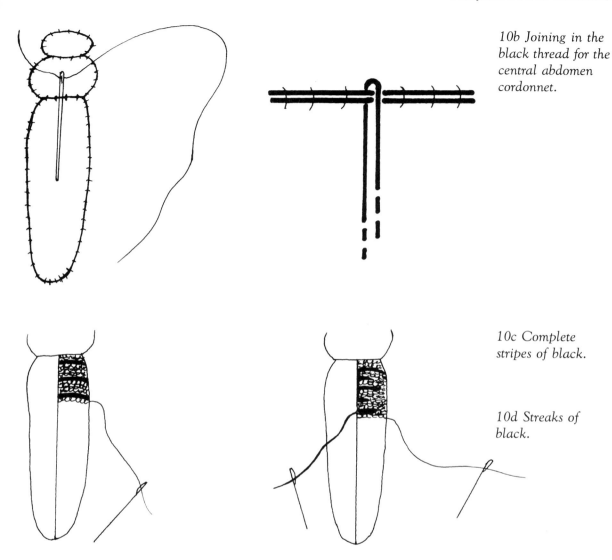

10b Joining in the black thread for the central abdomen cordonnet.

10c Complete stripes of black.

10d Streaks of black.

going around it at fairly regular intervals. These may either be worked in as complete stripes [10c], or you can use two needles to alternate long and short streaks of black on the blue body [10d].

Do not work a cordonnette.

3 Couch down the silver wire cordonnet outline for the wings, making sure that you have a good overlap and interlocking each end to prevent any unravelling [10e].

Using the irridescent thread (cut enough to avoid having to join another length), work two rows of fairly spaced out whipped single Bruxelles stitches at the top area of the wing [10f]. Then complete the rest of the wing area in irregular spaced single Bruxelles stitches so

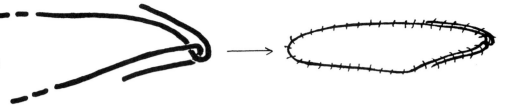

10e Interlocking
and overlapping
the wire cordonnet
at the inner wing
ends.

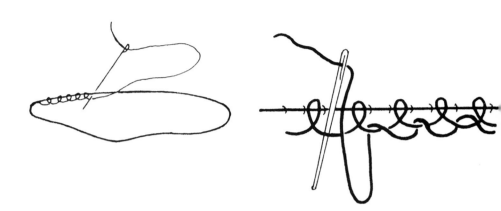

10f Whipped
single Bruxelles
stitches at the top
edge of the wing
(the whipping
stitches are shown
slacker for clarity
— they will be
tighter in the actual
work).

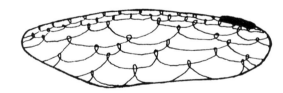

10g Position of
black buttonhole-
stitch marking on
outer wing tip end.

10h Gathering
stitches around the
worked body.

10i Sewing the
antennae thread to
the underside of the
head.

that it looks like the veined wings of a dragonfly. You might find it helpful to look at illustrations of these insects that show this veining.

Using a fine black thread, work a short length — 4–5mm ($\frac{1}{6}$–$\frac{1}{4}$in) — of close buttonhole stitches ('knots' facing outwards) along the top of the wing cordonnet near the outer wing tip [10g].

4 **Carefully** remove the completed body and wings in the usual manner (by cutting between the two calico foundation layers etc.).

5 Make up the dragonfly. Start at the head, and run a gathering thread of tiny running stitches around the body close to the edge [10h].

Next, cut the pipecleaner to a suitable length. It needs to fit inside the dragonfly's body. Add a small amount of cotton wool to the head and thorax portions of the pipecleaner as necessary.

Gently draw up the gathering thread, positioning the pipecleaner and cotton wool stuffing inside. When it is completely drawn up, catch-stitch the edge carefully — this will be positioned centrally underneath the body — so that the dragonfly body is formed.

Sew the two small black beads near the side of the head as eyes and add a short length of the stiff black thread to form antennae. I did this by sewing it in firmly [10i].

Carefully attach the four wings to the underside of the thorax with a few firm stitches at the inner wing ends.

Use three short (about 3–5cm or 1$\frac{1}{4}$–2in) lengths of the stiff black thread to make the six legs [10j]. If necessary, the thread could be waxed slightly to give it more body.

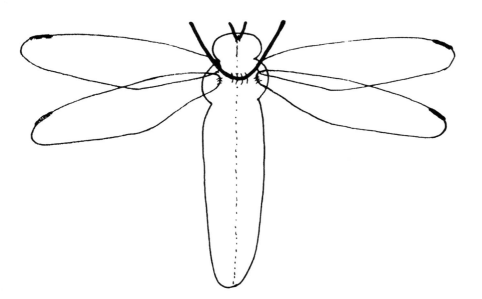

10j First pair of legs (one thread) attached to underside of thorax.

Finally, arrange the wings and body shape as desired. Try to make the dragonfly's position look as natural as possible.

The dragonfly illustrated was carefully attached to a painted silk background with a few tiny stitches.

Making a simple painted silk background

A painted silk background can really enhance a particular piece of lace. The dragonfly in project 10 is relatively small, but placed on a simple painted scene of soft colours (within a pale grey mount in a silver frame) it became quite an eyecatching picture (see back cover).

The following method is a simple and quick way to achieve an effective painted background using only a few colours. There are also many excellent books on the market which will give you the techniques of painting on fabric.

Method

A wide range of silk paints are available. The ones used in the dragonfly picture were Orient Express, painted onto a medium-weight white habutai silk.

1 Secure a piece of medium-weight habutai silk **tautly** in a plastic embroidery frame or over a plastic lid with an elastic band [1]. Make sure that the area will be big enough for your picture.
2 Put small quantities of the colours onto a china palette or an old saucer and have a jar of clean water ready, together with a medium and a slightly thicker painting brush (a wedge-shaped one is excellent for skies and large areas).

Useful hints

1 It really is simple so work with confidence and panache! Too much fussy 'painting' could spoil it.
2 You do **not** need to be able to draw, just have a rough idea of the basic scene you intend to convey.
3 Keep the silk taut in a plastic embroidery ring, or, if it is small, secured over a plastic box or lid with an elastic band.
4 Try a small background first, so that you can see what the silk and paints do. Always refer to the instructions on the type of fabric paints you choose.
5 Since a picture is not going to be washed, you do not need to 'fix' it with a chemical fixative. (Some silk paints are 'fixed' by ironing to make them permanent.)

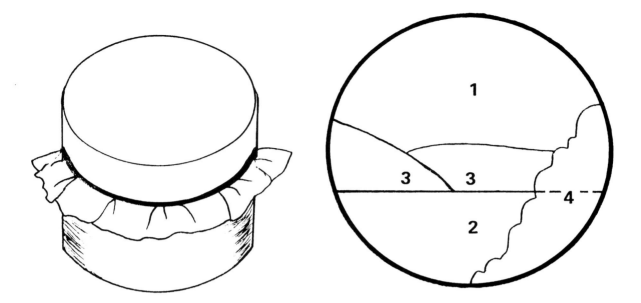

3 Decide on the order of painting. I usually do the sky first (1), together with any water (2), and then the foreground (3), together with any trees and hills (4) [2].

4 For the sky (and water) use blue, diluting it with water to make it fairly pale. Paint in the sky (and any water) **quickly**, then add a little more blue and (again quickly) stroke a few streaks of this colour across the damp, painted area. The colours should all blend and merge.

5 Using the desired colours, now paint in the main background and then the foreground. Remember that hills in the background will look paler and softer than features in the foreground. The colours can be used over each other whilst damp. You will soon learn how the silk and paints react together.

  If you want to halt the 'blending and merging' you can use a hairdryer to dry the silk.

  Trees and bushes can be added as 'blobs' or 'splodges'; to give a natural effect use two or more colour greens.

6 When the silk painting is dry, remove it from the ring or lid and iron

1 Silk held tautly over a plastic lid with an elastic band.

2 My own order of painting a background scene.

Useful hint

If you don't like your finished painting, don't throw it away. Small areas can probably be used for tiny greetings cards.

it on the back to smooth the silk (first putting an old piece of cloth or sheeting over the ironing board to stop any possible marking of your ironing board).

7 It is a good idea to hold a cardboard picture mount, or a mounting card's aperture over the painting, to see which colour surround looks best [3]. Generally, a soft or dark olive-green goes with a greeny landscape scene, and grey or blue with water, but try the effect of pale yellow, soft brown, etc. It will also depend upon the lace to be used.

8 Depending upon its use, the silk can be attached by lacing, double-sided sellotape or masking tape to the card that goes under the opening. However, these should not be attached too close to the painted scene.

When placing the lace on your mounted silk be fussy about it, since the position often makes a great difference [4]. Remember, you can often turn the mount sideways [5].

Attach the lace to the fabric with a few invisible stitches. A long beading needle is very helpful here if the silk background is mounted first.

3 Cardboard picture mount held over the painted silk to see the visual effect.

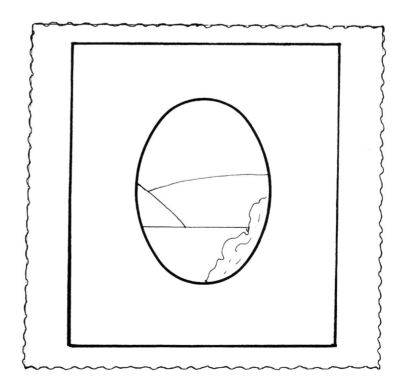

4 Upright mount.

5 Mount turned lengthways — a different perspective may be achieved.

Project 10: Further design ideas
The dragonfly could form part of an embroidered picture, which will thus add further three-dimensional interest. It could also be perched on a dried flower arrangement!

Bibliography

Clabburn, Pamela, *Beadwork*, Shire Publications, 1980
Grimwood, Valerie, *Starting Needlepoint Lace*, Batsford, 1989
Hills, Ros and Gibson, Pat, *Needlework Stitches: Classic and Contemporary*, Batsford, 1989
Kieboom, Ineke van den and Huijben, Anny, *Naaldkant*, Terra
Thompson, Angela, *Embroidery with Beads*, Batsford, 1987

Book suppliers

The following are stockists of the Batsford/Dryad Press range:

England

AVON
Bridge Bookshop
7 Bridge Street
Bath BA2 4AS

Waterstone & Company
4–5 Milsom Street
Bath BA1 1DA

BEDFORSHIRE
Arthur Sells
Lane Cover
49 Pedley Lane
Clifton
Shefford SG17 5QT

BUCKINGHAMSHIRE
J. S. Sear
Lacecraft Supplies
8 Hillview
Sherington MK16 9NJ

CAMBRIDGESHIRE
Dillons the Bookstore
Sidney Street
Cambridge

CHESHIRE
Lynn Turner
Church Meadow Crafts
7 Woodford Road
Winsford

DEVON
Creative Crafts &
Needlework
18 High Street
Totnes TQ9 5NP

Honiton Lace Shop
44 High Street
Honiton EX14 8PJ

DORSET
F. Herring & Sons
27 High West Street
Dorchester DT1 1UP

Tim Parker *(mail order)*
124 Corhampton Road
Boscombe East
Bournemouth BH6 5NZ

Christopher Williams
19 Morrison Avenue
Parkstone
Poole BH17 4AD

ESSEX
J.H. Clarke & Co. Ltd
2 Exchange Way ·
Chelmsford
Essex CM1 1XQ

GLOUCESTERSHIRE
Southgate Handicrafts
63 Southgate Street
Gloucester GL1 1TX

Waterstone & Company
89–90 The Promenade
Cheltenham GL50 1NB

HAMPSHIRE
Creative Crafts
11 The Square
Winchester SO23 9ES

Doreen Gill
14 Barnfield Road
Petersfield GU31 4DR

Needlestyle
24–26 West Street
Alresford

Ruskins
27 Bell Street
Romsey

ISLE OF WIGHT
Busy Bobbins
Unit 7
Scarrots Lane
Newport PO30 1JD

KENT
The Handicraft Shop
47 Northgate
Canterbury CT1 1BE

Hatchards
The Great Hall
Mount Pleasant Road
Tunbridge Wells

LONDON
W. & G. Foyle Ltd
113–119 Charing Cross
Road
WC2H OEB

Hatchards
187 Piccadilly W1V 9DA

MIDDLESEX
Redburn Crafts
Squires Garden Centre
Halliford Road
Upper Halliford
Shepperton TW17 8RU

NORFOLK
Stitches and Lace
Alby Craft Centre
Cromer Road
Alby
Norwich NR11 7QE

Waterstone & Company
30 London Street
Norwich NR2 1LD

NORTH YORKSHIRE
Craft Basics
9 Gillygate
York

The Craft House
23 Bar Street
Scarborough YO13 9QE

SOMERSET
Bridge Bookshop
62 Bridge Street
Taunton TA1 1UD

STAFFORDSHIRE
J. & J. Ford (*mail order*
& lace days only)
October Hill
Upper Way
Upper Longdon
Rugeley WS15 1QB

SUSSEX
Waterstone & Company
120 Terminus Road
Eastbourne

WARWICKSHIRE
Christine & David
   Springett
21 Hillmorton Road
Rugby CV22 6DF

WEST MIDLANDS
Needlewoman
21 Needles Alley
off New Street
Birmingham B2 5AG

WEST YORKSHIRE
Sebalace
Waterloo Mill
Howden Road
Silsden BD20 0HA

George White
   Lacemaking Supplies
40 Heath Drive
Boston Spa LS23 6PB

Just Lace
Lacemaker Supplies
14 Ashwood Gardens
Gildersome
Leeds LS27 7AS

Jo Firth
58 Kent Crescent
Lowtown, Pudsey
Leeds LS28 9EB

WILTSHIRE
Everyman Bookshop
5 Bridge Street
Salisbury SP1 2ND

Scotland

Embroidery Shop
51 William Street
Edinburgh
Lothian EH3 7LW

Watertone & Company
236 Union Street
Aberdeen AB1 1TN

Wales

Bryncraft Bobbins
(*mail order*)
B. J. Phillips
Pantglas
Cellan
Lampeter
Dyfed SA48 8JD

Hilkar Lace Suppliers
33 Mysydd Road
Landore
Swansea

Equipment suppliers

England

BEDFORDSHIRE
A. Sells
49 Pedley Lane
Clifton
Shefford SG17 5QT

BERKSHIRE
Chrisken Bobbins
26 Cedar Drive
Kingsclere RG15 8TD

BUCKINGHAMSHIRE
J. S. Sear
Lacecraft Supplies
8 Hillview
Sherington MK16 9NJ

Winslow Bobbins
70 Magpie Way
Winslow MK18 3PZ

SMP
4 Garners Close
Chalfont St Peter SL9 0HB

CAMBRIDGESHIRE
Josie and Jeff Harrison
Walnut Cottage
Winwick
Huntingdon PE17 5PP

Heffers Graphic Shop
(*matt coloured transparent*
adhesive film)
26 King Street
Cambridge CB1 1LN

Spangles
Carole Morris
Cashburn Lane
Burwell CB5 0ED

CHESHIRE
Lynn Turner
Church Meadow Crafts
7 Woodford Road
Winsford

DEVON
Honiton Lace Shop
44 High Street
Honiton EX14 8PJ

DORSET
Frank Herring & Sons
27 High West Street
Dorchester DT1 1UP

T. Parker (mail order,
general and bobbins**)**
124 Corhampton Road
Boscombe East
Bournemouth BH6 5NZ

ESSEX
Threads 'n Things
60 Arnold Road
Clacton-on-Sea CO15 1DG

GLOUCESTERSHIRE
T. Brown (bobbins**)**
Temple Lane Cottage
Littledean
Cinderford

Chosen Crafts Centre
46 Winchcombe Street
Cheltenham GL52 2ND

HAMPSHIRE
Needlestyle
24–26 West Street
Alresford

Richard Viney (bobbins**)**
Unit 7
Port Roval Street
Southsea PO5 3UD

ISLE OF WIGHT
Busy Bobbins
Unit 7
Scarrots Lane
Newport
PO30 1JD

KENT
The Handicraft Shop
47 Northgate
Canterbury CT1 1BE

Denis Hornsby
25 Manwood Avenue
Canterbury CT2 7AH

Francis Iles
73 High Street
Rochester ME1 1LX

LANCASHIRE
Malcolm J. Fielding (*bob-
bins*)
2 Northern Terrace
Moss Lane
Silverdale LA5 0ST

LINCOLNSHIRE
Ken and Pat Schultz
Whynacres
Shepeau Stow
Whaplode Drove
Spalding PE12 0TU

MERSEYSIDE
Hayes & Finch
Head Office & Factory
Hanson Road
Aintree
Liverpool L9 9BP

MIDDLESEX
Redburn Crafts
Squires Garden Centre
Halliford Road
Upper Halliford
Shepperton TW17 8RU

NORFOLK
Stitches and Lace
Alby Craft Centre
Cromer Road
Alby
Norwich NR11 7QE

Jane's Pincushions
Taverham Craft Unit 4
Taverham Nursery Centre
Fir Covert Road
Taverham
Norwich NR8 6HT

George Walker
The Corner Shop
Rickinghall, Diss

NORTH HUMBERSIDE
Teazle Embroideries
35 Boothferry Road
Hull

NORTH YORKSHIRE
The Craft House
23 Bar Street
Scarborough

Stitchery
Finkle Street
Richmond

SOUTH YORKSHIRE
D. H. Shaw
47 Lamor Crescent
Thrushcroft
Rotherham S66 9PQ

STAFFORDSHIRE
J. & J. Ford (*mail order
and lace days only*)
October Hill
Upper Way
Upper Longdon
Rugeley WS15 1QB

SUFFOLK
A. R. Archer (*bobbins*)
The Poplars
Shetland
near Stowmarket IP14 3DE

Mary Collins (*linen by the
metre, and made up articles*
of church linen)
Church Furnishings
St Andrews Hall
Humber Doucy Lane
Ipswich IP4 3BP

E. & J. Piper (*silk
embroidery and lace thread*)
Silverlea
Flax Lane
Glemsford CO10 7RS

Vycombe Art (*fabric
paints*)
High House
Parham IP13 9LX

SURREY
Needle and Thread
80 High Street
Horsell
Working GU21 4SZ

Needlestyle
5 The Woolmead
Farnham GU9 7TX

SUSSEX
Southern Handicrafts
20 Kensington Gardens
Brighton BN1 4AC

WARWICKSHIRE
**Christine & David
Springett**
21 Hillmorton Road
Rugby CV22 5DF

WEST MIDLANDS
Framecraft
83 Hampstead Road
Handsworth Wood
Birmingham B2 1JA

The Needlewoman
21 Needles Alley
off New Street
Birmingham B2 5AE

Stitches
Dovehouse Shopping
Parade
Warwick Road
Olton, Solihull

WEST YORKSHIRE
Jo Firth
Lace Marketing &
Needlecraft Supplies
58 Kent Crescent
Lowtown
Pudsey LS28 9EB

Just Lace
Lacemaker Supplies
14 Ashwood Gardens
Gildersome
Leeds LS27 7AS

Sabalace
Waterloo Mills
Howden Road
Silsden BD20 0HA

**George White Lacemak-
ing Supplies**
40 Heath Drive
Boston Spa LS23 6PB

WILTSHIRE
Doreen Campbell (*frames
and mounts*)
Highcliff
Bremilham Road
Malmesbury SN16 0DQ

Scotland

Christine Riley
53 Barclay Street
Stonehaven
Kincardineshire

Peter & Beverley Scarlett
Strupak
Hill Head
Cold Wells, Ellon
Grampian

Wales

Bryncraft Bobbins
B. J. Phillips
Pantglas
Cellan
Lampeter
Dyfed SA48 8JD

Hilkar Lace Suppliers
33 Mysydd Road
Landore
Swansea

Australia

Australian Lace magazine
P.O. Box 609
Manly
NSW 2095

Dentelles Lace Suppliers
c/o Betty Franks
39 Lang Terrace
Northgate 4013
Brisbane
Queensland

The Lacemaker
724a Riversdale Road
Camberwell
Victoria 3124

Spindle and Loom
83 Longueville Road
Lane Cove
NSW 2066

Tulis Crafts
201 Avoca Street
Randwick
NSW 2031

New Zealand

Peter McLeavey
P.O. Box 69.007
Auckland 8

USA

Arbor House
22 Arbor House
Roslyn Heights
NY 11577

Baltazor Inc.
3262 Severn Avenue
Metairie
LA 7002

Beggars' Lace
P.O. Box 481223
Denver
Colo 80248

Berga Ullman Inc.
P.O. Box 918
North Adams
MA 01247

Happy Hands
3007 S. W. Marshall
Pendleton
Oreg 97180

**International Old
    Lacers Inc.**
124 West Irvington Place
Denver
CO 80223-1539

The Lacemaker
23732-G Bothell Hwy, SE
Bothell
WA 98021

Lace Place de Belgique
800 S.W. 17th Street
Boca Raton
FL 33432

Lacis
3163 Adeline Street
Berkeley
CA 94703

Robin's Bobbins
RT1 Box 1736
Mineral Bluff
GA 30559-9736

**Robin and Russ
    Handweavers**
533 North Adams Street
McMinnville
Oreg 97128

**The Unique And Art
    Lace Cleaners**
5926 Delman Boulevard
St Louis
MO 63112

Unicorn Books
Glimakra Looms 'n Yarns
Inc.
1304 Scott Street
Petaluma
CA 94954-1181

Van Sciver Bobbin Lace
130 Cascadilla Park
Ithaca
NY 14850

The World in Stitches
82 South Street
Milford
N.H. 03055

Sources of information

United Kingdom

The British College of
Lace
21 Hillmorton Road
Rugby
War CV22 5DF

The Lace Guild
The Hollies
53 Audnam
Stourbridge
West Midlands DY8 4AE

The Lacemakers' Circle
49 Wardwick
Derby DE1 1HY

The Lace Society
Linwood
Stratford Road
Oversley
Alcester
War BY9 6PG

Guild of Needlelaces
Mrs June Dawkins
Netherlea
39 Moor Road
Breadsall
Derby DE7 6AA

**United Kingdom Director
of International Old
Lacers**
S. Hurst
4 Dollis Road
London N3 1RG

USA

International Old Lacers
124 West Irvington Place
Denver
Co 80223–1539

Lace & Craft magazine
3201 East Lakeshore Drive
Tallahassee
FL 32312–2034

OIDFA
(International Bobbin and
Needle Lace Organization)
Kathy Kauffmann
1301 Greenwood
Wilmette
IL 60091

Index

The GIY Diaries

Michael Kelly is the founder of GIY, a social entrepreneur, author, TV presenter and grower. He worked in the IT industry for 10 years before starting GIY in 2008. GIY is now a leading social enterprise, with its home, GROW HQ, in Waterford. Michael co-presented and produced three series of *Grow Cook Eat* for RTÉ and will present the upcoming series *Food Matters* in 2023. He writes columns on food for the *Irish Times, Irish Independent* and *Food & Wine Magazine.* He was the 2017 Local Food Hero in the Food & Wine Awards. He lives in Dunmore East with his wife, Eilish, and their two young children.

Sarah Kilcoyne is a painter-illustrator from Tipperary, Ireland. She moved to Berlin, Germany, in 2011 after graduating from the Limerick School of Art & Design, and has been working as a freelance illustrator ever since. She uses traditional illustration techniques, hand-painting in watercolour, ink and coloured pencil.

The
GIY
DIARIES

A YEAR OF GROWING AND COOKING

Michael Kelly

Gill Books

Gill Books
Hume Avenue
Park West
Dublin 12
www.gillbooks.ie

Gill Books is an imprint of M.H. Gill and Co.

9780717195077

Designed by Bartek Janczak
Illustrated by Sarah Kilcoyne
Edited by Jane Rogers
Proofread by Kristin Jensen
Indexed by Adam Pozner
Printed and bound by Białostockie Zakłady Graficzne S.A, Poland
This book is typeset in 11.25 on 15.5pt Minion Pro.

The paper used in this book comes from the wood pulp of sustainably managed forests.

A CIP catalogue record for this book is available from the British Library.

5 4 3 2 1

contents

introduction

It barely seems possible, but I've been growing my own food for nearly 20 years now. I don't quite know how that happened or where the time went. I'll save you from the monotony of my 'garlic story', which is how it all began, but I still remember the excitement of producing food – MYSELF and IN MY OWN BACK GARDEN! It seemed like magic, like a form of alchemy, that food could be coaxed from my unpromising soil and with my unpromising amount of growing knowledge. A (slightly diluted) version of that excitement still visits me each time I harvest veg in the garden all these years later.

Over the years, the soil has improved and my knowledge has grown. In some ways I find it remarkable that I've learned so much, and yet in other ways I find it strange that I still seem to have so much to learn. The veg patch remains as it has always been: my great teacher. It teaches me about food growing (and I learn equal amounts from my successes as I do from my failures), but it also teaches me about food more generally. In GIY, we talk often about how the real impact of food growing happens outside the veg patch – as our knowledge develops, we become more 'food empathetic' and we become more ethical consumers. We make different, better, more sustainable buying decisions.

Food growing has taught me about soil and how we can create healthy living soil by replacing the nutrients we take from it during the growing year. It has taught me about the connection between soil health, nutrition and flavour – in fact, I am now convinced that you can actually taste the life of the soil in the veg you grow yourself. Food growing has helped me to tap into the wisdom of nature when it comes to what to eat at different times of the year. It has taught me about the effort and skill it takes to grow food successfully, and therefore to value the genius of the growers and farmers who put food on our table and the importance of paying them a fair price for their produce.

It has taught me how much fun it is to eat more plants (and therefore less meat) and to eat more parts of the plants that I grow. It has taught me how tragic food waste is and how all food can be either preserved or turned into compost to feed the soil. It has taught me lessons about the role that the natural world plays in putting food on the table – how to work with nature rather than against it (and to never, ever use chemicals). At times, the veg patch has even taught me how to be more mindful – how to silence the endless chatter in my mind and appreciate the wonders around me. In some ways the veg patch is a lens through which I can understand the world better – or at least the food chain and my part in it. So I am grateful for all it has taught me, but I am also grateful that it has quietly, generously and without fail fed us as a family – countless delicious, wholesome meals served at our kitchen table, which looks out on the very place where the food is grown. I don't think you can live better than that.

For most of that 20-year journey, I have kept a diary of my efforts in one form or another, either through columns in various newspapers and magazines or as scrawled entries in mud-stained garden diaries. Reading them again to put together this book, I was struck by two things: the common threads that run through all the years (the progress of the seasons, the highs and lows, the vagaries of weather, etc.) and just how different every growing year is. As a single representative year, this diary is, I think, a highlights reel of sorts. I hope you enjoy reading it as much as I've enjoyed growing the veg (and eating it …).

Michael Kelly

january

A new year and a new growing season – we emerge from our winter hibernation brimming with foolish New Year enthusiasm. Don't forget, it's still the depths of winter, so while it's a good month to get yourself ready, hold off until next month to sow seeds if you can.

This month we're loving … parsnips.

Tough as old boots and often unappreciated in the kitchen. At this time of the year we love their earthy goodness.

New Year's resolutions sometimes get a bad rap because they seem to represent the folly and flightiness of the human spirit. We start off the year with grand intentions to eat only salads and run a hundred miles a week. But then by mid-January we've quietly and guiltily abandoned our good intentions and reverted to type.

This year, make a simple resolution that can transform your life: grow food. And before you think that sounds like a resolution that might involve significant effort, life changes or all-round hassle on your part, fear not – you won't have to buy a pair of Birkenstocks (though they are cool again in case you didn't know). It doesn't have to be a huge amount of food. We're not talking 100 per cent self-sufficiency or living off the grid. It's not scary or daunting.

Here are the Don'ts: Don't spend a load of money on expensive garden equipment, books or tools. Don't grow a goatee. Don't dig up your garden or sign up for an allotment. Don't learn Latin for reading the plant names. For now, we're keeping it small-scale, achievable, practical. Unlike most of our resolutions, this one is about working with (rather than against) our limitations – our lack of time, lack of space, lack of knowledge.

Just grow food. Grow some salad leaves in a container. Stick a pea in some potting compost in a pot. Grow your own garlic. Or some herbs on your balcony. Start small. Pick three vegetables that you like to eat and learn how to grow those. How about setting yourself the target of producing an entirely home-grown meal? Just one little meal. That's easy, right?

Keep this in mind as you start. Research shows that if you grow some of your own food (even if it's only a little amount), your food habits may change. And this is down to the deeper understanding of and connection with food and the food system you will have because of your food growing experience – in GIY, we call this *food empathy*. You will be welcoming optimism and happiness into your life and saving some money in the process. You will also be out and about in the fresh air, getting some exercise at the same time. And you will have access to the most delicious, nutritious, seasonal food.

So forget about the Bikram yoga. This year, just grow food.

I love how when the year turns from old to new, my GIY life gets turned on its head. The end of the year becomes the beginning. The wind-down becomes the ramp-up. A dwindling to-do list looks very busy again. The sudden shift in tone in early January is dramatic.

I have often found my enthusiasm waning as the new growing year begins. But this year feels different. I am itching to get started.

Whether you're enthusiastic about it or not, it's always advisable to hold off until February to get started with the bulk of your seed sowing. Even the zany Celtic calendar sees January as winter. The days are too cold and short for successful seed sowing. As a result, the January to-do list is usually filled with silly jobs that no sensible GIYer would ever really be bothered with, such as sharpening your hoe, cleaning plant labels and the like.

This year, inexplicably, I find myself searching for silly jobs to get stuck in to. I've already cleaned out the potting shed and the polytunnel, so today I decided to sort out my seed box in advance of getting my seed order done. Unusually for me, I decided to be brutal with a cull of unneeded seeds. Though it might seem thrifty to hold on to seeds perpetually, it's generally a false economy in a busy growing year, particularly with slow-to-germinate vegetables. For example, it might take three weeks to discover that out-of-date celery or carrot seeds are, in fact, dead, by which time the window for sowing them might have passed.

Apart from occasional trips to grab some food for the table, I don't spend so much time in the veg patch in January – generally speaking, the garden is a cold and uninviting place at this time of the year. Thankfully my absence won't do much harm. The work I did getting beds cleared and covered with compost or seaweed in November and December means that the veg patch is pretty much in lockdown and enjoying its winter slumber.

Later in the month I will sow some seeds in the polytunnel for early crops – carrots direct in the soil and beetroot in the potting shed for later planting out. There are also still some crops to be cleared from the veg patch that I really should have done by now (celery and Brussels sprouts that are far past their best). But there's nothing madly urgent or pressing, so I'm relaxing (sort of) and taking a break.

Thankfully, the hungry gap – that time between having no food left in store and waiting for new-season crops to harvest – is still a few months away; there's still an abundance of food to be had from the garden and in stores. In the house we still have plenty of onions, garlic, squashes and pumpkins perched high up on shelves or on top of the kitchen dresser. We've plenty of sauerkraut, pickles and chutneys in the kitchen; these are a god-send, particularly for school lunches – a simple slice of ham or cold chicken can be turned into a serious sandwich with a good dollop of some chutney or pickle. We also have loads of tomato sauces, celery and beans in the freezer (a little bag of frozen broad beans is a lovely taste of summer in the depths of winter). In the garden we have carrots, leeks, celeriac, sprouts and parsnips in the ground; kale, spinach, chard and oriental leaves in the polytunnel; and some beetroot in a box of sand in the garage.

So, all in all, life is good.

You will often read in veg-growing books that it's a good idea to lift veg from the soil before the worst of the frosts. This is how I usually approach over-wintering veg: **5 january to lift or not to lift?**

1. **Carrots:** I generally leave them be, which admittedly means we lose some of them to munching from slugs later in the season. But honestly, I am happy to chop off any bad bits in the kitchen and I haven't had a great experience of storing carrots.
2. **Beetroot:** better to lift and store them. They store very well in a box of dry sand.
3. **Parsnips:** leave them in the soil. They are as tough as old boots, so go with it. The very odd times we have a hard frost or snow means you can't dig them out, but that's increasingly rare with our mild winters.
4. **Celeriac:** leave them in the soil. I've eaten celeriac direct from the soil as late as May, which is around the time I start sowing the next season's crop!

5. **Leeks:** leave them in the soil. With constant freezing and thawing they are inclined to go a little mushy in the long term, but leeks don't store well once lifted. Try to use them up by the end of this month.

Remember, as you clear beds, cover them with compost, well-rotted farmyard manure or seaweed, and then a protective cover like cardboard or reusable sheets of black polythene (weighed down with stones). Bare soil is not common in nature for a reason – valuable nutrients will be washed away during wet weather.

kale and smoked cheddar risotto

JB Dubois, our head chef, does this recipe on the Vegetarian Cooking course at GROW HQ. The idea is to show people that introducing a couple of veggie dinners into your repertoire each week can be healthy and delicious. Don't be put off by the idea of making your own stock – you can make it in half an hour, and it makes all the difference to the flavour of the risotto.

Serves 4
ingredients:
For the vegetable stock:
— 1 small carrot
— 1 small leek
— 1 stick of celery
— 2 cloves garlic
— 1 sprig thyme
— salt

For the risotto:
— 100g kale
— 1 carrot
— 1 clove garlic
— 100g Knockanore cheese (or other smoked cheddar)

- 20g butter
- 250g Arborio rice
- salt and pepper
- 1 litre veg stock
- toasted sesame and poppy seeds, to garnish
- squeeze of lemon juice, to finish

directions:

First make the veg stock. Wash, peel and roughly chop the vegetables and garlic. Place them and the thyme in a pot, cover with 1.5 litres of cold water and a pinch of salt. Bring to the boil and simmer for 20 minutes. Remove from the heat and allow to infuse for another 10 minutes, then pass through a fine sieve.

For the risotto, wash and chop the kale. Peel and grate the carrot. Peel and chop the garlic. Grate the smoked cheddar. Sweat the garlic with the butter in a large pot on a low heat for 2 minutes. Add the rice and sweat it off for 2–3 minutes (keep stirring to prevent it sticking). Add a good pinch of salt and pepper. Add the veg stock little by little, stirring every few minutes. The rice should be cooked when all the stock has been absorbed (15–20 minutes). When the rice is cooked, add the kale, the grated carrot and the grated cheese, give it a quick stir and serve immediately. Garnish with the toasted seeds. Add a squeeze of lemon juice.

7 january
seed
acquisition
disorder
(SAD)

Ordering seeds is always an enjoyable experience for me, since it marks the official start of the growing year. I am not a naturally acquisitive person and I only go shopping for clothes and things when I absolutely have to (and I will be grumpy for the entire time I'm there). But I absolutely love ordering seeds. In fact, I love it so much that pretty much every year I go dramatically OTT, ordering way more than I need. How could you not, with visions of exciting food-growing projects swirling around in your head? So many possibilities! Such wonderful names!

A couple of years ago, my seed box got damaged (long story) and I had to order seeds of every vegetable and herb that I grow. The order came to an eye-watering €300 … ouch! In my defence it's important to look on these things as a good investment, which of course it is. I've never accurately worked out the value of produce coming from the veg patch in a year, but some research I found a few years back indicated an approximate tenfold return. So, by that rule of thumb, €300 worth of seeds could yield €3,000 worth of food. And if that seems fanciful, bear in mind that a single courgette plant yields over 40 courgettes (worth €40) from a seed worth about 30 cents – that equates to produce worth 130 times the value of the seed! Of course, that doesn't take into account the incredible investment that food growing has on your health and wellbeing (and that of your family), never mind the sneaky carbon sequestering you are doing in the soil.

Before you start, sort through the seeds you already have to see what's usable. If you mind your seeds carefully (resealing the packet after use) and store them in a cool, dry place, they should be fine to reuse this year, as long as they are still in date. Discard any seeds that are out of date. I keep my seeds in a Tupperware box with a lid and keep it in the house in a relatively cool room. At least I do now, after the aforementioned accident …

My annual seed order is a thing of beauty, a perfect creation. The harsh realities of my ineptitude in the veggie patch and the crushing impact of pests and weather have yet to impact on its pristine brilliance. It is full of hope and expectation, a dream of a perfect GIY year. Long may it remain so.

Why am I advising you to wait until February to really kick on with seed sowing? Low heat levels are the main reason that we can't sow seeds successfully in January – most seeds just won't germinate when soil and air temperatures are low. But that can be fixed using an artificial source of heat. Low light levels are also an issue and can't be fixed so easily. Because there are only

8 january
the
problem
with
january
sowing

about 8–9 hours of daylight per day in January, a key problem with seeds sown at this time of the year is that the seedlings tend to become straggly or 'leggy', as they are literally straining for light. I know how they feel. Having said that, I often can't wait to get started and at least plant *something* – perhaps some oriental salad leaves and the like. You might get lucky and have a bright, warm January this year.

If you are going to sow at this time of the year, it might help to get your hands on a propagator, which is designed to increase the temperature for seedlings so that you can start your seed sowing earlier. A propagator is a shallow container into which you put your seed pots and trays – it has a removable plastic lid (often with a vent) that you take on and off depending on the temperature.

Propagators can be (a) unheated (b) heated or (c) heated with a thermostat control. An unheated propagator can be used indoors on a sunny windowsill at this time of the year, but it would probably be too cold at night to use in a greenhouse. A heated propagator is more beneficial (though more expensive). A unit with a thermostat control will automatically set the temperature to the desired level – a sensor will detect when it's too hot or cold and raise or lower the temperature accordingly. The Rolls-Royce version, if you will.

If you are raising a lot of seedlings and finding space in your propagator is an issue, it might be worth investing in a heating mat. It's a similar idea, but has a far larger surface area. My heating mat in the potting shed is about 2m long and has a heating element in it (much like an electric blanket), so the whole surface warms up. The mat rests on the work bench in the potting shed and I place pots and seed trays on top to keep them warm. If it's really cold, you can then cover the individual pots with upcycled plastic covers – I find old fruit punnets or freezer bags useful.

Of course, a windowsill in a very warm south-facing room in the house can often be a successful propagation space too (although kids and dogs put paid to that set-up in our house).

14

If ever there were a reason *not* to grow your own, the incredibly complex jargon that accompanies the hobby would surely be it. Books and courses and experienced GIYers talk about fine tilths, broadcasting, ridges, brassicas, legumes, furrows, modules and blocks – and that's only the start of the gobbledygook. To my mind these terms only achieve one thing: they make food growing sound more complicated and less accessible than it really is.

Of course, there are lots of things that can go wrong when you try to grow your own – there's a high chance slugs will eat half the stuff you grow and rabbits might get the rest. Your carrots might be zany-shaped and your cabbage leaves might have holes in them. Your courgettes will be too big and your tomatoes too small. Some veg won't grow and you won't know why, others will grow phenomenally well and you won't know why either. Let me assure you – even after growing food for around 17 years, I still have these problems. I still have epic failures. But *every* year (including the first year), I get to eat the finest of fresh, nutritious, delicious homegrown food.

Remember, at a basic level, seeds *want* to grow. That's the good news. Stick a seed in the soil and it will turn into a seedling and then eventually a plant, and finally the plant will produce some vegetables that you can eat. A leek seed is hardwired with all the information it needs to become a leek – you don't need to give it any special instructions on how to do so. All you need to do is provide it with the correct conditions and it will reward you with some lovely grub.

Polytunnels are a brilliant addition to your growing area, if you have the space and can afford to buy one. A polytunnel is basically just a big piece of clear plastic that creates a little patch of always-dry, always-warm veg garden, which means polytunnel owners can extend their season at both ends – starting a little earlier and keeping going a little later than you would if growing outside. This is, in fact, the main benefit of owning a tunnel.

So, even though it's far too wintry to be sowing seeds outside, the polytunnel is a place that doesn't abide too rigidly to the vagaries of the Irish climate. Despite being tempted to get stuck into seed sowing now, I'm practising patience and won't start sowing in earnest until next month, and it will be March before there is any sowing direct in the veg patch outside. In previous years I've started aubergines off this month from seed, using a heated mat in the potting shed. In fact, an early start with aubergines is often the difference between success and failure with this tricky-to-grow crop. But from experience, I know a very cold snap could wreak havoc on any January-sown seeds.

In other years I've also had success with direct sowings of carrots and potatoes in the polytunnel in January. With the carrot sowing, I had tender young carrots ready to eat in early May. That is a useful thing indeed, particularly as I tend to sow my maincrop carrots in May and they're not ready until September. January-sown spuds will most likely need a fleece cover to protect emerging plants from frost, even in the polytunnel. If it works, and temperatures don't dip consistently, you could be rewarded with a crop of new potatoes in early May, which could be two whole months before the outside crop. Don't plant too many, though – they might take up space needed in May for other, more valuable, crops like tomatoes, which will be ready to be planted out around then if sown in February.

It's also a great time of the year for some polytunnel love. No, not *that* type of polytunnel love – it's way too cold for that. Prevent tears and rips in the plastic turning into something more serious by applying special polytunnel repair tape. Clean your polytunnel and get rid of any build-up of dirt and green mould, which will reduce the amount of light available to plants over time. A long-handled soft brush with a bucket of hot soapy water is the best job for this. A ladder might be needed for getting to the top of the tunnel. Use a hose to rinse. Repeat on the inside, although you will need to wear rain gear! Recently someone told me that they clean the top of their polytunnel using a big sheet of bed linen, with a person on each side of the tunnel holding on to an end and pulling over and back as if it was a giant hanky. I'm officially intrigued.

In some ways, the great revelation of food growing is the importance of healthy soil and its connection to our own health. Healthy soils are not only the foundation for producing food, fuel and medical products; they are also essential to our ecosystems, playing a key role in the carbon cycle, storing and filtering water and improving resilience to floods and droughts. Soil is our 'silent ally'.

Our soils work hard. We will work them even harder in the decades to come – population growth will require a 60 per cent increase in food production – but instead of working to conserve and protect this precious resource, we're literally treating it like dirt. The world's soil is under immense pressure – it takes a thousand years to form a centimetre of soil, but we're losing it permanently (and at a dizzying pace) to relentless urbanisation to accommodate the expanding population. An area of soil the size of Costa Rica is lost every year, and here in Europe 11 hectares of life-giving soil are sealed under expanding cities every hour. Globally, a third of all our remaining soil is degraded by erosion, compaction, nutrient depletion and pollution. Given the role it plays in feeding us – with 95 per cent of our food coming from it – Indian environmental activist Vandana Shiva says that our determined destruction of the soil globally represents a 'species-level act of suicide'.

As GIYers we play an important part in the management of this critical resource, not only by our gentle stewardship of the soil in our own gardens, but also by developing a deeper understanding of how soil works (and sharing that knowledge with others). Of all the things I have learned about food growing, a deeper understanding of the soil has been perhaps the most important (and certainly the most satisfying). I am starting to understand that food growing is not about growing plants at all: it's about growing soil. If you get the soil right, the plants really look after themselves. Of course, that means many mucky, sweaty hours spent turning compost heaps, lugging barrows of farmyard manure or collecting seaweed, but that's okay too – you won't need a gym membership when you're a GIYer.

Gradually my soil at home has come to life – it's no longer the heavy potter's clay we had when we arrived here first, but friable and teeming with life. We GIYers are like 'nutrient shepherds', which sounds a little pretentious (okay, it sounds very pretentious), but it is indeed our job here – shepherding nutrients from the compost heap to the soil, to the plants, to the kitchen table and back to the compost heap again.

So this year, let's love our soil. Pick up big handfuls of it in your hands. Smell it. Stand in it in your bare feet. Care for it. Nurture it. It is literally where all life begins.

winter frittata

You can pretty much throw any combination of veg at this recipe and it will stand up to the abuse quite happily. It couldn't be simpler or more delicious. Serve hot or cold (a great lunchbox filler when cold).

Serves 6

ingredients:
— 600g mixed vegetables, such as onions, celeriac, carrots, squash or pumpkin, parsnip, beetroot, potatoes
— 1 large garlic clove, finely chopped
— 3 tbsp olive oil
— salt and pepper
— 6–8 large eggs
— a handful of mixed herbs (e.g. parsley, rosemary and thyme), finely chopped
— about 20g strong-flavoured hard cheese, grated (cheddar or Parmesan will do fine)

directions:
Preheat the oven to 180°C. Prep the veg: peel the onions and slice them thickly or cut into quarters; peel the carrots, parsnips, celeriac, beetroot, spuds and squash and cut into roughly equal chunks (about 2cm on average). Put in a lasagne dish, add the garlic, oil and plenty of seasoning and bake for about 40 minutes, until the veg are tender. About halfway through that time, it's a good plan to take the dish out and turn everything over with a spatula.

Beat the eggs together with the chopped herbs and some more salt and pepper. Take the dish from the oven, pour the egg evenly over the veg and scatter over the grated cheese. Return to the oven for 10–15 minutes, until the egg is set and the top is starting to colour. Leave to cool slightly, then slide the frittata out onto a plate or board. A slice of this is really a meal in itself, but for dinner I would serve with chips/baked potatoes and fresh salad leaves if you have them (or a celeriac remoulade or coleslaw).

A very simple way to think about soil fertility is this: each year we have to return the nutrients to the soil that we took from it the previous year when growing the veg. In practical terms that means covering the soil with a layer of one of the following each year: homemade compost, farmyard manure or fresh seaweed. While it would be great if I could produce enough compost at home to 'close the gate on fertility', in reality, I need a mixture of compost, seaweed and green manures (a sowing of grasses, like rye, that you grow specifically to protect or feed the soil) to cover all the beds in the veg patch. I have used farmyard manure over the years (from cows and horses) but have needed it less as I've increased the amount of compost I produce.

Homemade compost is the gold standard from a nutrition perspective, and happily it's something every one of us can produce easily at home (even the smallest garden can support a compost heap). I don't always get it right, but every year I think I am getting a little better at making compost. The key, I think, is to treat your heap (or heaps) not as a place where you can happily dump all manner of stuff from the kitchen and garden, but as if you were making a loaf of bread – you have to make sure you have the right mix of ingredients, bake it well and treat it with a little love.

I used to have some God-awful compost heaps– slimy, smelly, sludgy yokes that festered away in the corner of the garden. I had to avoid making eye contact with them each time I made a trip there. Part of the problem is that composting is always explained in a way that makes it sound highly technical. It's all carbon and nitrogen ratios and one would think you need a PhD in chemistry just to get involved. Any time anyone tried to explain the process of making compost to me, my eyes would glaze over and I would hear soothing music in my head while they talked.

So, let's get the science bit out of the way. In order for the material you've dumped on your heap to turn into compost, there has to be a mixture of nitrogen and carbon – roughly a fifty/fifty split, but it doesn't need to be too precise. The green stuff in the heap is high in nitrogen, while the brown stuff is high in carbon (see tips below). If you have a good mix of both, you will have the right balance and it will break down and turn into compost quickly. Too much green and you will get a really wet, sludgy heap – like many of my efforts over the years (the result of adding too much grass clippings). Too much brown and you get a really dry heap that won't rot quickly (but will rot eventually).

How long it takes to turn to compost depends on what's in it – it could be three months, but you will know when it's ready by the fact that you have dark, crumbly compost with no smell. You will get about 20–30 wheelbarrows of compost from a 1m x 1m compost heap, perhaps twice a year if it's functioning really well and making the compost quickly. That might sound like a lot of compost, but bear in mind that each winter you will need a wheelbarrow of compost for each square metre of veggie bed.

18 january
compost
tips

1. The smaller the materials and the layers you put on the heap, the quicker it will break down. Think of it like your own digestive system – if you chew your bread, it will be easy for your stomach to break down. If you swallow it whole, it won't. So, as a rule of thumb, chopping the materials with clippers will help. If you have bigger items, like cabbage stalks, bash them up with a sledgehammer first.

2. After that, the key is layering. Spread the layers out – don't put it all in a big mound! Add about an 8cm (3-inch) layer of brown material and then an 8cm layer of green material on top until you get a heap that's about 1–1.2m (3–4ft) high and then leave it alone to rot down (i.e. don't add anything else to it). That means you probably need a minimum of two heaps. In practical terms, I often have far more green materials than I have brown – I usually end up dumping some greens in a pile beside the heap and waiting until I have a brown layer before adding them.

3. It's counter-intuitive, but regular turning (monthly) will aerate the heap, which will help it to decompose – the more often you turn it, the quicker it will rot. A well-layered heap will heat up quickly, rot down fast and uniformly, won't smell and should be easy to turn.

4. The brown layer can consist of straw, wood ash, cardboard, newspaper, small twigs, leaf mould, soil or garden 'sweepings'. The green layer could contain seaweed, grass clippings (but not too much), veg plants and hedge clippings. I don't add any kitchen waste (even peelings) to make sure I am not attracting rodents. Put kitchen waste in the brown bin or, even better, feed them to your hens if you have them.

5. You can have a completely open heap, or construct sides for it with timber or timber pallets (this makes turning a little easier). It should be about 1m (3ft) wide and deep. Start with a brown layer, such as straw or twigs. Cover the materials with cardboard or old carpet to keep the worst of the weather off them.

spiced parsnip burgers

JB occasionally serves these parsnip burgers at GROW HQ and they go down a treat. They shouldn't work, but they do. A fantastic and delicious way to use up a parsnip glut.

ingredients:
— 400g peeled and grated raw parsnip
— a pinch of salt
— ½ tsp cumin seeds
— ½ tsp coriander seeds
— 75ml rapeseed oil and a little more for frying
— 1 clove garlic, finely chopped
— a pinch of cayenne pepper
— a pinch of ground turmeric
— 80g organic gluten-free flour, plus a little more for coating the burgers

directions:
Preheat the oven to 180°C.

Put the grated parsnip in a large mixing bowl and add a pinch of salt. Massage for few minutes until you feel the grated parsnip soften under your fingers. In a small frying pan on a medium heat, toast the cumin and coriander seeds for 2 minutes. Add the oil, finely chopped garlic, cayenne pepper and turmeric and cook for 2 more minutes.

Add the spice mix to the grated parsnip, mix well, add the gluten-free flour and mix again. Portion into generously sized burgers. Coat the burgers lightly with the remaining flour. Warm a little rapeseed oil in a large frying pan on a medium heat, fry off the burgers for 2–3 minutes on each side, then cook in the oven for 10 minutes.

GIYing in raised beds is becoming increasingly popular, mainly because it overcomes the problems of poor soil quality and drainage. Raised beds are an ingenious way to provide good-quality, deep, fertile soil that's perfect for planting.

If you have never grown anything at all and are starting with an area of lawn, here's one way to get started. Build a raised bed from salvaged or purchased timber by nailing together four planks – a 4ft square (1.2m) bed is considered ideal, as you can reach the centre from all sides and therefore never need to stand on the soil, which compacts it and makes it hard for plants to grow. Make it at least 25–30cm (10–12 inches) deep.

Lay the frame on the grass. Pick somewhere sunny and sheltered. Put down a layer of cardboard and newspaper on the grass inside the timbers and wet it thoroughly – this will rot down and kill off the grass in the process. Fill the bed with a mix of approximately 60 per cent soil and 40 per cent well-rotted compost or manure. Cover it with black plastic for a few months so the soil is nice and warm, ready for your seeds and seedlings in April/May.

The path between your beds should be just wide enough to take a wheelbarrow and to allow you to kneel comfortably. I generally keep the path to a rake's width, which is narrow enough that you are not wasting valuable ground. You can leave the paths as bare soil if you want – it will need to be hoed regularly to prevent a build-up of weeds, but on the plus side you can use soil from the path if you need it for earthing up in the bed. Alternatively, you could put in a more permanent (weed-free) path using Mypex (weed-suppressing membrane) and pea gravel or bark mulch.

I've become a major fan of celeriac as a grower. Although it's relatively unknown as a veg here, I reckon it deserves far more notoriety than it currently enjoys. Celeriac looks similar in size and shape to a turnip, but as the name suggests, it basically tastes like celery (with a slightly nuttier flavour).

I love celery, but it doesn't keep well in the ground, so it's not possible to store it fresh (although you can freeze it, which I do – aiming to get 20 bags of it into the freezer so I can grab handfuls for soups, stews and trivets). Celeriac, on the other hand, is a big knobbly (and, truth be known, butt-ugly) root vegetable and courtesy of its thick skin it will sit very well in the soil through the harshest winter.

You can use celeriac as an alternative to celery – for example, you can dice it and lob it into a stew or soup – but it's tasty enough to stand on its own two feet too. It's delicious mashed into potato or even grated raw. My absolute favourite way to eat celeriac is to eat it raw in a slaw or salad. A celeriac remoulade is delicious and simple – the celeriac is left raw and simply cut into *very* fine strips. This is a great way to get some raw veggies into you without it feeling like you are eating raw veggies (if you know what I mean).

Celeriac is one of those vegetables that is easy to grow, but hard to grow well. The key is that it has a very long growing season – you start it from seed in March and it can take two to three weeks to germinate. When the seedlings are hardy and about 10cm (4 inches) tall, you plant them out. Celeriac loves constant moisture, so a soil with plenty of well-rotted compost or manure added is vital, and it will need watering in dry weather. In a 5m x 1.2m (16ft x 4ft) veg bed you will produce enough celeriac to last 24 weeks (eating two of them a week). That's a good investment for your winter store cupboard.

Celeriac is ready to harvest when the swollen root is 7–10cm (3–4 inches) across. Use a fork to ease it out of the ground. Don't forget that the leaves can be used to add celery flavour to soups, stews and trivets.

improving wet soil

For many GIYers (including this one), wet soil can be a real dampener (see what I did there?). Our garden is at the foot of a large hill and our soil is a heavy clay that doesn't drain well. The result? Our soil gets very boggy with even a hint of rain. When we first moved here, it was more suitable for growing rice than vegetables. Vegetables grown in a wet, sodden soil never fare well, but thankfully, this is a problem that can be fixed, albeit not necessarily quickly.

The obvious place to start is to raise the level of the soil above the ground. Increasing the depth of the soil and lifting it up above ground level means that it will drain more quickly and stay drier. Raised beds made of timber are an inexpensive way to achieve this – they have another benefit too as they allow you to stay off the beds, meaning the soil will be less compacted. A raised bed 25–30cm (10–12 inches) deep filled with a mixture of soil and compost will work a treat.

Adding plenty of farmyard manure or compost in the winter or early spring each year will improve the soil and make it easier to work with. It will be less sticky and more fibrous. I have been doing this for about 15 years now, and each year I see an improvement in the soil structure. When I first started out, my soil was like potting clay. It's not any more.

Each year, I cover my beds with black polythene (I reuse the same sheets each year), held in place with bricks, which prevents it from being blow away (in theory). I have always been in two minds about this since the accepted wisdom is that it's good for soil to be exposed to the elements in the winter – a good frost is said to kill off any nasty stuff in the soil and also break up large clods of soil. But on balance I believe this has played a major role in drying out my soil and it prevents nutrients being washed away in heavy rain.

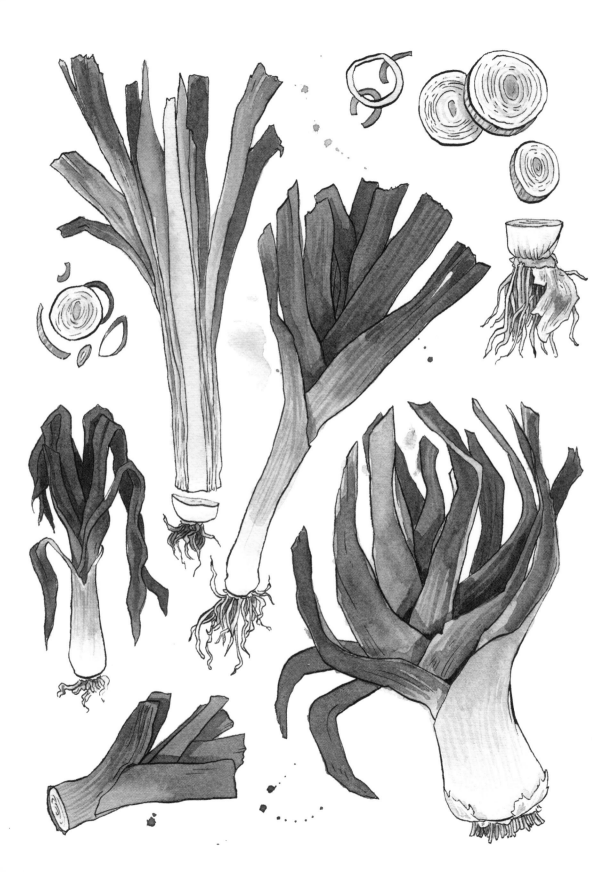

february

Winter continues in the veg patch, but the first seeds are sown inside as we try to coax little seeds into becoming seedlings. We're sowing some of the great long-season veg like tomatoes and peppers.

This month we're loving … leeks.

They stand in the ground all winter and bring their goodness to many a soup and stew.

1 february
St Brigid's Day

Though St Brigid's Day is considered the start of spring in the Celtic calendar, unfortunately it's still winter outside in the veggie patch. By the beginning of February, I am always itching to get started with my seed sowing – you can get lots of vegetables started in seed trays on a sunny windowsill indoors at this time of the year. The problem is that when they are bursting from their pots and ready to be planted out in a month's time, it may still be too cold to do so. Patience is the ultimate virtue for the GIYer.

Though winter stores are looking increasingly bare, I'm glad for the full freezer and the work we did chopping, shelling, podding, blanching and cooking the last harvest. Having your own produce is a fantastic boon at this time of the year, when supermarket shelves are laden down with imported, unseasonal produce. I saw a cellophane-wrapped tray of veg in a supermarket the other day that had little portions of asparagus, beans and broccoli from three different countries (Kenya, Peru and Spain) on three different continents – all in the one container! That's as good a metaphor as any for the lunacy of the modern food chain.

As we move further and further from the winter solstice, we gain about five minutes of daylight at either end of the day and comparable dollops of optimism. It seems (whisper it) to be getting a little warmer too. Roll on spring!

2 february
buying a polytunnel

I regularly extol the virtues of having a polytunnel, especially as having one will extend the growing season at both ends and bring a warmer, drier climate to a corner of your garden – win–win! Here are my top tips if you are considering buying one:

- A typical tunnel for home gardeners is 3m x 6m (10ft x20ft) with a height of about 2m (6ft).
- Get as big and tall a polytunnel as you can possibly afford and have space for. You will always want more space for growing and the extra headspace will be appreciated for

growing climbing plants like tomatoes and cucumbers and to save your back.

- It should be positioned on well-drained soil and on level ground, in a sunny spot, oriented east–west.
- Choose a warm, dry day to erect the tunnel. This will make the polythene supple and therefore easier to pull tight. Get lots of help (or, better still, get the company that you're buying from to do it). Anchoring the plastic really firmly in the soil is vital, otherwise the whole thing could blow away in a gale.
- In the summer there can be extreme heat in the tunnel. Therefore, you should build in as much ventilation as possible, i.e. wide doors at both ends with ventilation panels. Get galvanised steel frame sliding doors if you can afford them – they will last longer than timber ones, which tend to rot or eventually get blown off their hinges.
- If well fitted and maintained (with the plastic washed each year with a soft brush and warm, soapy water), the polythene can last 15 years. The original small tunnel I bought when I started growing still has the original plastic on (some holes are taped up in places, but that's okay).
- Watering is essential, especially in summer. Having a tap in the tunnel, or at least close enough for a hose connection, will save a lot of effort! A drip-feed hose so you can give the tunnel a good soak once a week in the summer is also a great investment.
- A bench, shelf or table in a polytunnel provides a great location for propagating seeds and bringing on seedlings. Even better if you can get power to it, so you can have a heated bench for bringing on seeds at this time of year.

3 february
sowing seeds

It's wonderful to be back in the potting shed this week doing my favourite thing: sowing seeds. It's February, so it's still relatively tentative sowing and almost exclusively confined to vegetables

.

and herbs that will be planted out in the polytunnel, as opposed to outside, e.g. chilli peppers, aubergines, spinach, beetroot, spring onions and some herbs (coriander and dill). For now, I'm holding out getting started on sowing my numerous tomato seeds, but as they need a long growing season, like chilli peppers and aubergines, they'll be next on my sowing to-do list.

The weather has been arctic with some snow on the ground this week, all of which makes it more challenging to persuade the little seeds that it's a good plan to come out of the ground. Basically, success at this time of the year is about cheating them into thinking it's spring. First of all, I use an electric heating mat, which gives the seeds some 'heat from beneath' to help them on their way. It's important to keep a close eye on watering when doing this, as the compost can be inclined to dry out on a sunny day with the extra heat.

I also put some horticultural fleece over the trays and pots – always at night and often in the daytime as well if it's particularly cold outside. It's better if you can leave it off by day so the seedlings get plenty of light (which they also need as well as decent temperatures). I find it's an added bonus if you can bring the water for watering them up to room temperature. I use a 2-litre water bottle with some little holes in the lid as a nimble watering can at this time of the year – it's ideal for watering seed trays. I leave it on the heating mat so the water warms up too. They seem to appreciate it – well, you wouldn't like a cold shower at this time of year, would you?

It's impossible not to feel buoyant, hopeful and full of springtime enthusiasm when you see signs of life emerging in a seed tray. Let's hope the winter cold snap moves off soon to enhance the experience.

Parsnips are as tough as old boots and at this time of the year **4 february** I always have a decent batch in the ground outside in the veg **tough as** patch, despite the inclement weather. As spring progresses, they **old boots** will start to sprout – confirmation that they are, of course, a root – and at that point they are not so good to eat. So if you have any left in the ground, you need to start using them up. Incidentally, if a parsnip is left to grow it produces a very beautiful and surprisingly tall plant – worth doing just to see the full life cycle of this wonderful veg.

parsnip chips

There's not often much culinary experimentation with parsnips, which is why they've never become a much-loved veg. This is a very simple recipe and the secret ingredient is Parmesan cheese – it tarts them up no end.

ingredients:
— 500g parsnips
— 2 tbsp plain flour

- — salt and pepper
- — a handful of Parmesan cheese, grated
- — 1 tbsp olive oil

directions:

Preheat the oven to 200°C.

Peel the parsnips and chop them into big chip-like chunks. Place the parsnips in a pot and cover with cold water. Bring the pot to the boil and simmer for a few minutes. Drain the parsnips into a colander.

Spread the parsnips on a baking tray and add the flour, seasoning well with lots of salt and freshly ground pepper. Add the Parmesan cheese and drizzle with olive oil, then mix it all together, ensuring that the parsnips are evenly coated in the flour, cheese, oil and seasoning.

Pop them in the oven and roast for 30 minutes or until golden brown.

5 february
how to sow
different
veg

I've discovered as I get older that I am a person who loves to square things away. And that applies equally to food growing. I'm constantly looking for things that simplify what can be a fairly complicated life skill. Over the years I've deployed all sorts of little nerdish tricks, categories, tables, Post-it notes, spreadsheets and all manner of other organising devices to try to break it down and make it easier for me to understand.

When it comes to seed sowing, I always thought that almost every vegetable seemed to start in a slightly different way, which just added to the general confusion. In fact, there are only two categories: those that are sown direct into the soil, and those that are sown in a pot or tray to be planted out later. So, let's break it down (use a spreadsheet if you want!).

First, we start with veg that are sown direct in the soil outside (or in a polytunnel or greenhouse). This category can be broken down into three different types of seed:

- **Tubers**, e.g. potatoes, where the 'seed' is an actual potato. In a similar vein are artichokes, yacon, oca, etc.
- **Sets**, e.g. onions and shallots, where the 'seed' is a small, immature onion that someone else has grown from seed; or garlic, where the 'seed' is a clove of garlic from last year.
- **Seeds** that are best sown direct in the soil, e.g. peas, French beans, parsnips and carrots.

Second, we have the veg that are sown in pots or module trays for later planting out into the soil. In this category I include pretty much everything else, e.g. tomatoes, peppers, aubergines, celery, celeriac, salads (including oriental greens), cabbage, kohlrabi, swede, chard, turnips, kale, beetroot and so on.

Admittedly there are quite a few veg that I include in the latter category (sowing in module trays for later transplanting) that could just as easily be sown direct outside. A good example of this is beetroot. So, the question is: why would I do this when it would save time to sow them direct? The answer is that I find it more successful to start them off inside and plant out later. (And besides, I just love spending time in the potting shed.)

The reason it is more successful is that plants are at their most vulnerable (to frosts and slugs, for example) when they are seedlings, and it is generally more successful to plant a plant than to sow a seed. Sowing seeds in pots/trays also allows you to get a head start on the growing season as you keep the pots/trays indoors or under cover during February/March/April, when it is generally too cold to sow outside.

Here's a rough, but not exhaustive, guide to how to sow different veg. In some cases, it comes down to personal preference – for example, I sow beetroot in module trays, but I know some people like to sow them direct.

- **Sow in pots:** cucumbers, squashes, pumpkins, courgettes
- **Sow in module trays:** beetroot, chard, kohlrabi, lettuce, spinach, tomatoes, peppers, onions (seeds)

- **Sow in pots or trays for later 'pricking out' into module trays:** cabbage, cauliflower, celery and celeriac
- **Sow direct** (where they are to grow): carrots, parsnips, peas, beans, garlic, onions (sets).

Of all the skills I have learned as a GIYer, being able to make my own compost has been the most useful. The compost corner at the end of the garden is not a pretty or quaint place – but it is pivotal when it comes to the food producing that occurs in my garden. And without it, very little food would grow at all. Over the years I have learned to see these two parts of my garden (the veg patch and the compost corner) as intrinsically linked and part of a natural cycle of growth, decay and regrowth that is essential to growing.

I use two different compost systems in my garden: a plastic composter and homemade open compost bays for garden waste. The plastic composter is the standard unit you get from local authorities or from your garden centre. It's not terribly easy to get compost out of (even with the hatch in the front), but by alternating layers of food waste and newspaper you can produce quite good compost (albeit slowly).

For garden waste, I have a three-bay compost system made from old timber pallets – it's my attempt at the 'New Zealand Box' compost design and the idea is that it acts like a compost conveyor belt. You fill one bay and when it's time to turn the compost you tip it into the next bay. So if the system is working right, you should have compost at various stages of decomposition in each bay.

6 february
making black gold

You will probably remember from your science classes back in school that seeds need specific conditions to germinate and thrive. It's very helpful to keep these basic needs in mind at this time of the year. Most seeds need these three conditions:

7 february
the needs of seeds

1. **Heat:** Seeds need a decent temperature to germinate. A warm windowsill in the house or a heated bench in the potting shed is ideal for starting seeds off, particularly at this time of the year when it's cold and dark. There are exceptions, but it's a good rule of thumb.

2. **Light:** Once germination begins, light is essential. Positioning the seed tray as close to full light as possible is key. For example, seed trays placed on the windowsill will do better than a seed tray placed a few feet away from the window. Some veg, like celery and lettuce, need light to germinate in the first place, so don't cover them with compost when sowing. Most seeds need 12–14 hours of light to thrive, and we don't generally have that in February. Some growers use artificial lighting to compensate for the lack of natural light early in the year, but I'm happy to work with the seasons a little more.

3. **Humidity/moisture:** When it comes to watering seeds, the key is that they need uniform moisture. They shouldn't be waterlogged, and certainly never allowed to dry out. Gentle watering with a fine rose is essential to ensure you don't wash the seeds away (or push them too deep into the soil to germinate). It goes without saying that we generally need to water less at this time of the year because the colder/darker conditions mean less moisture is lost to evaporation.

Every now and then a supply chain issue breaks through into the public consciousness and shakes us out of our apathy about our food chain. In recent years there have been occasional Covid- and climate-related breaks in the seemingly faultless supply chain of veg from southern Europe, and while we obsess about running out of iceberg lettuce or rationing courgettes, we often miss the real issue.

The focus should not be on the fact that Spain's south-eastern Murcia region supplies 80 per cent of Europe's fresh produce during the winter, but rather on why we are so obsessed with unseasonal veg. Courgettes, aubergines, tomatoes and iceberg lettuce are not currently in season. To restore some sanity to the food chain, we should be removing these veg from our diet in winter and instead turning to crops our own climate – and our own growers – can provide us with.

Now, before you say that I am just being contrary and trying to drag us back to the 1960s, let me offer three solid reasons why this would be a good idea. First, a shift to seasonal eating is better for our health – our bodies don't need thirst-quenching, water-filled vegetables like tomatoes at this time of year. Second, eating food that is in season in our locality means eating food that is at its freshest and tastiest. Third, our reliance on unseasonal food locks us into an unstable reliance on foreign food imports. Eating unseasonably might be great news for growers in Murcia (and I am sure they are fine people indeed), but it is terrible for Irish agriculture and jobs. Irish growers are leaving the industry in droves because they cannot compete with our taste for unseasonal food or the climate and labour advantages of their continental competitors.

These occasional crises are a timely reminder that we have become far too 'recipe-led' when it comes to feeding ourselves. Open any magazine or newspaper this weekend and you will see celebrity chefs touting recipes that are laden with unseasonal ingredients. Your local supermarket – a place where there are no seasons – will support this by ensuring that these veg are

available 365 days a year. This is unquestionably a marvel of modernity and logistics, but it does no favours to our palate, our health, the health of our planet or to local farmers and growers.

ribollita

Do you have a school lunchbox meal from your youth that still horrifies you? I remember being mortified that my mum put cold burgers in my school lunchbox when I was kid. Thinking about it now, I am sure they were perfectly lovely, but all I wanted was a ham sandwich like the other kids. So I feel a little bad for my kids when I send them to school with flasks of ribollita in the winter months. But hey, what's a parent for if it's not to embarrass the crap out of you? In the winter months, I make a giant pot of this on Sundays and reheat it each morning for flasks. Effectively this is a vegetable stew, so you can add other veg if you have them.

ingredients:
— 4 tbsp olive oil
— 1 onion, finely chopped
— 1 sprig of thyme, leaves removed
— 2 carrots, finely chopped
— 1 celery stalk, finely chopped
— ½ celeriac, peeled and chopped
— 1 leek, trimmed, washed and finely sliced
— 400g tin of chopped plum tomatoes or homemade passata
— 75g pearl barley, washed
— 800ml vegetable stock
— 1 sprig of rosemary, leaves removed and finely chopped
— 300g kale or chard, tough stalks removed
— salt and pepper

directions:
In a large saucepan, heat the olive oil and sauté the onion over a medium–low heat for 10–15 minutes, until softened. Add the

thyme leaves and give it a stir. Add the carrots, celery, celeriac and leek and cook gently with the lid on for 5 minutes, stirring. Now add the tomatoes with their juice, the pearl barley, stock and rosemary and simmer gently for about 45 minutes. Chop the kale or chard leaves, add to the soup and cook for 10 minutes more. Season with salt and pepper.

12 february the tomato adventure begins So the great tomato adventure starts all over again. A 10-month odyssey begins with sowing seeds in a cold potting shed with Child Number 2 chatting incessantly in my ear. Growing tomatoes is a labour of love. Unlike, say, herbs or salads, which are quick and easy to grow, tomatoes take time and plenty of work. But my, oh my, is it worth it. The variety, the flavour, the utter deliciousness. There is simply nothing like a homegrown tomato. It's bleak and cold and wintry, but I'm hankering after the flavours of summer.

I am somewhat obsessed with tomatoes. Most people who grow them are the same. For years I grew around 20 plants in my first polytunnel in the garden, and that was enough to give us plenty of fresh tomatoes from July to October and sauces for the freezer. Then I got the mad idea that if I had a big commercial tunnel I could grow way more plants and stock the freezer with sauces (enough to last right through until the first fresh tomatoes come again in July). It was this hare-brained notion that led to us buying a big commercial tunnel for the field beside the house and growing about 80 plants a year. What can I say? It seemed like a good idea at the time.

When it comes to timing the start of the tomato season, you are balancing the need to get started (they need a long growing season) with the reality that they like a Mediterranean climate (and 18–20°C to germinate), which is sadly lacking in Ireland in February. To protect them against the cold, the tomatoes are on a heated bench in the potting shed and I have fleece at the ready for chilly nights. It would be best of all to wait until March to sow them, but I am keen to get started.

For the last two seasons I've grown around 80 plants and my summers have become a never-ending scramble to keep up with the abundance of tomatoes flowing from the garden. To put it in context, a single tomato plant could produce up to 200 tomatoes in a season. No family of four could keep up with this amount of fresh tomatoes. Instead, it's about processing them immediately into a sauce for the freezer, effectively packing up some flavour for the future. Last year I put around 50 bags of tomato sauce into the freezer. Of course, I could just stop growing so many plants, but what would be the fun in that?

In terms of varieties, I aim for a good mix of shapes, sizes, colours and flavours. There are old reliable ones and new experiments, along with some new purchases and seeds found down the bottom of the seed box. Here are 10 of my favourite tomato seeds:

1. **Sungold:** My favourite tomato – a beautifully sweet, yellow/red cherry tomato, top of the taste tests.
2. **Beefsteak:** Huge, slightly flattened tomatoes are the mainstay of our tunnel crop – cut big thick slices of it in the summer and top with a poached egg. Delish.
3. **Shirley:** A popular hybrid for early production with large trusses of medium-sized fruit.
4. **Sweet Million:** A sweet, shiny red cherry tomato and a prolific cropper.
5. **Tigerella:** Red fruits with orange-yellow stripes and a fine flavour.
6. **Gardeners' Delight:** A solid worker – produces bite-sized, tangy tomatoes.
7. **Golden Sunrise:** Medium-sized golden yellow fruit with a sweet, distinctive flavour.
8. **Alicante:** Another favourite of ours – a prolific cropper that produces medium-sized red fruits.
9. **Albenga:** Produces large and distinctive pear-shaped beefsteak-style fruits.
10. **Sweet Aperitif:** Another taste test topper, a prolific red cherry with thin skin and excellent flavour.

16 february
mindful
chores

I picked up a fascinating little book a few weeks back called *A Monk's Guide to a Clean House and Mind* by Shoukei Matsumoto, and it has sort of reset how I view some of the mundane jobs that need to be done around the house and garden. Using the word 'chores' to describe these jobs is probably deeply unhelpful, since it has such negative connotations. In his book, Buddhist monk Matsumoto suggests that keeping the house and garden clean is not a chore at all, but a route to enlightenment. Who knew?

The key to transforming these tasks from repetitive, annoying 'must-dos' into something a little more spiritually useful is both simple and infuriatingly tough at the same time: they must be done mindfully. I've been practising, trying to stay in the moment while pottering around the kitchen or the veg patch, and it is surprisingly calming. Staying in tune with your breathing while you are working gets rid of the mental chatter (if only briefly) as well as removing the sense of impatience that often accompanies mundane jobs.

Take sweeping the floor as an example. Since reading the book I've started sweeping the floor every morning in a mindful way. It takes about three or four minutes (yes, I timed it) and is delightfully old school and calming at the same time. My daughter thinks it's hilarious and jests about my 'mindful sweeping', which she always says disdainfully while making air quote marks with her fingers.

Out in the potting shed I try to stay mindful while seed sowing. A bag of compost opened and tipped out on the sowing bench. Cold black plastic seed trays filled with even colder, blacker compost. Seed labels lined up awaiting a scrawl of information. Seed packets fished out from my big box of tricks and opened carefully to reveal their bounty.

While I work, I find myself wondering how many growing seasons I have ahead of me. Maybe 30, if I am lucky? I pull myself back from such existential thoughts and try to stay in the moment. I listen to the wind whistling around the potting shed. I plug in the heated cable to start the process of warming the sand beneath the seed pots. I realise I am whistling.

I have shelter from the elements in the potting shed, but I feel my feet are numb in my wellies and the tips of my fingers are cold. I can see my breath while I work. I would like to luxuriate over this process, particularly today since it's the first sowing of the year, but it's too damn cold – so I move quickly. Sow a seed, label it, move on. Before I finish, I make a cloche over the pots with some rubber pipe and a layer of clear plastic over them, tucking the plastic in beneath them. I am creating a little hothouse for these seeds, which need heat to germinate. It feels a little artificial, but my growing year always starts like this – coaxing Mediterranean conditions from a cold February and trying to warm up the world.

borscht

In this recipe, GROW HQ head chef JB Dubois uses cooked beet-root (traditionally, borscht uses uncooked) to retain a brighter pink colour.

ingredients:
— 3 beetroot
— 3 medium carrots, coarsely grated
— 2 medium potatoes, peeled and finely diced into approx. 5mm cubes
— 2 cloves garlic, crushed
— 1 small onion, finely diced
— 1 stick of celery (or half a fennel bulb), finely sliced
— 2–3 tbsp rapeseed oil
— a generous pinch of salt and pepper
— 1 sprig of thyme
— 1 bay leaf
— 1 large tomato, roughly chopped
— 1.5 litres water or stock
— a few drops of raw cider vinegar
— sour cream and fresh dill, to garnish

directions:
Cook the beetroot in salted water for 1–3 hours (depending on the size of the beetroot and the season – summer beets cook faster than winter ones). Check with a pointy knife if the beetroot are soft all the way through. Drain and leave to cool, then peel and dice into 1cm cubes.

Prep the rest of the vegetables. Put the carrots, potatoes, garlic, onion and celery in a large saucepan with the rapeseed oil. Add the salt and pepper and sweat the vegetables on a low heat for 7–10 minutes, checking them from time to time, until the vegetables start to soften slightly. Add the thyme, bay leaf, tomato and the stock or water. Simmer for 15 minutes, until all the vegetables are entirely cooked. Add the beetroot and simmer for a further

5–6 minutes. Add a few drops of vinegar to taste. Check the seasoning and serve with sour cream and fresh dill.

18 february
the last
carrot

My last carrot from last year's harvest was used up on Sunday as part of a tasty roast lunch. There was no fanfare, pomp or ceremony, but I felt sad because it's back to shop-bought carrots from here on in – with the associated ongoing quest to find decent Irish organic carrots and wondering what the non-organic ones are sprayed with.

Though I say so myself, I did pretty well with carrots last year. They are not an easy vegetable to grow well, needing a decent depth of good-quality and fertile topsoil to thrive. Many a GIYer I have spoken to will mention carrots as one veg they often really struggle with.

It helps to think about the science of what happens when you sow a carrot. Once the seed germinates, the root starts to grow beneath the surface. As it winds its merry way down into the soil, if it meets hard soil or a stone, it will either stop (resulting in stunted carrots) or fork to get around the obstacle. So basically, your carrot bed is one bed where it pays to make sure you have at least a spade's depth of good deep soil. I'm not a big fan of digging, but last spring I did some heavy-duty soil-turning with a fork in the bed where I was going to sow my carrots and parsnips. It was hard work – although I confess that I did enjoy it; there's nothing more satisfying than the tired, sore feeling you get after a morning's toil in the veg patch – but the result was that the bed produced fine, long roots.

This weekend I am doing a sowing of early carrots in the polytunnel – they should be ready in about early May, so I won't have to make do with shop-bought carrots for too long.

Most of us like the idea of having little bees buzzing around the flowers in our garden and we may even be aware that all their activity has a purpose. Few of us stop to think about just how vital these industrious pollinators are to our very survival as a species. And vital they are. In fact, of the 100 crops that provide 90 per cent of the world's food supply, 71 are pollinated by bees. In Europe alone, 84 per cent of our crop species are animal-pollinated and 4,000 vegetable varieties exist thanks to pollination by bees. In Ireland, it is believed pollinators contribute some €53 million annually to the Irish economy (and of course the honey bees produce all that lovely honey). If bees were to disappear, commercial agriculture as we know it would most likely disappear too and humankind would face an uncertain future.

So the fact that pollinators are in a major decline globally is serious news indeed. More than half of Ireland's bee species have undergone substantial declines in their numbers since 1980, with 30 per cent considered threatened with extinction. Total honey-bee colonies in Ireland are thought to have declined significantly since the introduction of the parasitic mite *Varroa destructor* in

1997. The reasons for the decline of pollinators are many and varied but can be summed up under the headings homelessness (loss of habitat); hunger (loss of biodiversity); sickness; and poisoning. It wouldn't be over-egging things to say that humans are either wholly or partly responsible for all four of these factors. We are literally biting the hand that feeds us, and that's not clever.

For growers, the loss of pollinators means lower crop yields and reductions in quality. For consumers, it means reduced choice and higher prices for the fruits and vegetables that are essential in our diet, as producers must find alternative methods of pollination. One would imagine that if any other important cog in our food chain were under such serious threat, it would be a major news story. But you rarely hear this issue discussed.

There are practical and proven steps we can take to reverse this decline. Whether you have a 10-acre smallholding, an allotment, a small back garden or even a windowbox, all GIYers can play our part in providing an environment where pollinators can flourish. Here are some top tips:

1. Avoid using chemicals in the garden to control weeds or pests.
2. Let the grass grow – it saves you time and money, and the pollinating insects will be thrilled.
3. Embrace untidy. Provide plenty of different habitats – don't be so quick to lift and tidy.
4. Plant pollinator-friendly plants that flower from spring to autumn.
5. Get comfortable with weeds – plants like dandelion, clover and nettles are important food sources.

20 february
the
meitheal

I love the earthy, rural Irish tradition of the meitheal (pronounced meh-hill), where people on neighbouring farms used to come together to help with a time-sensitive task like saving hay or harvesting. The meitheal was effectively a co-operative labour system

– it was a cashless transaction, with the meitheal members (mei-thealers?) expecting no payment in return for their work, but safe in the knowledge that when their time came to have a job completed, the meitheal would visit its largesse on them too.

Meitheals also created community spirit, but at a time when communities were already pretty tight – it's safe to say that community building wasn't the primary reason for having one. It was simply an entirely efficient, speedy and cheap way to get a major job of work done.

Today a meitheal visited my own garden. Our neighbours, John and Bridget, agreed to help with some of the work needing to be done in the big tunnel to prepare for this season's tomato growing in exchange for some fresh produce during the summer. Both are at retirement age (well, you don't ask …) and although they still have some raised beds in the garden, they don't bother with a polytunnel any more. They are fond of tomatoes, so were enthused by my hare-brained project to grow 80-odd tomato plants in a large commercial polytunnel.

In exchange for the produce, we get access to their time. This is needed very rarely at this time of the year, except for the occasional big winter project like turning soil, but much more frequently in the summer months when the tomato plants require watering and side-shooting every week. John and Bridget are meticulous side-shooters! It's a great swap – produce for labour. And, truth be told, we probably couldn't manage the big tunnel without them. Both are experienced growers and had an organic box scheme way back before such a thing was trendy. That means we can always swap notes, and I learn a lot from them while they are here. I've never seen a man as useful or as elegant with a shovel as John, and he's probably fitter than most men half his age. They often arrive by bicycle to do an hour or two of tomato side-shooting or digging before disappearing off on their bikes again.

Today we removed the Mypex from the tunnel and turned over the soil inside it. Given the size of the tunnel and how long it would take me, the job would haunt my mind for weeks, but with the three of us working on it, we finished in an hour.

A meitheal really is ideal for work of this nature and I was struck by its brutal efficiency – a daunting piece of work made simple by extra hands. Of course, we also used the time to chat about everything and anything, and it's the sense of camaraderie that brings us all back together for the next time more hands are required to make light work.

21 february
toms

To my delight (and it really was delight), the tomato seeds germinated quite quickly and quite suddenly midweek – one day it was bare soil, and the next about half the seeds had germinated and surprisingly tall seedlings had pushed out of the soil. I always marvel at the idea that when tomato seedlings emerge from the soil, they *really emerge*. It's hard to believe that these tiny little seedlings will grow up to 3m or more during the summer months and will (we hope) be laden down with hundreds of tomatoes. With the heated mat helping to dry the soil out, I am having to water the trays every other day.

24 february
prepping
the spud
beds

My potatoes for outdoor planting are currently 'chitting' in the potting shed. In about three weeks' time I will be sowing the early varieties, so it's time to consider whether the beds where they will be sown are ready. Potatoes will benefit from lots of fertility in the soil, so a good covering of homemade compost, farmyard manure or seaweed will help.

I don't have any compost left in my heaps, so I had to go off in search of fertility for the spud beds. A local farmer friend of mine gave me access to an old cow manure heap in one of his fields, from which I was able to extract 10 bags of well-rotted manure – perfect, crumbly black gold. Shhh! Don't tell anyone. This was enough to put a decent covering on the beds, which are now ready for the spuds.

If you don't have much space, you can still grow potatoes quite successfully in large pots or containers. The pots will need to be relatively deep: 50–75cm (20–30 inches) deep so the spuds have the depth of soil they need to grow. Put a 10cm (4-inch) layer of compost in the bottom of the pot and place the seed potato on it, then cover it with another 10cm layer of compost and water in. Each time the top of the leaf pops out over the soil, cover it over again – you can continue with this until the pot is full. This plays a little trick on the poor potato plant because it has to grow more stem to get out of the soil – more stem growth means more space for the potatoes to grow. If sowing them at this time of the year, cover them with fleece at night.

Alternatively, you could try growing spuds in a compost bag. Buy a bag of peat-free compost (three bags usually cost about €15), open it carefully along the top (don't rip the bag) and empty out the compost. Make about 8-10 drainage holes in the bottom of the bag (a garden fork is ideal for doing this). Roll the top of the bag down about halfway. Put a small layer of compost back in the bottom of the bag and put two or three seed potatoes on top (spaced as far apart as you can). Cover them with another layer of compost. Store the remaining compost – you will need it later for earthing up. Each time you see a shoot appearing above the soil, cover it up with more compost and unroll the bag slightly. Keep adding compost every time a shoot appears until you have used up all the compost and the bag is fully unrolled and full of compost again. You will need to water the plants daily as there is a risk with this type of growing that the compost will dry out – make sure it doesn't. When the plants have finished flowering, empty the bag carefully and harvest your lovely spuds. You can spread the compost in the vegetable garden, but don't reuse it for growing spuds. You can sow early spuds under cover (i.e. a polytunnel or greenhouse) from now. If you will be leaving the container outside, wait until mid-March to sow.

27 february
a word
on food
packaging

Right at the time when our planet is at its most vulnerable to the vagaries of climate change, there seems to be an explosion in the amount of food packaging we're using. Everywhere you look there are examples of entirely unnecessary food and beverage packaging that takes serious energy to produce and dispose of. Thanks to our relatively new-found obsession with coffee-on-the-go, we now dispose of over 200 million coffee cups in Ireland every year. Globally, the figure is over 500 billion – that's one million cups a minute. Though many of these cups are labelled as recyclable, in reality they are very difficult to recycle due to the mix of plastic and paper used in their production. Most of them end up in landfill or incineration. I can't help thinking that our descendants will look back at this time in human history and think that we had completely and utterly lost the plot.

There's a similar problem when it comes to food packaging. I've seen supermarkets where there are packaged and loose parsnips on the shelves side by side (the former in rigid plastic trays and wrapped in cellophane, presumably to save the consumer the extraordinarily time-consuming job of popping the loose ones into their shopping trolley or a paper bag). When I contacted Tesco about this, they responded (kudos for responding) that this is about offering consumers a choice and directed me to a page on their website where it states that they are committed to making all their packaging recyclable or compostable by 2025. This is commendable, but there are no guarantees that recyclable packaging will get recycled. It also misses the point. While there are certainly types of food that need packaging to prevent damage, parsnips are not one of them – courtesy of their thick skins, they are incredibly durable.

But it's not just parsnips. No vegetable or fruit, it would seem, is safe from spending its final days suffocating in a plastic sarcophagus. I've seen everything from packaged apples to aubergines, bananas (fecking bananas!), cabbages, celeriac and oranges. Recently, a well-known supermarket withdrew a plastic-packaged cauliflower 'steak' from shelves after being ridiculed on social media. The steak-shaped piece of cauliflower was for sale for £2 when a full cauliflower was available in the same supermarket for less than £1! Our planet and our wallets are paying a hefty price for our sheer laziness.

It's easy to indulge in supermarket bashing, but supermarkets are nothing if not responsive to consumer demand. The veg and fruit aisle can be plastic-free if we vote with our wallets. When you go shopping, bring a bag and fill it with loose veg and fruit, leaving the packaged ones behind. When you go for your morning coffee, bring a reusable cup. Ultimately, this is our fight.

march

Spring arrives with a whimper rather than a bang and the first big outdoor sowings – potatoes and onions – happen later in the month. Seed-sowing activity ramps up, but beware of those cold snaps.

This month we're loving … rhubarb.

The first and most welcome new-season crop for crumbles and tarts aplenty.

1 march
spring is in
the air

'Grand bit of spring in the air,' the lady said to me as we stood waiting for the pedestrian lights to go green. 'It's lovely,' I said and smiled back at her. And it *was* lovely to be walking along the quays in brilliant sunshine carrying my jacket under my arm. The combination of brighter mornings, longer evenings and mild weather has put a spring in my step and I'm feeling chipper. I suspect I'm not alone. But there's also an underlying sense of unease about it being 20°C on a sunny afternoon in Ireland in March, even though technically it's the start of meteorological spring. Does it make me a climate change curmudgeon to worry about these things? Should I enjoy it or feel absolutely terrified when climate breakdown leads to unseasonably pleasant weather?

Over the past few years, we've experienced worrying extremes of weather in Europe. Record-breaking highs of 20.6°C were recorded in Wales in February – the first time ever that temperatures exceeded 20°C in a winter month in the UK. The same time of year, but a few years earlier, a once-in-a-hundred-years snowstorm – the 'Beast from the East' – hit swathes of the UK and Ireland, leaving us shivering in Siberian air. And in one year Ireland suffered through six weeks of unseasonably warm weather, leading to drought conditions, during the summer, only for Dublin airport to record its coldest October night since records began later in the year. Topsy turvy doesn't begin to describe it. The new normal, it seems, is for our weather to be entirely abnormal.

Meanwhile we continue to whistle as we walk past the graveyard. On the news there are nice puff pieces about people enjoying the summer-like temperatures (eating ice creams and wearing short sleeves!), with not a mention of climate change. Increasingly I think adults seem to be on the wrong side of history on this topic and teens and children are the ones talking sense. I walked past a group of teenage climate change protestors in Cork City Hall last week – they looked angry (as teenagers tend to), but perhaps that's the only appropriate response.

While we waste time thinking about frivolities like who wore what to the Oscars and who won extortionate amounts in the EuroMillions, nature is screaming at us in every way it can that we need to fundamentally change the way we live. All aspects of our lives – food, transport, energy, waste – will have to change – dramatically, unthinkably – if we're to avoid catastrophe.

So perhaps in considering how we should feel about the unseasonably warm weather, we should channel the uncompromising attitude of Greta Thunberg, who lambasted investors and bankers attending Davos: 'I want you to feel the fear I feel every day,' she said. 'Act as if your house is on fire. Because it is.'

There's a wise old GIYer I know who says that the 'sap starts to rise' in gardeners in March. It's an odd expression, yet I completely get what he means by it. The sap is, of course, starting to rise in plants, but it feels like something is stirring inside us GIYers too. Spring is in the air everywhere we look and the desire to get out there and stick our hands in the soil is palpable.

3 march
the sap is
rising

They say that when soil is broken by a spade or fork, it releases endorphins. This might explain why GIYers are such a happy bunch – we're basically high on soil all the time. Whether or not this is true, there is something I've noticed over many years of GIYing – I have started to be more in tune with the seasons. When you grow your own vegetables, you must be. Mother Nature has her own pace, and it is a slow, methodical, inexorable one – she refuses to be rushed or to slow down. Every year my excitement gets the better of me and I sow seeds in January and February, but it is only now that they will germinate and sprout into action. It's GIY time, folks.

Back in mid-February I sowed batches of 10 tomato seeds in 10cm (4-inch) pots (one pot for each variety). The seeds have all germinated – thanks to the heated bench in the potting shed – and the pots are bursting with seedlings. But it's too early to plant them out in the polytunnel. So today I moved each seedling into

4 march
pricking
out

its own module in a module tray (or you could use small 5cm (2-inch) pots).

This process is called 'pricking out' – a term that would put me into a fit of the giggles if I was immature, which, I might add, I am not. In a nutshell it's the act of moving very young seedlings from the pot they've germinated in to another container or bed to provide more space. It's a little different from transplanting, which is where we move a more established seedling to its final growing position in the soil or a container.

Pricking out is a delicate, mindful little operation and you must be very careful not to damage the root or stem of the seedling. Having filled the module tray with seed compost and banged it a few times to settle the compost, I make a decent-sized hole in the compost in one module with my finger. Then, using a plant label, I ease one of the seedlings out of the pot, holding it very gently by the leaf. I then place the seedling into the hole in the module, sprinkle a little compost around it, firm it in gently and water.

It's important to keep a close eye on seedlings at this time of year – a daily check-in to see if they need watering (particularly if they are on a heat source) is important at this very vulnerable stage in their development. With the cold nights, I am also covering my seedlings with fleece at night. I'm struck by how quickly space on the heating mat becomes prime real estate.

From just 10 small pots of toms, there are now a couple of big module trays there. Spring is hotting up.

PSB time

If the fact that we've put February behind us wasn't reason enough to be cheerful, along comes March and purple sprouting broccoli time. I love this vegetable, not least because it provides some wonderful greens for the kitchen at a time when we're just about tiring of the root crops (like carrots and parsnips), and other veg (like beetroot and celeriac) have disappeared altogether.

Purple sprouting broccoli – let's get on first name terms and call it PSB – is an amazing vegetable to eat, but it's also somewhat of a veg-growing oddity. It bucks the 'sow in spring, harvest in autumn' convention and instead spends almost a full year in the ground, surviving all but the toughest of winters and becoming 'sow in summer, harvest in spring'. This makes it supremely useful for the home grower because it means it's providing food in the difficult 'hungry gap' months of March and April. This early arrival brings it in ahead of pretty much everything else in the veg patch – it will be May before early peas, potatoes and even salad greens make much of an appearance.

Unlike regular broccoli (properly known as calabrese), which puts all its efforts into producing one big, densely packed and, dare I say, relatively tasteless, central head, PSB is an altogether more gradual and nuanced affair. The part we eat is, in fact, the flowering shoots. And happily, the more we harvest, the more it produces. Let's just say we will be eating lots of it over the next two months. That will also be a great tonic for our sluggish post-winter bodies.

From a taste perspective, the home grower has all the advantages when it comes to PSB. Cooked immediately after harvesting, its flavour is exquisite and it needs just a few minutes of gentle steaming or boiling. We generally have it as a side veg, but we also put it centre stage in a pasta dish or as a starter, dipping the shoots in a tangy dressing (tahini is a great base for a PSB dressing, as are anchovies).

If you are buying PSB, seek out local and recently picked produce. Try a local farmers' market or good supermarket. Don't bother with the cellophane-wrapped 'fresh'-from-Kenya alternative. The flavour will disappoint.

8 march
salad
sowing

Now we're into March, today I began my first sowing (on a heating mat indoors in the potting shed) of lettuce and out in the polytunnel a short row of oriental greens (mizuna, red mustard, pak choi, rocket). This is the start of my monthly succession sowing of salads, which I will sow at the start of each month between now and August. I generally sow two eight-module trays of lettuce and a couple of short rows of oriental greens each month. I've found this is enough to give me a consistent supply of each without any major shortages or gluts. Sixteen heads of lettuce a month (four a week) and plenty of oriental greenery should be enough for most households.

I also did a clear-out in the salad polytunnel, mostly to clean up the paths that had become suddenly carpeted in weeds and to clear out the autumn-sown pak choi that had bolted. The hens were delighted to receive these plants. We still have some oriental greens, winter purslane (claytonia) and spinach in the tunnel, but probably only enough for a few weeks more, which is why I was spurred to start my annual salad sowing process.

9 march
first
rhubarb
harvest

I was out and about pottering in the garden a lot this week, feeling like I was finally emerging from a long winter hibernation. It felt really good to be outside. With the slight stretch in the mornings and evenings we've effectively gained 10 hours a week of potential GIY time, and it no longer has to be a weekend-only activity.

My heated propagation mat in the potting shed is getting a bit crowded now, so I switched on the power to the propagation bench (a heated coil running through a 15cm (6-inch) bed of sand) to get it warmed up. It takes three to four days for the sand to heat up. The heated propagation units allow you to cheat the return of the cold weather by giving the seed trays heat from beneath. It does the same job as the heated mat, just on a bigger scale.

I still haven't planted anything outside yet. I thought about sowing broad beans, but time ran away from me. There's no rush, as I can sow them later in the month.

I was also able to harvest the first new-season crop of the year this week: rhubarb. I put a good covering of compost on the rhubarb plants back in November and they seem to have really benefited from that. Not only did it nourish the plants, it also effectively acted to 'force' them to come on early. I was surprised to see how much there was available to harvest even at this early stage. I made and enjoyed a delicious rhubarb crumble, which was a real first taste of spring. I also like to melt down chunks of rhubarb and a little sugar and water in a saucepan and store it in the fridge to add to yoghurt pots for our school/work lunches.

Nicky Kelly's rhubarb crumble

After harvesting the first of our rhubarb yesterday, we celebrated with this lovely crumble.

ingredients:
— 600g rhubarb, chopped into chunks
— 100g golden caster sugar
— 140g self-raising flour
— 85g butter
— 50g light brown sugar

directions:
Preheat the oven to 200°C.

Put the rhubarb in a saucepan with the caster sugar. Cover and simmer on a very low heat for 15 minutes. When it is soft, pour the rhubarb into a medium baking dish.

To make the crumble, rub the flour and butter together with your fingers until you have a soft, crumbly topping. Now add the brown sugar, mixing it together with your hands. Scatter the topping over the rhubarb and bake for 30 minutes, until golden brown on top. Serve piping hot – some custard on top is nice.

11 march
dealing
with leggy
seedlings

Seedlings can become 'leggy' when there's not enough light available and they are essentially reaching to get to whatever light there is. As well as the 'legginess', they will veer in the direction of the light. But here's an interesting tip for dealing with seedlings that have become leggy: simply run your hand gently through the seedlings each day, up to 20 times at a go, to encourage a bit of hardiness in the seedlings – much as a light breeze would do.

If you have leggy tomato seedlings you can address this when re-potting them by planting them up to their lower leaves, so if they are a couple of inches tall due to stretching, bury them deep and the seedling stem develops roots. You can do this anytime you 'pot on' tomatoes and it ensures a sturdy plant. This approach is unique to tomatoes, though.

12 march
sow leeks

If you want a continuous supply of leeks throughout the winter, do three sowings each year: one now, in mid-March, a second in late March and a third in May. This method provides leeks from autumn this year to spring of the following year. I generally do all my sowing in one go, though, to save time, enough to give me three leeks a week from October to March – that is 72 leeks. I think you need to time the first harvest for around October/November, when we start to crave winter foods.

Leeks are super easy to grow from seed in module trays (three or four seeds per module) before being transplanted to their final growing position later on. I could go on for pages about the approach to transplanting seeds – there's a right palaver about 'puddling in' leeks (only a horticulturalist could come

up with these phrases), which involves creating a little hole with a dibber, popping in the leek and, instead of firming it in with soil, pouring water into the hole to create a puddle. The soil then gently falls in around the seedling without damaging it. I've also planted out leeks as you would a normal seedling and it's worked fine too. I think the key is to make sure it's deep enough to ensure there will be plenty of the white part of the leek when you harvest.

If you are space-constrained in your growing, it's worth considering this fundamental point when deciding what to grow: not all vegetables are the same. They don't all give you the same bang for their buck, so to speak. The great Joy Larkcom talks about a 'value for space' rating in her seminal book *Grow Your Own Vegetables*.

First, it's worth considering that some vegetables are incredibly fast-growing and therefore give you a very quick return from the space you have allocated to them. This means you can very quickly start growing something else in the same space once you've harvested them. For example, you can be eating white turnips about two months after sowing them. Radishes will be ready even quicker than that, usually within a month. Other vegetables are very slow-growing and will monopolise a piece of ground for ages before giving a return. For example, garlic is sown in winter and is not ready to eat until the following summer, while purple sprouting broccoli is growing for almost a year before you get to eat it.

Second, different vegetables take up different amounts of space in the ground. Each carrot needs only 3–4cm (1–1½ inches) in your soil, while a Brussels sprout plant needs to be planted 1m away from its nearest neighbour. On top of this, there is the question of yield. Some vegetables return a lot of food for the space they take up. Others really don't. At the end of a very long growing season, a well-grown sweetcorn plant will probably give you only two cobs for all your effort. You will most likely get only four sweetcorn plants in a metre of growing space (since they are planted about 50cm (20 inches) apart), so eight corn on the cob from a metre is a pretty poor return. Take that same metre of growing space and plant it up with beetroot and you will get about 40 beetroot (four rows with the plants spaced 10cm (4 inches) apart in the rows). Or if you sowed an oriental green, such as mizuna, in the metre of space, you will get to harvest food from the plot on multiple occasions, since oriental greens are what are known as 'cut and come again' vegetables (that is, you cut the plant down to about 5cm and it grows back again to give a second, and sometimes a third, harvest).

It's also worth thinking about growing vegetables (or vegetable varieties) that are difficult to source in the supermarket (e.g. Jerusalem and globe artichokes, celeriac, yacon, purple sprouting broccoli, fennel, endive, chicory and oriental salads) or difficult to source fresh (e.g. peas, broad beans, French beans and runner beans).

Finally, some vegetables can be considered particularly valuable because of the time of year when we can harvest them. Any vegetable that is available to eat fresh from the garden in the tricky 'hungry gap' months (March–May) is worth its weight in gold. Purple sprouting broccoli is an example of this, which is why we're generally willing to allow it to monopolise space in the vegetable patch almost all year round.

**16 march
outdoor
seed
sowing**

By mid-March, things really start to ramp up a gear in terms of seed sowing and today my thoughts turned to the outdoor seed sowings. Theoretically, right now I could sow potatoes, onion sets and broad beans outdoors. I say theoretically because it's always impossible to be definitive about when to start outdoor sowing – we are still susceptible to harsh night-time frosts and low soil temperatures, so play it by ear and if in doubt, hold off!

French farmers apparently have a failsafe – and decidedly Billy Connolly-esque – method for working out when to start sowing outside: it involves dropping one's trousers and sitting with your bare arse on the soil in the veg patch. If it's too cold to leave your bum on the soil, then it's too cold to sow seeds! A thermometer is a slightly more scientific approach and has the advantage of not upsetting the neighbours. My tip is to hold off on outdoor sowings until day-time air temperatures are consistently above 7°C.

Still, it's exciting to see that we are moving steadily away from 'tentative/hopeful' sowings towards the bulk of our spring sowing. It's truly the most wonderful time of the year (sorry, Christmas).

**17 march
the humble
spud**

Honestly, I could take or leave some of the traditions of St Patrick's Day, but one tradition that I do love is sowing early potatoes. Having sown my early spuds today, we should have our first delicious potatoes in mid-June (around 14 weeks after growing).

I do two sowings of potatoes each year. Early potatoes are sown on or around St Patrick's Day, while maincrop potatoes are sown in late April. Early potato varieties are faster-growing than maincrop ones and are harvested before they have had a chance to form skins (which is why you can effectively just wash off the skins rather than peeling them before cooking). Maincrop varieties take a whole month longer to mature and develop thick skins, which means they store well. I think about it this way: early potatoes are for eating in the summer, while the maincrop potatoes are for winter (and storage).

Potatoes are grown from 'seed potatoes', which are potatoes saved from the previous year's crop. It was traditional for Irish GIYers to save their own seed potatoes, but this is generally out of favour now – better to buy certified seed potatoes each year in case your own potatoes carry a virus.

Fundamentally, potatoes are not difficult to grow – all you are doing is basically sticking a seed potato in the soil, which sprouts into a plant, which produces lots of other potatoes. So a single potato is magically transformed into anything from five to 15 potatoes, which, you must admit, is sort of miraculous. Traditionally, Irish people put their spuds in the ground on or around St Patrick's Day, believing it to be an auspicious day on which to do so. Since it's always the first outside sowing I do each year, it's always exciting after a long winter hibernation.

When it comes to planting time, it couldn't be easier. Simply mark out a row with some twine and place a seed potato on the ground every 25cm (10 inches). If you are adding a second row, make sure the rows are about 50cm (20 inches) apart. Then, with your hands or a trowel, make a hole for the spud about 15cm (6 inches) deep, pop the seed potato into it and cover back over with soil. And you're done!

Today I sowed three 5m (16½ft) rows of early potatoes, varieties Orla and Arran Pilot. That's about 60 spuds in total, yielding hopefully a kilo of spuds per plant or so.

The most important thing to remember is that potatoes form along the stem between the seed spud and the surface of the soil – so the more space you have between the two, the more spuds you get. So that means sowing the spud deep in the soil and 'earthing up' once the plant comes out of the ground (i.e. drawing soil up around the stem to force it to grow longer).

Potatoes won't really mind if your soil isn't great – in fact, they will do a good job of helping you to improve it. Sowing spuds is an almost universally accepted method of helping to turn an unpromisingly poor piece of ground into a vegetable patch. When you grow your own potatoes, you also get to try out lots of varieties that aren't so readily available in the shops (where the Rooster and Kerr's Pink dominate) – you can literally grow whatever variety takes your fancy, for example Home Guard, British Queen, Duke of York, Setanta, Cara, Sarpo Mira and more.

I think it's weird that we've become obsessed with imported sweet potatoes as a so-called superfood when the humble spud is just as nutritious – what's more, it's a seasonal, fresh, local food that also supports Irish jobs. It's one of the most versatile ingredients we have at our disposal in the kitchen. Very few dinners (in our house at least) do not contain potatoes in some form, whether boiled, baked, roasted, fried, mashed, chipped or, if we're feeling sassy, au gratin or dauphinoise. And if you think supermarket spuds are convenient, well, in my view it's even more convenient to wander down to the veg patch and dig some spuds fresh from the soil – you don't even have to get in the car. The act of harvesting spuds is pure GIY joy. Rummaging in the soil underneath a potato plant and finding lots of lovely tubers is a moment that gives opening presents on Christmas morning a run for its money.

potato, kale and roast garlic soup

This is JB's recipe from GROW HQ. Roasting the garlic beforehand gives it a lovely flavour.

Serves 4

ingredients:

— 1 whole head of garlic
— a drizzle of olive oil
— 300g green curly kale or cavolo nero
— 1kg potatoes (any type will do)
— 1 leek
— 1 small onion
— 50g butter
— a small pinch of ground nutmeg
— a pinch of salt

directions:

Preheat the oven to 120°C.

Roast the whole head of garlic (skin on) covered with a drizzle of olive oil for 30–45 minutes, until the garlic softens. Let the garlic cool. Cut the bottom part of the garlic head and squeeze out the roast garlic pulp. Smells delicious …

Cook the kale in a large pot of boiling salted water for 3–4 minutes. Strain the kale and cool it straightaway in iced water. Squeeze the cooked leaves and chop them roughly. This process will fix the chlorophyll and will keep your soup vibrant green. Peel and roughly chop the potatoes, leek and onion and sweat them in the butter, nutmeg and salt on a low heat in a large saucepan for 5 minutes. Cover with 1.5 litres of cold water and simmer for 20–30 minutes, until all the vegetables are cooked through. Add the blanched kale and the garlic pulp and blend. Check the seasoning before serving.

19 march
lazy beds

There was certainly a feeling of spring in the air today and I spent a pleasurable, though back-breaking, couple of hours working on new lazy beds in the veg patch. Lazy beds are a traditional way of creating what are effectively raised beds without the timber sides. Given the work that goes into maintaining them, I always smile at the idea of calling them 'lazy' beds. It is, in fact, a complete misnomer, because they are much harder work to construct and maintain than a timber-framed raised bed.

The lazy bed was traditionally used as an attempt to overcome poor, shallow, infertile and often boggy soils that were difficult to grow in. They were particularly effective in mountainous regions where the short growing seasons made holding soil warmth a problem. Poignantly, the remains of famine-era lazy beds can still be seen on the side of mountains in many parts of the West of Ireland, particularly in County Mayo. The fact that they have survived intact suggests that they were abandoned suddenly – in that sense, they are an agonising snapshot of death and devastation similar to the grisly casts of Vesuvius victims in Pompeii.

Though I have some timber-framed raised beds in the veg patch, I also have a large lazy bed area measuring 10m long and 5m wide (32ft x 16ft). Within that space I have parallel banks of beds each about 1.2m (4ft) wide and separated by trenches 30cm (1ft) wide. I sow crops in rows in the long beds, while the trenches are used as paths and for drainage. The trenches are exactly a rake's width, as regular raking keeps them weed-free and creates a fine tilth of soil, which is then drawn up onto the beds and raked in. This simultaneously deepens the trenches and raises the beds. Several years of cultivation using this method has created good soil quality.

Though I get a kick out of the fact that I am helping to preserve a once-widespread growing tradition, lazy beds are not purely nostalgic, as they enjoy all the practical benefits of a timber-framed raised bed but with no cost. They are well suited to areas that lack deep soil or where drainage is a problem. The beds are drier and therefore warmer than the flat land around them. They warm up more quickly in the morning and retain their heat longer into the evening. The effectiveness of lazy beds for drainage can be seen in my garden on very wet days when the trenches on either side of the beds can often be filled with water.

20 march
in the
throes of
spring
sowing

Today's fine, dry weather allowed me to get out into the garden and get a major start on the year's GIYing. Though it was undoubtedly cold overnight, it warmed up considerably in the afternoon, and when the sun shone it certainly *felt* like spring.

Out in the vegetable patch I finished sowing my early potatoes. I sowed one bed of Duke of York and the other of Home Guard – about 40 seed potatoes of each. I'm also trying a small experiment – covering one of the potato beds with fleece and leaving the other exposed. I'm hoping that the fleece covering will give me potatoes a week or so early.

In the polytunnel, I sowed a long row of early carrots after first raking the soil to a fine tilth and creating a little ridge to increase the depth of the soil for them. Good deep soil equals nice long carrots. I also sowed about 10 seed potatoes in the tunnel – hopefully these will be ready a few weeks before their counterparts outside. And finally, in the potting shed I did the first sowings of celeriac and celery and a further 'succession' sowing of beetroot. I'm certainly getting stuck into the meat and veg of the spring sowing now. And you know what? It feels great! By the evening my body was weary, but my mind and soul were entirely contented.

22 march
sowing
broad
beans

Broad beans can be sown outside pretty much as soon as you can get the ground ready. They are a super hardy vegetable that will withstand the worst weather that nature can throw at them. Certain varieties of broad beans, such as Aquadulce Claudia, can even be sown before Christmas for an early, early crop. If I am not sufficiently organised for that, this is a great time to sow them. Do make sure to get a spring sowing variety if you are sowing at this time of the year.

After raking the bed to get it relatively flat, I use the handle of the rake to mark out a straight line (you could use some twine between two sticks if you want to be super straight) and lay the beans on the soil at 20cm (8-inch) spacing. Then I simply poke them down into the soil to the depth of my finger

(4–5cm/1½–2 inches). Today I sowed roughly 50 beans in three short rows 50cm (20 inches) apart. It's probably way too many plants and no doubt I will be cursing myself in months to come as I struggle to keep up with the crop of beans. But they freeze well, so they are never really wasted. Last year I decided I didn't really like broad beans and I wasn't going to grow them again, but spring exuberance always wins out in the end.

I've been taking some steps to sort out the big polytunnel and get it ready for the season ahead. Last year I grew around 80 tomato plants in our large commercial tunnel, but like most growers I was battling the twin evils of too much work and not enough time. I struggled with weeding and watering all season long, although I did seem to stay on top of the harvesting and sauce-making!

25 march managing the workload

I have a cunning plan to try to reduce the workload some-what for the season ahead. First, I am going to use Mypex (a tough weed control membrane that suppresses the growth of weeds by blocking the light) on the paths to ensure I don't have weed problems. It's a pricier route to go than regular hoeing, of course, but needs must and at least it's reusable year after year.

Second, I am going to invest in a proper seep-hose water-ing system so that I don't have to water each plant. Tomatoes are thirsty plants, requiring up to 11 litres (2½ gallons) of water per plant per week. Typically, I've done that watering every other day (a few litres to each plant), which is obviously tremendously time-consuming. At GROW HQ, our head grower, Richard Mee, turns on the seep-hose system once a week instead – he's worked out how long it takes to deliver around 11 litres to each plant with the seep hose (about two hours). Amazingly, the plants seem to get used to the weekly watering regime and thrive on it.

Of course I must also sort out the fertility in the soil, adding some dried seaweed and poultry manure pellets to ensure that the tomatoes have enough feed to see them through their six months in the soil. Apart from an occasional comfrey tea feed during the summer, they shouldn't require any other feeding. The dried seaweed and poultry pellets will be sprinkled on the surface and raked in before laying the seep hose on top. Thankfully I still have some time to get this job done – the tomato plants were only sown in mid-February and are still growing in the toasty warmth of the potting shed. They will not be going out into the polytunnel until May at the earliest.

Today I also sorted some other issues. I had a few tears in the plastic to fix (with an adhesive polytunnel tape – available from good polytunnel suppliers) and a new door to put on (the old one blew off in a storm last autumn). I also got a trench dug around the tunnel to fix a drainage problem due to poor soil – after heavy rain the paths *inside* the tunnel would fill up with water. I was always torn between feeling this was a terrible thing or perhaps a good thing in terms of reducing the amount of watering needed! All the work will be worth it when the first tomatoes start to make their way to the kitchen around mid-July.

26 march
an early
spring
round-up

I've been pleasingly busy in the veg patch over the last few weeks and absolutely loving it – there's something about this time of the year that just gladdens the heart.

In the potting shed, I've an array of module trays to look

78

after every day now – covering them with fleece at night (if it's forecast to be cold) and watering them in the morning, as on a heated mat they are inclined to dry out, particularly on sunny days. The aubergines, chilli peppers and peppers, which were sown in February, are slow to grow and don't need to be 'potted on' just yet. Along with these Mediterranean veg, I'm also nurturing trays of salad greens (oriental greens, lettuce and annual spinach), beetroot, baby turnips and little pots of celeriac and celery.

Outside, the winter-sown garlic is growing well – there's little to do there apart from ensuring the bed is hoed every couple of weeks to prevent weeds. Like everything else in nature, weeds are about to go mental, so this is a good time to get on top of them so that you enter the busy spring period with a clean veg patch.

The purple sprouting broccoli plants needed some tending, but are producing well (as always, the more you pick, the more they produce). The rhubarb plants are producing reasonably well, but as they did last year the plants have quickly started to run to seed. Our head grower at GROW HQ, Richard Mee, tells me that this is probably due to the plants being a little old or under stress. His advice is to take them out and split them or plant new ones for next year.

raw kale salad

This recipe will open your eyes to the potential of kale for salads. Massaging the kale with lemon juice and salt in effect cooks it and makes it far more palatable while retaining its nutrients. I was sceptical about the culinary merits of a kale salad until I tasted this – it's delicious. It will keep for three days in the fridge.

Serves 4
ingredients:
— 250g kale
— juice of 1 lemon
— 2–3 pinches of salt
— olive oil

- 1 small red onion, finely sliced
- 25g dried cranberries, finely chopped
- 50g cashew nuts, roasted and chopped
- 2–3 stalks of celery, finely chopped

directions:

Remove the stalks from the kale and chop the leaves into fine strips. Place in a large bowl and add the lemon juice and 2–3 pinches of salt. Massage the kale with the juice and salt until it starts to soften a little. Sprinkle with olive oil and leave it to sit for another 10 minutes. Add the red onion, cranberries, cashew nuts and celery and mix well. Later in the year you could add some cherry tomatoes or cucumber to this salad.

28 march sowing cucumber seeds

Today I sowed cucumber seeds. I start them off in 8cm (3-inch) pots, putting just one seed in each pot and placing the pots on a heating mat – a warm, sunny windowsill will work if you don't have a heating mat.

Cucumbers really are an amazing veg to grow. Of all the episodes of our TV series *Grow Cook Eat*, the cucumber episode was my favourite – the cucumber plants are just visually stunning and it still blows my mind that from a tiny seed you get this Jack and the Beanstalk experience with vast gluts of fruit to harvest. One or two cucumber plants will satisfy the needs of most households. I'm always harping on at GIY talks about the thriftiness of growing your own cucumbers – a single plant will churn out up to 40 or 50 cucumbers over the season. Each cucumber would cost you €1 to buy in the supermarket, while a packet of cucumber seeds containing 20 seeds will cost about €2.50, which means that there's potentially over €1,000 worth of cucumbers right there in a single packet of seeds! Now, admittedly, you won't want to grow 1,000 cucumbers, but you get my point. And don't forget that cucumbers store incredibly well in a pickle, which means you can enjoy them all year round if you

grow enough of them. My cucumber pickle recipe, which you can read about in August (page 199), is a real go-to in our house – I stock up the presses in the kitchens with it and we use it for the kids' lunches for almost the full school year.

29 march
a sudden
cold snap

It's hard to believe that this time last year we were basking in 20°C heat and headed for the beach over the Easter holidays. This year, it's a case of wrapping up well and trying to endure persistent freezing temperatures. It does all seem rather unnatural, particularly since it feels like it should be spring now that we've planted the potatoes. People shake their heads and say that the world has gone mad and that climate change is wreaking havoc, but then again, March has a track record of throwing up unpredictable weather. So perhaps this is just normal.

Either way, the cold weather has caused things to slow down in the veg patch after a couple of productive weeks. Growth of my seedlings in the polytunnel has slowed almost to a stop – the lack of sunlight means I am not even having to water them all that much since the potting compost is not drying out. One suspects that the newly planted spuds aren't doing a whole lot in the cold ground outside either. Rhubarb, the only thing that was starting to be very productive, seems to have been knocked back too, with the leaves looking burned. I fret that it's frost damage and wonder whether they will bounce back.

This growth 'pause' couldn't come at a worse time, really, considering that the larder is now starting to look very bare. This week we used up the last of our stored carrots, onions, shallots, squashes and pumpkins (though I have to say that I cheered up immensely when I cut open the last pumpkin and saw the beautiful vibrant orange colour of the flesh). Anyway, with the exception of some chutneys and pickles, some frozen veg in the freezer and the stalwarts of the polytunnel (oriental greens) and the winter veg garden (purple sprouting broccoli, perpetual spinach and chard), pickings are slim indeed.

I've worked out that I spent 10½ hours this March in the veg patch or potting shed, which is under three hours a week. That's not too bad when you consider that we're in a busy time of the year. Today I spent about three hours in the potting shed with a glorious sun beating in on top of me.

I did a good batch of seed sowing: basil, coriander, calabrese, cauliflower, celery and celeriac. All of these (with the exception of celeriac) are 'succession sowings' – that is, small but regular sowings of a vegetable to maintain a steady supply. I sowed one eight-module tray each of basil, calabrese and cauliflower and two trays of the leeks. I also sowed one 9cm pot each of celery and celeriac. It's important to get the celeriac sown early – the mistake people make most often is sowing it too late. To get nice big celeriac they need to be out in the ground by May, and that means getting them started now. Celeriac is a fantastic storage veg that will do very well in the ground next winter – I grow about 40 each year, which will see us through from November to late March next year.

I do three sowings of celery during the year, as it doesn't tend to do so well in the ground (although I did manage a very late harvest in February this year from last year's crop!) and needs to be used almost immediately after it's picked.

april

The days lengthen, the ground heats up and all living things (including seedlings and weeds) are growing by the day. The level of activity increases as we balance seed sowing and transplanting, but we don't grumble – we love it.

This month we're loving … purple sprouting broccoli.

We took care of the plants for nearly a year, and now they repay us with spring deliciousness when there's very little else to eat.

1 april
april fool!

Today started with Mrs Kelly playing her annual April Fool's Day trick on me and (as is the tradition), I swallowed it hook, line and sinker. 'Oh my God!' she screamed. 'There's a fox in the hen run!' I tore out of the door and sprinted down the garden, mentally preparing for battle. But there was no fox, of course, and when I looked back at the house, she and the kids were looking out of the door in convulsions of laughter.

Anyway, fooling (and being fooled) aside, today I was grappling with a map of the veg garden and deciding how much space to allocate to the different veg families. Generally speaking the crop rotation plan will pretty much dictate what's to be grown where, but this year the luck of the crop rotation draw sees my onion family (garlic, onions, shallots and leeks) get the short straw in terms of allocated space. That's a problem for a veg family that is so valuable in the kitchen – particularly onions and garlic. So then the question is, do I stick to the plan or bend the crop rotation rules a tad to try to snaffle a little extra space from another veg family?

If I'm honest, the obvious candidate to have some space taken back is the brassica family (cabbages, kale, Brussels sprouts, PSB, etc.). This would be more a commentary on how much heartache brassicas cause rather than on the veg themselves, which are very fine indeed. The little seedlings of the brassica family are particularly vulnerable to slugs and then, of course, you have to grapple with the menace of caterpillars from the cabbage white butterfly and all the palaver over netting. If there was a 'heartache index' for vegetables (and there should be), the brassica family would surely top the table.

Still, I certainly don't want to cut the brassicas out completely. Though I've never been much of a fan of cabbage, in recent years I have become *obsessed* with sauerkraut (it's a long story) and eat a little of it every day (I swear, I physically crave it). Red cabbages are also great for late-summer slaws, so having a few decent heads of cabbage is a must during the growing year. Kale is a brilliant veg too, particularly the chef's favourite cavolo nero variety, but really, two or three healthy kale plants is plenty. Brussels sprouts and sprouting broccoli are also fantastic veg to have for winter and early spring, but both take up a lot of space because of their wide spacing – so one or two plants of each should do the trick.

So I guess I can scale back the brassicas just a *little* and allocate another bed to onions. Onions are also a far more easy-going vegetable, so hopefully this will reduce the overall heartache index for this year's growing.

Timing is always important in the veg patch, but with the growing of tomatoes it is even more so.

Tomato seeds are sown in February and coaxed and nurtured along various phases of growth with a view to planting out into a greenhouse or polytunnel in April or May. A healthy cherry tomato plant can produce literally hundreds of tomatoes – it goes without saying that it takes a lot of energy to produce that much food, so the plant has a lot of growing to do before it can undertake this super-human task. Growing tomatoes successfully in Ireland is about cheating our climate and starting them indoors in February so the plants have enough time to grow big and strong before producing fruit in July.

My tomatoes are in module trays now, having been 'pricked out' of the pots they were sown in. At this time of the year it's a slightly anxious affair as you try to figure out when it will be warm enough to plant them in the ground in the tunnel. Myself and Richard, our head grower at GROW HQ (formerly a commercial organic grower), occasionally have nerdy horticultural conversations over lunch – they are the types of conversation that only veg obsessives could ever really enjoy. Today we were chatting about transplanting tomato plants and specifically whether to plant them out or pot them on at this stage. My plants are now outgrowing the trays they are in, so I need to decide what to do – it seems a little risky to put them out in the polytunnel given

**2 april
timing is
everything**

the weather we've been having. He says he sowed his tomatoes a whole month later than me, so he wouldn't have the problem that I now face. With a glint in his eye, he calls me a 'premature germinator'. He loves a bit of veg innuendo.

So why not leave them in the module trays? Well, when tomato plants are in trays tightly jammed together and getting bigger, they are competing for light. This can result in you losing the early fruit as the plant wisely decides it won't have enough light for the first fruit truss. This is where the timing issue comes in. Richard, in his wisdom, waited until March to sow his tomatoes, which means his will be fine in module trays until late April, when they can be planted out in the tunnel. In my eagerness, I sowed mine in mid-February and potted them on in early March, which means they are now bursting out of the trays, but it's still too early to plant them out. For now, all I can do is wait (or if I'm very worried about them running out of food, I could give them a plant feed), but it's another lesson in the importance of patience in the growing process.

sausage and beer stew

So many of my recipes at this time of the year focus on the available root crops that I have either in the ground or in storage, such as carrots, parsnips, celeriac and beets. This recipe was inspired by a frantic last-minute search for ideas to make dinner when all I could find in the fridge was a tray of sausages. Though I was tempted to go for a simple plate of sausage, eggs and chips, I had some veg in the basket and decided to concoct a stew. I would generally pair sausages with cider in a stew, but all I had in the fridge was a bottle of non-alcoholic lager left over from Dry January. Never mind, it seemed to work in this delicious and warming meal. Don't worry too much about sticking to the veg ingredients too rigidly – you could use celery instead of celeriac, swede instead of squash, etc.

Serves 4

ingredients:
— olive oil
— 6–8 good-quality dinner sausages
— 2 onions, diced
— 1 leek, trimmed and finely chopped
— 4 cloves garlic, diced
— 2 large carrots, diced
— ½ celeriac, diced
— 1 330ml bottle of beer
— 500ml beef or chicken stock
— 400g tin of tomatoes or 2 tbsp tomato purée
— 2 tbsp chopped herbs (parsley, rosemary and thyme)
— 1 bay leaf
— 1 tbsp mustard (I used Dijon)
— ¼ squash or pumpkin, peeled and chopped into large chunks
— salt and pepper
— crusty bread or baked potatoes, to serve

directions:

Heat a little oil in a frying pan. Cut the sausages into chunks and fry them for a minute or so on each side, until browned. Remove from the pan and set aside on a plate. In the same frying pan, fry the onions, leek, garlic, carrots and celeriac on a gentle heat for about 10 minutes, until soft. Transfer to a heavy saucepan or casserole.

Pour the bottle of beer into the frying pan to deglaze the pan, scraping any nice brown bits off the pan with a wooden spatula. Bring to the boil and let it simmer for about 10 minutes to reduce down a little. Add it to the veg with the stock, tomatoes, herbs, bay leaf and mustard. Bring to the boil and then add the squash or pumpkin. Cook for 15 minutes with the lid on.

Add the sausages to the saucepan and cook for another 15 minutes. Taste and season with salt and pepper. Check the consistency – leave to simmer for another 10 minutes if it needs to be thickened or add a little boiling water if it's too thick.

Serve with crusty bread or baked potatoes.

5 april
start small
and keep it
simple

Here's a confession. In my first few years of GIYing, I was completely and utterly useless at it. Voracious reading on the subject left me feeling none the wiser. A veg-growing guide might, for example, tell you that you start growing garlic by sticking a clove in the soil. I would immediately wonder, 'Which end do you stick in the soil?', and riddled with indecision, I would be reluctant to even try. The first time I sowed carrots, I ended up weeding the little seedlings away because I had no idea which were weeds and which were the carrot seedlings.

Most people start their GIY journey by buying a book – usually some sort of a vegetable growing guide that has an A–Z listing of all the vegetables one can grow. This seems sensible and I'm all for people buying books (particularly if they are mine … ha ha), but I always think that starting with a comprehensive guide to growing is like using the Kama Sutra to learn the basics

of sex. What one really needs, of course, is to keep it simple – start small and focus on vegetables that are easy to grow (like herbs and salad greens). A couple of early quick wins will give you the confidence to keep going.

Incidentally, I wince whenever I hear the phrase 'green fingers' – the idea that you are either born with an ability to grow things or you aren't is deeply unhelpful. In reality, growing things is a skill, and like any skill it takes time to master. All of us have to go through that phase where we are novices, and we have to accept the fact that we will most likely kill a lot of plants while we wait for our ability to catch up with our enthusiasm. Once we've accepted that fact, it somehow doesn't seem so scary.

Let's be honest – in the grand scheme of things a couple of plants sacrificed for the greater good is not such a big deal. Don't let yourself get derailed by occasional mishaps. Get back on the horse and try again. The most important thing is that we show up each spring ready to try another season.

6 april the art of seed sowing On any course I run at GROW HQ, I always spend a lot of time on seed sowing. It's such an important part of GIYing, and I think that once you've seen it done right and practised it yourself, it's a skill you'll have for ever.

Though some seeds (tomatoes, aubergines, celery, etc.) are best started off in pots, most of my seed sowing is done in module trays. A module tray is a tray with individual compartments or modules in it. A decent-sized tray will measure 335mm x 515mm (roughly 13 x 20 inches) and contain between 80 and 150 modules. They are made from rigid plastic so they can be used again and again. I have five of them at home, which I've had for ever. The beauty of a module tray is that the roots of seedlings are kept apart, which means you don't upset them when you are transplanting them.

Before you fill the tray with compost (make it peat-free), it's important to work with the compost a little first. Break up any larger clumps – this is important because smaller seeds might fall through the cracks and fail to germinate because they're too deep in the compost. I start by completely overfilling the tray with compost and working it into the modules with my hands. Banging the tray against the bench a few times will help the compost to settle down into the container. Overfill it again, then use a flat stick or piece of timber to 'slice' the excess compost off the top, leaving a flat, clean surface on the module tray.

Before sowing the seeds, I make a 'divot' in each module with my fingers. This is the little recess in the compost into which you will drop the seed. I usually use two fingers from each hand to make the divots in four modules at a time to speed things up. How deep you make the divot depends on how deep the seeds need to be. A good rule of thumb is that you sow the seed roughly twice as deep as the seed's size. So a tiny lettuce seed is almost on top of the surface, while a larger seed like a squash or pumpkin would be much deeper.

Depending on the size of the seed, you can either pick one up and drop it into the divot or use a plant label to move it off the palm of your hand and let it fall into the divot. With most vegetables, you will be sowing one seed per module, but with others (e.g. oriental greens or leeks) you might be sowing three or four

seeds per module. It's important to label the tray – I use white plastic labels and a pencil so they can be washed off and reused. I always write on the label the name of the veg, the variety and the date it was sown. That way, if germination is slow, you can check how long it's been since it was sown – and make an executive decision to wait a little longer or cut your losses and start again.

To cover the seeds, I then overfill the tray with compost again and slice the excess off with my trusty stick to leave a flat surface. I then bring the trays outside and water them on the ground by the potting shed. I use a fine mist setting on the hose, but a fine rose on a watering can is just as good.

9 april
hoeing

Today I was out and about, hoeing in between the over-wintered onion sets here at home. One of the most common reasons we hear from people as to why veg growing hasn't worked for them is that they couldn't cope with the weeds. This is entirely under-standable since there are times when the persistence and speed at which weeds take over can be incredibly demoralising. It can help, I think, to reframe how you think about weeds – it's certainly not helpful to view them as an adversary that has to be beaten down. Though they will compete with your veggies for nutrients, they are first and foremost just a plant that happens to be growing in the wrong place. Some of them are even edible (like chickweed and dandelions) and in the winter they can even be beneficial since they provide valuable cover to protect the soil. So in general, I've learned to be a little more circumspect about them.

I do like to at least start the growing season with a weed-free patch (at this time of the year weeds will compete with seeds and seedlings) and then do my best to keep on top of them during the peak weed season from spring to midsummer. For me, the only way to do that is through regular hoeing, so from April to August I try to run over the entire veg patch with a hoe each week. Its enjoyable work if you do it right, standing upright with a long-handled hoe and moving it forward and back just beneath the soil surface. An oscillating hoe is a good investment to make lighter work of it.

Ideally you want to hoe to prevent weeds as opposed to having to get rid of them. So, strange as it sounds, I will even hoe the soil if there are no weeds at all. Although you may have to pull weeds if they get well established, it's preferable not to have to, since it upsets soil structure and fertility. So it's far better to hoe weeds, which basically dislodges the roots and forces them to die – they then rot down and add to soil fertility. Hoeing is eight times faster than pulling weeds (clearly someone measured that!).

In addition to hoeing, mulches and green manures will prevent weeds from becoming established, as will coverings of Mypex, plastic, etc. It's also important to keep the grass around your patch short, otherwise it's a great seeding environment for weeds.

I've heard some of my fellow growers argue that you shouldn't bother growing onions on the grounds that they are so cheap and ubiquitous. Why, they sniff, would you allocate precious growing space to such a mundane vegetable when you could be growing something cool and exotic, like asparagus or salsify or globe artichokes? Onions … pfff … sure, they are practically a condiment, darling.

11 april
why bother growing onions?

Okay, so yes, onions are cheap and plentiful. And yes, it's true that if all you are using them for is as the starting point for your spag bol, then it probably won't matter a whole lot whether they're homegrown or from a Dutch mega-farm. But I'm convinced that the flavour of homegrown onions is better than shop-bought onions, so having your own means you're starting almost every meal with a better-tasting foundation. And they can be venerated in their own right, too – why not make an onion tart or a proper French onion soup and put them centre stage? Although I can't prove it, I also think homegrown onions make you cry more. I've often wondered why shop-bought onions don't make me cry any more. Am I just getting used to chopping them? Are my tear ducts drying out as I get older? Am I an emotional wasteland? Or is there something fundamentally different about the modern, commercial onion?

With the transition into April, today I was out sowing my onions. I find onions easy to grow. There are basically two ways of growing them: (1) from seed or (2) from 'sets', which are basically immature onions that someone else has grown from seed.

You should sow your onion sets between mid-March and mid-April (to sow from seed, you need to start them in February), but it's best to wait until the soil has warmed up a little. If you do want to go ahead with them, a fleece cover will keep them a little warmer and has the added benefit of keeping the birds away (crows and pigeons are inclined to pick at the sets). You will need to remove the cover once the sets start to grow.

I get seriously geeky when it comes to sowing onions – I have a bed 5m (roughly 16ft) long to sow them in and I get four rows in the bed. The onions are sown at 10cm (4-inch) spacing in the rows, which means I get 200 onions from the bed. I use the handle end of the rake to mark out the row and then space

the onions at 10cm. There are several reasons for being so nerdy about this. First, it just looks so damn pretty when they start to grow. Second, the spacing is important: 10cm gives you the perfect, in my opinion, medium-sized onion – you could go to 15cm (6 inches) and get giant onions or pull back to 7cm (3 inches) for smaller ones. Third, having an ordered grid like this makes it easier to run the hoe between the rows to keep on top of weeds.

To sow the sets, you simply push each set into well-prepared soil so that the tip is just showing above the surface. Try to find nice round sets; avoid the oval, tapered ones, which are more inclined to bolt. If birds pick the sets out on you, dig them up and plant them again carefully – don't push them back in, as you might damage the roots.

Onions are also a highly effective 'storage' crop. If I am lucky, onions will be perfectly content hanging in a braid in the kitchen until around February or March of the following year – at which point they start to get soft and sprout. So, harvesting from September, we will have 30+ onions a month until February next year. If it's not exactly a high-value crop in the way that others might be, that's still a return not to be sneezed at.

13 april
container growing

Viewers of *Grow Cook Eat* will know I was always sniffy about Karen's container growing in the TV series – honestly, it was just all part of the banter we had going on. But I've been forced to eat my hat a little on the issue over the years as I saw the success of GROW HQ's Container Corner and how well it worked for growing veg like carrots, peas, beans, beetroot and so on. It's such a sunny, sheltered little spot by the front door and some of the veg did better in Container Corner than they did in the ground in the veg patch.

Using containers, GIYers can grow great vegetables on decks, patios, terraces, flat roofs, balconies, in conservatories or even on a kitchen shelf or windowsill. We had a guy speak at a GIY festival years ago who grew £900 worth of veg on an apartment balcony in London (I always wondered why he couldn't have redoubled his efforts and got to an even thousand pounds).

Pretty much any container can be used to grow vegetables – pots, trays, troughs, window boxes, grow bags, wheelbarrows, old watering cans, tyres, etc. They should be a minimum of 15–25cm (6–10 inches) deep and there must be drainage holes in the base. Put in a 1cm (½-inch) layer of small stones to aid drainage. Most vegetables will grow well in containers – try lettuce, carrots, radishes, spring onions, cucumbers, Swiss chard, courgettes, beetroot, chillies, aubergines, strawberries and tomatoes. In fact, the single failure we had in Container Corner was broccoli – only because it wasn't covered properly with Bionet and the caterpillars destroyed it.

14 april
winter
greens

Though I've had a polytunnel for over a decade now, I still find it amazing that we can enjoy greens all year round from it. From a sowing back in the autumn of last year into the central bed of the polytunnel (when the tomato plants came out), we've had access right through the winter to oriental greens like mizuna, mibuna and pak choi and other winter greens, such as lamb's lettuce.

The plants are dormant over the winter, so it's just as well that one tends not to have such a great appetite for green things in the winter months. They are used only sparingly, but it's nice to know they are there. With spring in the air come February and March, and the polytunnel warming up to the point of being balmy by day, they burst into life. Over the last few weeks, growth has been phenomenal – which, although nice to look at, tends to make for slightly more stalky and bitter leaves. It's a good idea to get them out of the soil before they run to flower.

Thankfully, just as last year's winter sowing is starting to run past its best, the new-season oriental greens are going into the soil and should be ready for the first cuttings in just a few weeks. I sowed the seeds (of red and green mustard, mizuna, mibuna, pak choi and rocket) in early March and they germinated within a few days (on a heated propagator). Just over a month later, they are ready to be planted out. Interestingly, lettuce and annual spinach sown on the same day are not quite ready to be planted out yet, which shows just how quickly the oriental greens grow.

The speedy turnaround (about six weeks from seed sowing to eating) and winter-hardiness of oriental greens makes them one of the most reliable and useful crops in the garden.

We were blessed with beautiful weather today. It was simply glorious to be out working with the sun on my back (and in a T-shirt to boot) – all felt right with the world. Though it's not beyond the bounds of possibility that cold weather could return, for now it's definitely spring and I'm loving it.

**16 april
sowing
peas**

Today I got the peas sown, which (along with onions/shallots) are one of the major springtime outdoor sowings. I sow peas twice a year: once in mid-April and then again at the end of May, with the second crop appreciated later in the summer. Podding peas can be somewhat of a palaver – fun and romantic at first, but rather tiresome after a while. So, this year, to reduce the amount of podding required, I am growing more sugarsnap peas (which are eaten whole, pod and all, and have a wonderful, sweet crunch) and mangetout (which are similar).

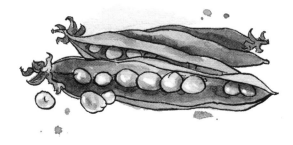

I sow my peas direct in the soil by using a hoe to make a shallow (4cm/1½-inch) trench about 15cm (6 inches) wide and placing the peas in a zigzag line along the row, spacing them about 5cm (2 inches) apart. I then simply rake the soil back over the peas and tamp the soil down with the back of a rake. I also sow some in 1m (3ft) lengths of guttering. This is a very handy way to sow smaller quantities in the controlled environment of the potting shed. Once the little plants are ready for planting out, I will simply dig a shallow trench and slide the soil and plants out into the trench.

Pea plants are tall and willowy and will need support when growing – a length of chicken wire between two posts works well, or you can buy rolls of pea support netting in your local garden centre. You can also use twiggy sticks instead if you want to avoid plastic. It's a good idea to put your support in place at sowing time, as it can be more difficult to do when the plants start to grow. You can enjoy fresh peas from May to October if you succession sow.

17 april
beetroot
fan

If I had to pick a favourite veg to grow, beetroot would come out on top (with a little competition perhaps from squashes, leeks, carrots, tomatoes, garlic … oh, sod it). Beetroot, how do I love thee? Let me count the ways. First of all, it's easy to grow – it is rarely troubled by pests or disease and, grown in module trays for later transplanting, I find it almost 100 per cent reliable. Let's be honest, there aren't many veg you can say that about. Second, it's great value for space – because beetroot is sown quite close together, you will get 40 beetroot from just a metre of veg bed (in four rows, with the beets 10cm (4 inches) apart in each row).

Third, beetroot is incredibly good for you – the betacyanin in beetroot can help detox your liver and reduce high blood pressure. It is packed with nutrients like folic acid, phosphorous and magnesium and is particularly high in vitamin C and iron (this is a great combination since vitamin C increases iron absorption). Finally, and perhaps most significantly, beetroot stores really well, making it possible to become self-sufficient in this superfood all year round.

I generally do three sowings of beetroot each year to maintain a consistent stash: an early crop sown in February for the polytunnel, a second crop sown around now for the summer months and then a final 'storage' crop sown in July for lifting in October or November. I store beetroot in a box of sand in the shed, from which we can enjoy fresh beetroot from October until May. Eating three a week on average, we chomp through about a hundred beetroot in this time.

Today I sowed a tray of beetroot in the potting shed. I sowed a full 84-cell module tray with one seed per cell and a selection of varieties (Detroit Globe, Pablo F1, Bulls Blood, Chiogga Pink).

beetroot and goat's cheese salad

I had no time at all for beetroot until I started growing it myself and realised that freshly cooked beetroot actually tastes great (particularly when paired with goat's cheese). It's the ultimate GIY vegetable – incredibly good for you, easy to grow and stores well. Cook beetroot whole in the oven (wrapped in tinfoil) or in a large pot of boiling water – they will take 30–45 minutes to cook depending on the size. Check with a skewer to make sure they're cooked. A beetroot and goat's cheese salad is practically a cliché at this stage, but that doesn't take away from the fact that it's a brilliant pairing.

Serves 4
ingredients:
— 500g beetroot, cooked, peeled and chopped
— a good handful of parsley, chopped, plus a little more to garnish
— salt and pepper
— 100g St Tola goat's cheese or equivalent, crumbled
— 75g walnuts, toasted (cashews, pecans or hazelnuts are also good)
— 70g leaves – oriental greens, baby spinach, small beetroot leaves or a mixture

For the dressing:
— 2 tbsp lemon juice
— 80ml olive oil
— 1 tsp Dijon mustard
— salt and pepper

directions:
First make the dressing. Whisk the lemon juice, olive oil and mustard together in a small bowl and season well.

Place the beetroot in a large bowl, mix in the parsley and season with a little salt and pepper. Add the goat's cheese and toasted walnuts (you can use untoasted walnuts, but you get a little extra flavour hit from toasting). Add the salad leaves and gently combine. Add the dressing and mix again. Garnish with a little more parsley.

19 april
earth up
spuds

As your potato plants grow, you need to 'earth them up' – this is the process of covering the stem (called a 'haulm') with soil. Since the potatoes grow along the haulm, the more of it that is buried beneath the soil, the more spuds you get. Use a draw or ridging hoe to bring loose soil from around the plant up against the stem (or use a spade if you don't have a draw hoe). When the stems are 20cm (8 inches) high, draw the soil up, leaving just 10cm (4 inches) of foliage above the surface. Repeat once or twice during the summer, particularly if you see spuds popping through the soil – spuds go green if exposed to the light and this makes them inedible.

Drawing soil up around the stem will also protect them from frosts, which are still very much a feature at this time of the year. In fact, at the moment I am simply covering the tops of the stems with soil as they appear, rather than covering them with fleece. With the amount of growth that is suddenly apparent, I am having to do this every other day.

A common question we are often asked at GROW HQ is, 'How do I know when my seedlings are big enough to transplant outside?' Like all the best questions, this one is hard to answer. It is critically important to get your timing right. If you transplant too early, the plant won't be able to survive the elements. Too late and the seedlings may become 'pot-bound'.

All vegetables are different, so there is no standard size at which you should transplant. However, there are a few general rules of thumb that can help you identify the right time (but be careful – this doesn't apply to all situations). First, size: if the plant is about twice as tall as the pot it's in, then it's usually ready to move on. Second, time: typically, you will be moving the seedling on six to eight weeks after sowing.

Third, look at how many 'true leaves' your seedling has. You have probably noticed that when a seed germinates first, you get what look like baby leaves on it – these are called cotyledons and they look different from the leaves that will grow later (e.g. with a tomato seedling, the cotyledons don't look like tomato leaves at all). The cotyledons provide stored food to the seedling during its infancy. Shortly afterwards, the 'true' leaves emerge – these are the plant's proper leaves and generate energy through photosynthesis that will feed the plant. Since the true leaves are evidence of a degree of maturity in the plant, they can provide a good indicator of when a plant is ready to be transplanted. When the seedling has developed three or four true leaves, it can usually be planted out.

Bear in mind, however, that no matter how big or small your seedling is, you should harden it off for at least a week before planting it out. Confused? Don't be. 'Hardening off' is the process of acclimatising seedlings that have been grown indoors or under cover to the colder temperatures outside. So, here's the deal: if you take seedlings that have been grown in the snuggly warmth of a sunny windowsill inside in your kitchen and put them straight out in the ground, they will probably die.

The key is to get them gradually used to the lower temperatures over the space of a week to 10 days. On the first day, put them out for a few hours, then bring them in again. The next day, leave them out for a few more hours and so on. As the week goes on, leave them out for longer and longer, until by the end of the week they should be out for almost the full day. At this stage, they should be ready for life in the great outdoors (including the night-times). If you're too busy for all that toing and froing, you could always just go ahead and transplant them and cover with some fleece instead.

Isn't it just the most wonderful time of the year? All of nature is in major growth mode – the most detested weeds and the most beloved seedlings are growing almost in front of our eyes. Leaves are emerging on trees and flowers are appearing in the garden practically overnight. I am spending night and day in the veggie patch at the moment and if I was asked, I couldn't tell you whether it's because there's so much work to do or because I love it so much.

21 april
the most wonderful time of the year

There *is* a lot to do. I'm still sowing loads of seeds, getting ground prepared in the veg patch for outdoor sowing, watering the tunnel, keeping on top of weeds and hardening off seedlings. I find the best way to stay on top of all the work is to sneak in some time in the garden every day, rather than leaving it all until the weekend. I'm an early riser anyway, so I'll happily spend half an hour in the morning before work – this morning I had three neat little rows of beetroot sown by 7.30 a.m. and got to listen to the birds in full song as a bonus! I ran around a few beds with a hoe too, which takes about 5 minutes and means that weeds don't have a chance to take hold. And, of course, with the long evenings I feel guilty about sitting down to watch TV when I could be out forking over a bed to get it ready for seedlings. I've done so much digging lately that I feel like an 80-year-old man today – but even though the body is tired, the soul is content.

26 april
planting for
winter

It seems strange to be thinking about winter, but around now is the time when you sow seeds for one of the stalwarts of the winter garden: Brussels sprouts. These plants will produce lots of food at a time when there is very little else cropping. If you could get four or five good plants going, you will have no shortage of healthy sprouts over the winter months.

A Brussels sprout plant will produce about 2kg of sprouts over a two-month period. Succession sowing is a good idea so that you have a steady, constant supply of sprouts, rather than them all coming at the same time. You can sow a couple of seeds now and then again in mid-May – try to aim for a total of five or six plants between the two sowings. Sow in module trays – one seed per module about 2cm (1 inch) deep. They will be ready for transplanting about four or five weeks later.

The Irish spring can bite you in the bum. Lulled into a false sense of security by the longer days, the growing grass, the emerging leaves and the blossoms on trees, I've been in full-on spring mode over the last few weeks.

Earlier this week I finally planted out the 80 tomato plants in the big tunnel – I also transplanted a load of spinach and beetroot seedlings in the veg patch outside. And then? I went outside this morning and was alarmed to discover a thin layer of frost on the windscreen of the car. Temperatures had plummeted overnight, with a blast of polar air bringing colder air temperatures. Though it seems like a temporary blip and warmer temperatures are on the way this weekend, we were down as low as 0°C at night this week. For most of today I've been fretting about the tomato plants. It's not the end of the world if I lose a few dozen beetroot or spinach seedlings, but the tomato plants are an altogether more valuable affair. From a purely monetary perspective, they are probably worth €5 per plant at this stage, and from an end produce prospective, they are worth far more than that. Let's say that a healthy plant can produce 300 cherry tomatoes and that a punnet of 20 organic tomatoes would cost you €3. That means each plant can produce €45 of tomatoes in a season. That means the crop is worth over €3,600. Yikes!

Of course, the monetary value is only part of the appeal. The sheer deliciousness of the tomatoes and the fact that I can 'store' them as sauces (in the freezer), sun-dried tomatoes and tomato ketchup gives them a value way beyond what they are worth if I had to buy them. So I'll be keeping a close eye on the plants this week, ready to roll out some fleece on top of them at night, if needs be. At least the sunny weather during the day is a bonus; the polytunnel will hopefully retain some of the day's heat into the night to keep the temperatures up a few degrees.

So let's hope that's the end of the cold nights for this year.

Horticultural fleece is a useful piece of kit for the home grower, particularly in the spring when you are trying to get seedlings established outside and we're still vulnerable to frost. Aside from frost protection, fleece can simply help plants to grow more quickly in the spring when temperatures are relatively low. It will generally increase temperatures by about 2°C, which can bring plants along by about two weeks.

Fleece is white, light and soft to the touch. You can buy it in small quantities (cut to size) in garden centres or in larger rolls if you need a lot. You can cover a row of seedlings with a layer of fleece, using some soil to weigh down the sides. They can be used with or without hoops. For frost protection, I generally just lie the fleece on top (it's very light). Fleece can be bought in different grades. Light fleece gives less protection but better light penetration (and is cheaper). But it is more inclined to tear than heavy-duty fleece. Fleece can also be used for pest protection. For example, I often use fleece to cover my carrot crop to keep the carrot root fly away or to keep the cabbage white butterfly off brassica (kale, cabbage, etc.) plants.

chargrilled cauliflower steak with cauliflower leaf gazpacho

A well-known supermarket got into trouble for charging ridiculous money for a single cauliflower 'steak' that was for sale on a tray and wrapped in cellophane. I suppose it says a lot about the modern world that people were willing to pay more for a cauliflower steak than they were for a whole head of cauliflower, which would, of course, be several cauliflower steaks if you took the time to chop it yourself! I love this recipe from GROW HQ head chef JB Dubois that makes a centrepiece of wonderful, in-season cauliflower and even uses the outer leaves to make a gazpacho to serve with the steak.

Serves 4–6

ingredients:
— 1 large cauliflower (with outer leaves)
— ½ tsp chopped chilli
— 2 cloves garlic, chopped
— about 160ml rapeseed oil
— 1 tbsp cider vinegar
— salt, to taste
— 1 tbsp smoked paprika

directions:
Peel the leaves off the cauliflower. Wash the leaves and chop them roughly. In a food processor, blend the cauliflower leaves with the chilli, garlic and a pinch of salt. Add 100ml of the rapeseed oil and the vinegar. Blend until smooth. Reserve in the fridge until ready to use.

Toast the smoked paprika for 30 seconds in a small saucepan on a low heat and add the rest of the oil. Take off the heat and allow to cool. Cut the cauliflower into steaks (keeping the centre stalk intact for each steak). Pour the smoked paprika oil over each cauliflower steak and sprinkle with a little salt. Leave to marinate for at least 20 minutes. Chargrill on both sides, 3–4 minutes on each side. You can finish cooking the steaks in a preheated oven at 180°C for 5–10 minutes if you don't want your cauliflower too crunchy. Drizzle the gazpacho over the cauliflower steak before serving.

30 april
sowing
parsnips
outside

Today I will be sowing my parsnips outside in the veg patch. Unlike carrots, they are relatively easy to grow (once you have persuaded them to germinate), and since they store well in the soil over the winter they are a valuable winter storage crop. I grow around 40 parsnips, which is more than enough to keep us happy between November (when we start hankering for root crops) and next March. To do this I allocate around 2m (6ft) of growing space. In a standard bed you will get three rows of parsnips.

Although I mainly practise a no-dig type of growing, I always put a bit of work into the root crop bed where carrots and parsnips will be sown. I start by turning over the soil with a fork (to a depth of a foot), which I think is the key to a decent crop since the roots can descend into the soil happily, with no obstructions such as hard soil or stones to thwart their growth. I then rake the soil well to even it off before sowing and break up any large clods of soil.

Most parsnip seed packets will tell you to sow them in February, but don't do it. It's far better to leave it until now, when germination will be more reliable thanks to warmer weather. To sow, make a drill 2cm (1 inch) deep – if the soil is dry, dampen it. Sow one seed every 5cm (2 inches) in rows 30cm (12 inches) apart and cover with soil. Germination takes up to three weeks. When seedlings appear, thin to 10cm (4 inches) apart for medium-sized parsnips. Once you have sown them, there is very little maintenance needed. Weed carefully until well established and watering shouldn't be necessary except in dry spells. Parsnips are ready to harvest when the foliage starts to die away in autumn, but the flavour improves after the first frosts. Lift them out of the soil carefully with a fork. Leave in the soil until you're ready to use them, but lift by March.

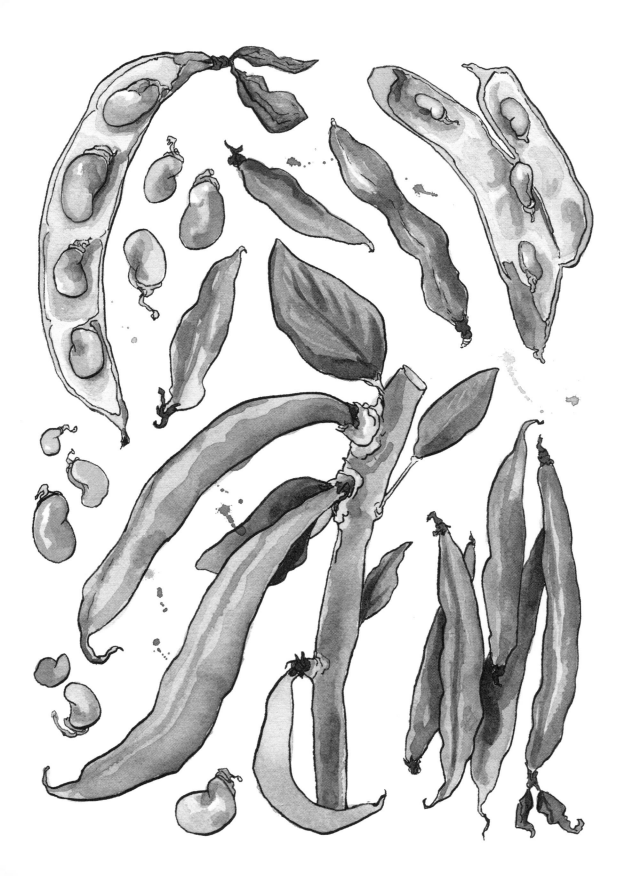

may

We're full on GIYing now, with every spare minute spent sowing, growing, watering or weeding. With the hungry gap at its peak, it's just as well that we don't have much longer to wait for new-season produce.

This month we're loving ... broad beans.

Sown last winter in the polytunnel, they are ready to eat now and it's a welcome return to fresh produce.

1 may
may day

Although May is, officially speaking, late spring, May Day, the first day of the month, is traditionally a celebration of the beginning of summer. It has been celebrated as a time of growth, renewal and fertility across Europe since pre-Christian times and is one of the two great celebrations in the Celtic year (the other one is Hallowe'en, which marks the onset of winter). Ancient May Day customs include may bushes, maypole and sword dancing, lighting bonfires, processions of chimney sweeps and comely maidens bathing in the dew of a May morning to retain their beauty (whatever you're into yourself, I suppose).

There's plenty to celebrate. After the long, lean winter in the veggie patch, things are growing at a dizzying pace, and keeping on top of things can be difficult. In addition to the routine tasks like weeding and watering, there's still sowing to be done, plants to be hardened off and (whisper it) even some gentle harvesting. In fact, there's so much to do that it's a good idea to occasionally take stock. Find a perch and sit down to take it all in – don't be tempted to read a paper or a book, just sit and stare at the beauty and wonder of it all for 5 minutes and see what it reveals to you. Try to be thankful and grateful for nature's abundance. As the colossal genius G.K. Chesterton once said, 'Wonder will never be lacking in this world. What is lacking is wonderment.'

3 may
parsnips

It's a testament to the year-round, cyclical nature of this pastime that in the same week I sowed my parsnips, today I was pulling out the last of last year's crop. Parsnips are a hardy old vegetable and they will sit quite happily in the ground through the worst of the winter weather. The constant frosts and thaws that wreak havoc (eventually) with your leeks and other winter crops have little impact on the tough old parsnip. Their foliage completely dies back over the winter months, to the extent that it can be hard to actually find the roots themselves when you go digging for them (usually on a Sunday lunchtime when my thoughts turn to preparing Sunday dinner).

In spring the plants start to grow again (parsnips are biennial) and produce another round of lush green foliage. Though this is undeniably pretty in an otherwise bare veg patch, it seems to spell trouble for the roots themselves, which on digging are found to be soft (and, worse, on cooking are found to be overly chewy). So today it was time to dig out what was left and consign them to the compost heap. Cue much soul-searching and gnashing of teeth about the waste and wondering why we didn't eat more of them while they were edible. Even the hens turned their noses up at them. Not to worry.

As I was pulling up the parsnips, I was reminded that at the garden show Bloom one year, one of the award-winning gardens had a most unusual plant that puzzled many garden designers as they couldn't recognise it. It was labelled *Pastinaca sativa*. It was a parsnip in its second year – an absolutely beautiful specimen plant that deserves a place in any ornamental garden. In fact, you could allow one of the plants to produce their pretty yellow flowers and harvest the seeds so that you don't have to buy more seeds. Parsnip seeds are notoriously perishable and given how long they take to germinate (three weeks or more), it's a good idea to buy fresh seed each year rather than taking a chance on last year's leftovers.

wild garlic pesto

Wild garlic is abundant right now and it's at its best in May. This recipe from JB uses wild garlic leaves instead of basil, which is not in season at the moment. Usually found in moist, shaded woodland areas, the leaves of wild garlic are relatively easy to identify by their overpowering smell of garlic.

Makes 2 jam jars (approx. 500ml)
ingredients:
— 150g wild garlic, washed
— 20g mature local cheddar (we use Knockanore)

- 30g sunflower seeds
- 400ml good Irish rapeseed oil
- a pinch of salt
- a drop of raw cider vinegar

directions:

Roughly chop the wild garlic. Grate the cheese. Put all the ingredients in a food processor (or, even better, a juicer). Blitz until smooth. Check the seasoning. If the pesto is too bitter, add more vinegar. This full-bodied pesto is a delicious dressing for salad, chicken, fish or pasta dishes and it's great as a simple dip.

Yes, it's the beginning of May, but I'm sitting inside while the wind howls and the rain falls outside, and I'm contemplating lighting the stove. But will I complain? No, I will not. Let the weather do what the weather does. I'm cracking on and promise not to mention it again … for now.

4 may
no more
moaning

Things have certainly gone up a gear lately. One could no longer describe the veg-growing activities as 'tinkering'. We're not quite at peak workload yet, but it's certainly busy. And you know what? I am absolutely loving it. In the potting shed, there's almost no space left on the benches, so full are they with seed trays and pots. That's always a good sign.

This week I sowed two vegetables that will only really come into their own next year: leeks and purple sprouting broccoli. I try to grow around 60 leeks. If this seems like a lot, bear in mind that leeks will stand happily in the ground right through the winter and spring. Amazingly, we're still eating the ones we sowed this time last year. That must be some kind of record. Purple sprouting broccoli has a very long growing season and takes up space in the garden for nine or ten months, but I think it's worth it considering it will be cropping when there's bugger all else to eat next March or April.

Carrots are a veg that cause a lot of problems for many GIYers, which is a great pity because the rewards are considerable when you get them right. They are great value for space and they store well. One of the most common problems that people have with carrots is that they end up with stumped or forked roots. Now, although the first couple might be fun to look at (particularly if they look rude), after that it is just plain annoying. The good news is that the problems that we have with growing them can be avoided. Promise.

First, carrots should only be sown direct in the soil as they do not transplant well – there's really very little point in trying to sow seeds in module trays for later transplanting or in buying carrot 'seedlings'. Working with such tiny seeds, planting depth is key, and because we're sowing direct, it's easy to end up sowing them too shallow or too deep. They are one of the only veg where I work hard on getting the soil to a fine tilth before sowing, so that you sow them into a nice flat, even surface.

Second, carrots are fussy blighters and need a deep, fertile soil. Think about the length of a decent carrot and ask yourself the question: are these seeds going to be able to push down into my soil and turn into nice long carrots? If the soil is heavy and stony, they probably won't. Ideally, the soil should be in decent nick up to a spade's depth. A hard, stony soil will result in stunted or forked growth. I generally aim to fork over the bed two to four weeks before sowing to make sure there is at least a foot of good, friable soil. I remove any stones and break up the clods with the fork before raking it to a fine consistency.

There's also a slightly different feeding regime when it comes to carrots. The usual advice of adding lots of compost, manure or seaweed to the beds over the winter does not apply in this case. In fact, although it might seem counter-intuitive, we want to be a little stingy with feeding and watering to encourage the root to grow into the soil in search of both. If there's too much nutrition in the soil, the root will often fork because it's getting distracted by easily available nutrients as it grows down.

So over the winter months I will generally hold off adding compost to the area where I am going to grow carrots the following year. However, I will add some seaweed dust to the soil before sowing to give it a little boost.

Timing your carrot sowing is also important. Although many growing books will tell you to sow carrots in March or April, I always wait until May or June to sow mine. Germination rates are far better if you leave it a little later to sow, and you also tend to have fewer problems with the dastardly carrot root fly (currently sniffing the air and taking off to fly to your veg patch at the mere mention of carrots). So that means I won't have carrots until later in the summer, but I don't mind waiting for what I think of as the quintessential stew/stockpot root crop. A careful covering with Bionet (a fine-grade horticultural netting) is really the only way to thwart the carrot root fly. The damage from the maggots of the root fly can be extensive to the point of ruining your crop.

Finally, I find that slugs can be a problem at sowing time as they eat the little seedlings when they emerge – as an example, one year I had an entire row of lovely carrot seedlings taken out by slugs. This is a double setback when you have waited two or

three weeks for them to establish and then find yourself behind if you have to re-sow. A sprinkle of organic slug pellets (iron phosphate) will help, as will the biological control Nemaslug (pricey, but maybe worth it to save an entire bed of carrots), which is watered onto the bed and gives you about six slug-free weeks.

So what about sowing? Having raked the bed flat, I make drills 2cm (1 inch) deep in rows 20–25cm (8–10 inches) apart and sow the seeds as thinly as I can. Cover back over with soil and then keep the seedbed moist to encourage germination. Don't be alarmed if nothing seems to be happening. It will take two or three weeks. Thin to 5cm (2 inches) when the seedlings are large enough to handle.

nettle tonic

Spring nettles are abundant right now, and they are at their best when young. They have all manner of health benefits: high in vitamins and minerals, blood-cleansing, anti-bacterial, anti-inflammatory, anti-allergy. A tea (really an infusion) made from nettles is a super tonic. Or you could try making nettle soup. Nettle tea has a rich and earthy taste that won't appeal to everyone, but you can sweeten it with some honey or stevia leaf.

ingredients:
—   a good bunch of fresh nettles, leaves and stems
—   boiling water

directions:
Obviously, if you are harvesting nettles from the wild, wear gloves or you will get stung! Choose young shoots and cut them rather than pulling (the plant will regrow). Rinse the nettles under a tap, then place them in a saucepan. Pour over boiling water and leave to infuse for 5 minutes or so. The ratio should be between a teaspoon to a tablespoon of nettle leaf to one cup of water – but you don't need to be too rigid.

The more GIYing I do, the more I become convinced of the merit of having good tools at my disposal. Every book on growing your own mentions this as being important, but as a novice grower you aren't always convinced of it. Either you stick to using the wrong tools for the job (and then take far too long as a result) or you buy cheap tools that always end up being a false economy. My garage used to be somewhat of a graveyard of cheap tool-buying folly, with various broken handles and tops piled in the corner. In more recent times, however, I've become more interested in buying quality tools and some of my favourite Christmas gifts of recent times have been garden tools (sad, I know) – like a copper rake that my sister bought me some years back. It's probably the sort of thing that is too expensive to buy for yourself but it makes the perfect gift and I always enjoy working with it. My sister told me that tiny bits of copper come off the head of the rake to improve the soil as you use it – I don't know if she was pulling my leg on that one. I also bought probably a half dozen pairs of cheap secateurs before I realised they were a waste of money and opted for a Felco pair (expensive at around €60 but worth it).

Seeing a tool being used properly by an experienced grower is often enough to convince you that you desperately need one. At a GIY event years ago I saw organic grower Klaus Laitenberger using an oscillating hoe and I was immediately hooked on the idea of having one, so easy did he make the job of hoeing seem with one in his hand. The oscillating hoe really is a useful tool to make light work of hoeing. The smaller head of a sharp Dutch hoe is ideal for more precision hoeing work – around onions and garlic, for example. I was also convinced to shell out for a really top-quality sharp, short-handled spade when I saw my neighbour John Carney using one to turn soil.

I also own a rarely used but supremely useful Chillington ridging hoe. It looks like a tool that the Grim Reaper would carry around with him, and it's a typically no-nonsense, sturdy piece of kit that will last a lifetime. It is a good example of a niche tool – perfectly suited to the job of earthing up spuds and making drills, and almost entirely useless for any other. Mine really does only get used a few times a year just for that very job, but it does the job brilliantly.

May is a frenetic month in the vegetable patch. Along with my longer sessions in the veg patch at weekends (usually two or three hours on either Saturday or Sunday), there's every incentive to get out there early in the morning and late in the evening during the week too.

8 may maincrop spuds in the ground

    With some fine weather holding firm, today I spent a good deal of time in the veg patch. I got my shallots and maincrop potatoes into the ground (varieties Sarpo Axona and Cara). I have also been trying to keep on top of the weeds, because it's around now (with perfect growing conditions) that things can go a bit pear-shaped and weeds can take over. Regular hoeing is the only thing for this – I try to do a bed or two every few days so that the time spent weeding is short and easy, standing upright and hoeing gently. The alternative? The heartache of a mass of well-established weeds that require back-breaking hands-and-knees effort.

    At this stage I have taken off most of the covers (that I use to keep the winter off the beds). You can use cardboard to cover beds as long as you use plenty of stones to stop them being blown off. I also got a sheet of silage plastic off a farmer years ago that can be reused every year – I am not wild about using plastic, but feel it's justified as it's not single use. Where the soil in a bed looks a little jaded, I bring over a barrow of compost from the compost corner and mix it in with the topsoil. In most cases, however, the layer of compost I put on the bed before covering it last winter is enough. The place looks wonderful in these bright, dry conditions – I just love this time of the year when vegetables like onions, peas and spuds are starting to establish themselves. It's a time of year full of hope – and it's great to be a GIYer!

disinfectant garlic spray

Here's a useful recipe for a disinfectant, anti-fungal garlic spray, which prevents pests from landing on plants (they don't like the smell of garlic) and enhances plant vigour. It can be used to spray tomatoes, aubergines, pumpkins, courgettes, basil and even on brassicas to guard against cabbage white butterfly. Spray once a week by putting the liquid in a spray bottle. Bear in mind that the spray will leave a slight tinge of garlic on plants – not a problem if you like the taste of garlic, obviously, but avoid using on plants that are going to be harvested within a week if you don't.

ingredients:
— 3 cloves garlic, crushed
— 1 tbsp vegetable oil
— 1 litre water
— 1 tsp liquid soap (hand soap or washing-up liquid, preferably something non-toxic like Ecover)

directions:
Add the garlic to the oil and soak overnight. Strain the mixture and add the water and soap. Shake well.

Apply liberally!

Generally speaking I like to work with nature in the veg patch rather than battling against it – that means not using chemicals to battle pests, but rather encouraging a healthy ecosystem where natural predators keep things in check. A good example of this is allowing ladybirds to deal with aphids on your broad beans. Occasionally, however, a particular pest such as slugs or wireworms do need to be dealt with if you are to have any success in growing food.

Wireworm is the larval stage of the click beetle and is the bane of my potato growing. The little worms burrow into your potatoes and create a network of tunnels – a reality that is typically only revealed after you've peeled the spud. The wireworm stays at the larval stage for up to five years, at which point it graduates to being a beetle and then leaves your spuds alone. I wonder what it eats then?

Anyway, I lost a third of my potato crop to them last year, and I've decided that it's just not on. Wireworm can be a particular issue if your veg patch is surrounded by grass, where the click beetle will lay its eggs (with the grass providing a good source of food for the larvae). Unfortunately, organic growing is particularly conducive to wireworm since the worms can survive using humus as their only food source.

Organic control options are limited. Turning the soil to allow the birds (particularly crows) at them will help. You can also try trapping them – the wireworm loves a good spud, and you can use their spud love against them. Cut some spuds in half and bury them a foot deep in the soil, remove a week later and you should have trapped some wireworms.

However, I suspect that's not going to deal with the wireworm population I seem to have, so this year I am going to try the bio-insecticide SuperNemos. These are microscopic nematodes that you spray into the soil, which the wireworm (and many other garden nasties, like vine weevils and leatherjackets, but not slugs, alas) feast on. In a demise worthy of the cheesiest horror movie, the nematodes then eat them from the inside out. Sometimes GIYing is not for the faint-hearted.

Along with the weeding and transplanting, the seed sowing continues at pace. It's this sort of activity that makes May so busy. This week, I've been out in the potting shed most evenings after dinner, sowing seeds of one type or another. It's a very pleasant hour, of course, and no great chore. I love how it clears my head. Last evening, I was accompanied by Child Two, which somewhat changes the dynamic from 'head clearing', as she updates me on developments in school. Though I would like to be more focused on the seed sowing to stay in the moment, I am receptive to her chatter. Childhood is fleeting, and there might come a time in her teenage years when she won't talk to me much at all, so I'm reminded how precious these moments are. She chats, I listen, we sow seeds together.

I had her sowing a tray of climbing French beans, which will be planted out in the big tunnel in a few weeks' time (they grow quickly). They could be sowed direct, but I like to give them a head start indoors to get ahead of the slugs. We fill a large module tray with compost, and she puts one seed on the surface of each module before pushing it down with her finger.

At the same time, I am pricking out celery and celeriac seedlings from a tray. The tiny seedlings, just a few centimetres tall, have now been transplanted into a module tray (one per module) in fresh compost. They will be kept inside for another month or so before being planted out. It's a delicate operation, holding the seedling by the leaf and carefully teasing it out of the compost with a plant label, making a little hole in compost in the module tray, popping the seedling in and firming it gently.

With the celery and celeriac finished, I then sowed some basil in module trays. In a few weeks' time, I will transplant them into individual pots in fresh compost, before planting out in the polytunnel. Finally, I also sowed a couple of trays of lettuce, one little seed per module. All the new trays and pots were then watered before we tried to find some space on the planting bench for them. We then headed back up to the house together to rejoin the world.

All around us, nature is in the process of a remarkable transition from brown to green. The potting shed is resplendent with emerging green seedlings; green leaves have emerged on the trees in our garden; brown soil is bringing forth rapidly growing green weeds. The decay and stasis of winter have been replaced by renewal and growth.

Barbara Kingsolver's wonderful memoir *Animal, Vegetable, Miracle* does a wonderful job of explaining why and how we should follow the arc of nature's plant growth if we want to eat the most seasonal, most nutritious food throughout the year. The arc follows a very specific trajectory through the seasons – from shoot to leaf to fruit and finally to root. To work out which foods are best for us at specific times of the year, we should simply look around us and consider what stage of development the plants around us are at.

Around now? Plants are bursting forward into life, producing green leaves that are nature's great and wise spring tonic and the most seasonally appropriate food one can eat at this time of the year. After a long season of earthy, heavy root crops, we are relishing revitalising nettles, baby spinach, chard and salad leaves.

A little later in the year, the plants will move beyond the leaf stage and start to produce seed pods (peas and beans) and flower heads (like broccoli). Then, in the summer, they start to set fruit. It starts with the small fruits like tomatoes and cucumbers, then later in the summer the fruits get larger with harder skins (to survive the oncoming cold), such as squashes and pumpkins. And then finally, as summer gives way to autumn and winter, the plants go down into the soil in search of nutrients and we get root crops.

Most of the food that the food chain serves up is no longer nutrient-rich, or at least not as nutrient-rich as it should be. This is because when it comes to nutrients, it all starts with the soil. If there are not enough nutrients in the soil (and there aren't – the world's farmland is between 75 and 85 per cent less rich in minerals than it was a hundred years ago), then there aren't enough in the food grown in it either. And then, of course, we pick food when it's not ripe and transport it halfway – or all the way – round the world so that it loses even more of whatever nutrients it had to start with. It's little wonder that there is such a chronic lack of human wellness and vitality.

Homegrown food, on the other hand, is nutrient-rich because it's grown in carefully maintained nutrient-rich soil, picked and consumed at the height of its freshness and, by definition, seasonally appropriate. That's a virtuous circle of fully nourished land, food and people.

18 may
chickweed I've been plagued with chickweed for well over a year now in the small polytunnel. God knows how it got in there, but clearly I unwittingly let some of it go to flower, and the result has been a persistent, interminable weed problem.

It's a formidable foe, with each flower being self-fertile and each seed pod producing up to 2,500 seeds. Once it starts to grow, it is rampant and has an extensive root system that makes it hard to knock back. Annoyingly, it seems to thrive and particularly enjoy growing right beside other seedlings, making it even harder to get at.

I covered the soil in the tunnel with black polythene for five months this winter in the hope of getting rid of it once and for all, but it's come back with a vengeance in the last few weeks. I recently read that its seeds can lie dormant in soil for four years. Persistent hoeing is the only way I can stay on top of it, and that's all I seem to be doing – staying on top of it, rather than getting rid of it.

There are upsides to chickweed. First, it is a sign of fertile soil, so I suppose you can console yourself with that fact as you weed it. Second, not only is it edible, it's considered to be (to use that awful phrase) a nutritional powerhouse. This is good news indeed since I regularly find it in the salad bowl with the oriental greens, among which it grows happily in the tunnel. The leaves have a mild flavour and can be added raw to salads and sandwiches. They can be tossed into soups and stews as well.

You can recognise chickweed by its oval leaves and starry white flowers, and if you pull the stem apart you find a second elasticated stem inside – our kids used to love that, but it makes it even harder to weed effectively.

I like growing all vegetables, but I love the ones that are sown once during the year and store well, for example carrots, parsnips, onions, garlic and so on. These are the real high-return crops, where it's possible to become self-sufficient (or close to it) with a single act of seed sowing. Squashes are another good example of this type of vegetable – thanks to their hard-as-nails outer skins, they will store very well from harvest time (around October) right through to the following May, an impressive eight months. Though we're in mid-May now, I still have a couple of squashes left in the kitchen from last year's growing. They are an incredibly versatile and delicious veg to have around – equally at home in a salad, risotto, stew, roast, tart or quiche – and the bigger ones have a serious amount of eating in them. It will be a bittersweet moment when the final one is hacked open and eaten.

20 may
sow once
veg

So easy are squashes to grow – and so well do they store – that I always find it strange that more commercial growers here don't get in on the act, particularly with the more unusual varieties of squash. Generally speaking, most supermarkets only stock butternut squash (and usually imported ones). It's a shame they are not more adventurous because there are far sweeter and more flavoursome varieties out there. My favourite of all squash varieties is the ghostly, grey-blue Crown Prince, which, despite its enormous size and pumpkin-like demeanour, has an incomparable sweet flavour. I've seen an imported version on the shelves of a well-known Dublin artisan supermarket for a whopping €12, but never an Irish one (and from then on treated my own stock with a new-found reverence).

It's a good time of the year to sow squashes, so today I got stuck in. If you start them off too early, they will positively shiver outside when you plant them out. I am growing the squash varieties Crown Prince, Delicata and Uchiki Kuri and the pumpkins Baby Bear and Rouge Vif d'Etampes. I have sown about 30 seeds in all, but will probably not have enough space to plant them all out. If I can produce about 40 or 50 fruits in total, I will be happy that there are many months of good eating ahead this winter.

25 may
feeding
toms

Rather than buying liquid feeds, for some years now I have been making my own organic version by soaking the leaves of the comfrey plant. Comfrey is a perennial herb with big, broad, hairy leaves that produce small purple flowers. It has long been used as a feed by organic gardeners, particularly the variety Bocking 14, named after the town of Bocking in Essex, the original home of the organic gardening research association Garden Organic.

Comfrey is a remarkably fast-growing plant and is one of nature's great 'miners' – that is, it sends its roots up to 2m into the soil and brings up nutrients, most notably potassium, from deep in the subsoil. It is this nutrient in particular which will be of benefit to all fruiting vegetables in the garden (tomatoes, peppers, pumpkins, courgettes, squash, etc.). The basic idea of making a comfrey tea is to harvest leaves and soak them in water for about a month. This potassium-rich 'tea' is then applied as a feed to fruiting plants. I use shears and literally cut the plant down to about 5cm (2 inches) from the surface of the soil. Use a pair of gloves, as the leaves are a little prickly. You can harvest mature comfrey plants three or four times each year. It grows back quickly and can be cut again about a month later.

You should be able to source the plants from a good garden centre and then plant them out about 60cm (2ft) apart. They will tolerate a shady, even damp, spot in the garden. Mine are thriving in a corner of the garden behind the tunnel. Keep the bed well watered until the plants get established and don't harvest leaves from them in the first year. Strangely, comfrey doesn't seem to be able to mine the nitrogen very well that it needs for itself, being a fast-growing leafy plant (similar to a brassica). I generally mulch the plants with lawn clippings when they die back in the autumn.

In addition to making a comfrey tea you can add comfrey leaves to the compost heap, where they will accelerate the decomposition of your heap and add potassium. You can also use the leaves as a mulch, putting a layer of leaves around a plant; they will break down and release their nutrients more slowly. I've heard of people putting comfrey leaves in a trench when planting potatoes and also planting comfrey underneath fruit trees as a companion plant.

There are two ways to make comfrey tea as a plant tonic. You can either make a concentrated tea that will have to be diluted, or a ready-to-use version.

1. **Concentrate:** Harvest comfrey leaves and shove them in a bucket with a lid. Weigh the leaves down with a brick or something else heavy. Drill a hole in the base of the bucket and place a container underneath. As the leaves rot down, a black liquid will start to drip down from the bucket into the container. This is your comfrey feed. Dilute 1 part comfrey liquid to 15 parts water.

2. **Ready to use:** Harvest your leaves and put them in a bucket. Fill the bucket with enough water to cover the leaves. Cover with a lid and leave for three or four weeks. This type of tea is ready to use without diluting.

April and May are peak hungry gap months, and it starts to really bite the closer we get to June, when the trickle of veg turns to a steady flow of broad beans, peas, beets and courgette. At GROW HQ, we always think that the hungry gap forces us to be more creative in the kitchen – this is undoubtedly true, but it doesn't change the fact that we're still very much looking forward to the influx of new-season crops next month.

I've a similar hungry gap problem here at home, though JB, our head chef at GROW HQ, would laugh at that idea – he has, after all, around 1,500 customers a week to feed, when I just have four. Still, things are getting awfully scarce here. The freezer is now empty of the three winter stalwarts: the tomato sauces, celery and French beans. All the spuds, garlic, leeks and onions from last year are finished. The last of the celeriac and parsnip have been pulled from the ground, the purple sprouting broccoli plants are finished and the last squash came down from the top of the dresser about two weeks ago. Even the chard, perpetual spinach and kale, which were so abundant from the tunnel over the winter and spring, have now bolted and I had to pull most of the plants up today. There are a few jars of cucumber pickle and courgette chutney in the press, but they hardly constitute a good meal (though they do help to make a fine sandwich).

There is one tiny saving grace. Remarkably, I still have a large bucket of carrots in the garage that we might get another few weeks from. These were sown last May and I lifted the last of the crop from the ground back in mid-February. Last year I grew some dark purple carrots as well as the standard orange ones, and they seem to store well. The key with them in the kitchen is to avoid some of the standard carrot applications such as stocks (they turn the stock purple) and soups (the flavour doesn't work). But they are brilliant roasted or as carrot 'chips', and indeed served raw.

Of course, where there are carrots, there can always be a slaw. Lacking any spring cabbage, I've been swapping in all sorts of brassicas as the 'cabbage' ingredient and, to be honest, pretty much any of them will work. Some thinly sliced kale or chard and/or the stalks from chard or pak choi bring a nice bit of crunch. The key to a good slaw is to season the veg really well before adding a little mustard (half a teaspoon, say) and use half and half yoghurt and mayo (homemade is best if you can).

There is a wonderful TED Talk by New York-based chef Dan Barber about a small farm in Spain that produces foie gras humanely (without the horrendous force feeding that the product has rightly been lambasted for). Raising his geese in a natural environment, farmer Eduardo Sousa rediscovered that if geese are allowed to forage at will, they will naturally gorge themselves in the autumn to build up fat for the winter. The result? A 'natural' foie gras. The important word there is 'rediscovered', because there is nothing new in this. Originally foie gras was invented simply as a timely slaughter of geese to take advantage of their fatty livers post-winter gorge. It was in a typically unthinking and cack-handed

**28 may
'take more,
sell more,
waste more'**

attempt to be the master or foie gras and have it all year round that humankind invented the 'gavage', or force-feeding, approach.

Although Barber's talk focuses on foie gras, it's actually a parable; there's a broader point in there about commercial food production. Eduardo Sousa calls modern methods of foie gras production 'an insult to history', a phrase that could equally be applied to all manner of food production methods from rearing thousands of chickens in unbearably cramped conditions in sheds, to growing tonnes of potatoes in the same field year on year using chemicals to 'cheat' nature, to strawberries from Israel on the shelves in a Wexford supermarket during the Irish strawberry season. So much of modern food production is an insult to life on earth, the planet and to human health. Barber calls it the 'take more, sell more, waste more' approach to food that just won't serve us in the future.

His advice is something that I think will resonate strongly with anyone who grows some of their own food. Listen to nature instead of imposing things on it. Work with it rather than against it. Accept that small is beautiful. Barber sums up by pointing to the happy coincidence that the most ecologically sensitive food production methods are also the most ethical and the most delicious. I would add that they are almost always the healthier and more nutritious choices too.

29 may
thinning
out
Just when we thought we might not get any summer at all, it looks like the weather is finally turning and we're going to get a little bit of heat and sunshine! Suddenly and without warning we've gone from worrying about whether the potato plants are going to get killed by frosts to worrying about whether we need to water the polytunnel and seedlings in the potting shed twice a day! Such is the life of a GIYer. One night last week temperatures in the polytunnel were as low as -2°C. One afternoon this week they soared to over 30°C – that's a serious jump in temperature. The plants must be *very* confused.

Today I've been doing quite a bit of 'thinning out'. Thinning out plants allows them the space they need to grow to full size. It's an important job at this time of the year as young seedlings are bursting into life and starting to compete for space. It can be a difficult discipline to grasp for a novice grower (well, it was for me anyway), because it seems such a shame to be throwing out these lovely seedlings. But if you don't do it the plants won't have the space they need to grow, and you will be left with a very poor yield.

Thinning out is only applicable to vegetables that are sown directly in the soil. Where you are sowing seeds in trays or pots and planting them out later, you will generally plant them at the right spacing and therefore won't need to thin. Good examples of vegetables that need thinning out are carrots and parsnips. With carrots we thin to 5cm (2 inches) apart when the seedlings are big enough to handle. Depending on how thinly (or thickly) you have sown the seed, you might have a fair amount of thinning out to do.

Now, you might well ask: why don't we just sow the seeds at 5cm spacing and avoid the need for thinning out altogether? Well, first, carrots are tiny seeds and it's difficult to be that accurate with them. And second, they are not reliable germinators – so if you did it that way, you might be left with lots of gaps in your row of carrots.

With parsnips, having sown the seeds at 7cm (3-inch) intervals, we then thin out to 15cm (6 inches) when the seedlings are big enough to handle – effectively that means removing every second one. Last year I forgot to thin my parsnips at the time I should have done it, so when I eventually got around to it, the parsnips I thinned out were actually a decent size and I had an early season feast of roasted parsnips!

roasted baby beetroot

If you sowed beetroot seeds for the polytunnel or greenhouse back in early spring, you might well be tucking in to your first new-season beetroot around now. These little beetroot (no larger than golf balls) are perfect for baking and will take just 20–30 minutes in a hot oven. Cooking them like this retains more of their fab health benefits than boiling. The tops here are edible too because they are so young and tender.

Serves 4
ingredients:
— 600–800g baby beetroot
— 4 tbsp olive oil
— 1 tbsp balsamic vinegar
— 1 tbsp Dijon mustard
— 1 tsp salt

directions:
Preheat the oven to 220°C.

Remove and wash the beetroot tops (twist them off rather than cutting, which will make them 'bleed'). Blanch them in boiling water for 1 minute, then drain and set aside. Put the beetroot on a baking tray and toss with 2 tablespoons of the olive oil and a little salt. Roast for 20 minutes, until cooked through. When they have cooled slightly, rub the skins off (or, if you can't wait, rub the skins off while holding the roots under a cold tap). Whisk together the remaining 2 tablespoons of olive oil with the vinegar, mustard and salt, then toss with the beetroot tops and roots. Serve cold.

june

The payback begins as the trickle of new-season veg turns into something more substantial. The big direct sowings – garlic, beans, onions, potatoes, carrots and parsnips – are complete now, so thoughts turn to protecting and nurturing the crops.

This month we're loving … peas.

Pods picked and eaten fresh in the garden. There's nothing quite like a homegrown pea.

It's hard to believe that we're now in the sixth month of the year already and that the longest day of the year is a mere three weeks away. At the risk of getting a slap on the head, let me say this much: it will be Christmas before we know it. We're just a week or two away from the first decent crops. In the small polytunnel, the broad beans, beetroot, kohlrabi, new-season spinach, chard and kale are just about ready. The outdoor-sown early potatoes should be ready in a few weeks. And today I earthed up the later-sown maincrop spuds.

The big tunnel is filling up nicely – all the tomato plants are doing well. Today I planted out the peppers and the climbing French beans. I sow the beans the same way as the tomatoes and cucumbers, with a string planted underneath the plants, which is then tied to a crossbar at the top of the tunnel. The beans will reach 3–4m (9–13ft) high (though you can stop them getting that tall by pinching off the growing tip if you wish). I start French beans in modules for later transplanting as it gives them a head start on the slugs, then I plant two seedlings at the base of each string (about 30cm, or 12 inches, apart). From two 3m (10ft) rows of plants we will have loads of beans – enough to keep us going for the summer and autumn, and plenty for the freezer.

Cucumbers are only a week or two away from being ready to eat, and I've more plants coming on in the potting shed. Cucumbers and tomatoes have slightly different watering regimes, which can be a challenge when you have them growing in the one place. The cucumbers like it steamy, which means watering the plants from overhead to create a humid atmosphere. Tomatoes, on the other hand, benefit from a drier atmosphere and need water deep to their roots.

From a sowing perspective we are moving on to the quick growers now. We're certainly not at last-chance stage for sowing, but June is probably the peak of it for this year. Today in the potting shed I sowed fennel, runner beans, basil, parsley and coriander, while out in the veg patch I planted out celery, courgette and summer squash and kept on top of the weeding. Phew!

Tomatoes are surely the most high-maintenance of all veg plants. At this stage of their development, it's all about pinching out side shoots. My tomato plants in the tunnel have suddenly taken off in the last few weeks and are now up to 1m (3ft) tall and growing literally by the day. There are even some early signs of tomatoes appearing on the vines and the plants are now in need of regular maintenance.

Pinching off tomato plant side shoots is one of those regular summer tasks that I get some pleasure from. It's understandably a source of considerable confusion to many newbie GIYers – which ones are the side shoots?! In fairness, there's a lot going on with tomato plants. The main shoot is the easy one to spot – that's the one growing up from the soil. Out of that, growing horizontally at intervals you get leaf stems (which have leaves on them) and fruit trusses (which will have tomatoes on them – though at this stage, they are likely to be flowers). Then finally, in the angle between the main stem and the leaf stems you get side shoots. These are the ones that must be removed.

The reason? Left to grow, these side shoots will literally become new tomato plants. Now you might be thinking that sounds great, but in fact all they will do is take energy from the main plant and reduce the amount of fruit you get. While your tomato plants are still quite small, this is a great opportunity to get familiar with what the side shoots look like. It won't be long before your plants will be 1.2–1.5m (4–5ft) tall and it will be more difficult to identify them amidst the tangle of leaves, stem and fruit.

Lots of GIYers I speak to have terrible problems growing basil successfully – this is a pity, of course, because basil is a tremendously useful herb to have around the place and delicious in a caprese salad, pastas or bruschetta. For the last year or two I have grown really good basil and I think I know why (I say 'I think' because like most things about growing I am never 100 per cent sure, and over-confidence is liable to come back and bite you).

Previously I used to sow basil in module trays, keeping them in the trays for five to six weeks after germination (which takes about 10 days) before planting out. I've since discovered that this was my problem – the seed compost that we use for seed sowing only has enough nutrients to support the seedlings for about six weeks, and after that the seedlings start to starve.

So the key is to treat basil a little more like tomatoes or celery, moving the plants on in three stages. Start by sowing in module trays (about four seeds per module). About a month after they germinate, you prick them out and pot them into 10cm (4-inch) pots with fresh compost. This effectively resets the clock, giving the seedlings access to another six weeks of nutrients at a crucial stage in their development. Having sown my basil in mid-May, today I potted them into individual pots. Fingers crossed I have another good crop of basil again this year.

The second key point with basil is to pay attention to how you harvest the leaves. Fight your instinct to strip the plant bare of leaves as soon as they appear. If you cut the growing tip just above the second set of leaves, the plant is forced to become bushy and will produce more leaves.

courgette salad

We had our first courgette of the season from an early-sown plant in the polytunnel. It was only finger-thick, but perfectly tender for a salad.

Serves 2

ingredients:
— 1–2 small 'fingerling' courgettes
— mixed salad leaves (rocket, red mustard, mizuna), washed
— 1 tbsp olive oil
— salt and pepper
— juice of ½ lemon

directions:
Wash and dry the courgettes and leaves. Slice the courgettes thinly, cutting them on the diagonal. If any of the leaves are large, cut them into two or three pieces. Toss the leaves and courgettes together, then add the olive oil. Season well and toss again, until the leaves are evenly coated. Finally, toss in the lemon juice and serve immediately.

5 june
watering tomato plants

Tomatoes can be difficult to grow well, but I think a proper watering regime is one of the keys to an abundant crop. The secret to watering tomatoes properly is that you need to water 'deep'. A healthy tomato plant is a thirsty beast, supported by a deep root system – so in other words, there's no point in standing there with the hose and spraying the plant or the soil around it with water. You need to get water right down where it's needed – at the roots. The more extensive the root system, the healthier and more productive the plant will be. There's an added benefit to a deep watering system in that by keeping water away from the plant itself, you minimise the chance of scorch on the leaves and avoid creating the wet conditions that could attract blight.

When I first started GIYing I happened across a handy method of deep-watering tomatoes, which involves upcycling used 2-litre milk cartons. Use a pair of scissors to cut the base off the carton and then bury the carton, upside down, in the soil beside the plant. You can angle it slightly so that it's 'aiming' at the plant and bury it deep enough so that only an inch or so of the carton is visible above the soil. Do this when planting the tomatoes out in the polytunnel so as not to disturb the plant's roots later on.

This is a good watering method for a smaller number of plants, as watering becomes a job of simply filling the container, confident in the knowledge that the plant is getting 2 litres of water where it needs it most. With 80-plus tomato plants the container system would be too time-consuming, as I've experienced in the past. So this year I've invested in a seep-hose watering system, which soaks the soil very effectively and will make the job of watering a lot more straightforward.

Watering tomatoes is all about balance. Under-water and you can end up with weak plants and a poor crop. Over-water and you can end up diluting the lovely sugars in the tomatoes, which give them their wonderful sweetness. Water irregularly and you can end up with split fruit. As a rule, water only when your plants need it. Don't get freaked out if your plants look a little wilted on a hot summer afternoon in the polytunnel or greenhouse – it's normal and they generally perk up again overnight. If they look wilted in the morning, however, they probably need watering straightaway.

In the early stages of growth, if watering manually into containers I water every two days to encourage the root system to develop. Later in the summer, when the plants are producing fruit, I will only water every three to four days. The surface of the soil may look quite dry, but that's fine – there's plenty of water underneath for the plant to survive between watering. Deep watering also prevents waste and cuts down on the amount of water lost to evaporation in a hot polytunnel. Watering early in the day also helps. Using the seep hose, I water only once a week – leaving the water switched on for two hours seems to work for me and the plants seem to get used to it.

We spend a lot of time listening to or identifying with the voice in our head. That little voice is constantly there and it's not always an amiable companion. It's always regretting the distant or not-so-distant past or fretting about some imagined future. It's generally pretty critical (of ourselves and others), often somewhat cruel and, occasionally, completely bonkers.

So if you can silence that voice for a little while and experience the present moment without it, it's an enlightening, liberating experience. The practice of mindfulness is about exactly that – creating little moments of what you could call 'no mind' where you are truly present and aware of the sensations, sights, sounds or smells around you. Not commenting on them, by the way (that would be the little voice returning); just being aware. It can be as simple as becoming aware of the in and out of your breath or noticing the contact between your body and the chair you're sitting on. In those brief moments of focus, the little voice is gone, if only temporarily. It will be back shortly, no doubt, to chide you from within. But for now, all is peaceful.

The little voice follows me to the veg patch. It's not big on praise and rarely focuses on all the work that's been done, instead reminding me of all the things I have yet to do. The bed that needs weeding, the peas that need staking, the potatoes that need earthing up. It's a hard taskmaster. But it generally must give way once I start a task and the focus shifts from my head to my hands. That's why the veg patch is a place of such calm.

Today I was down on my knees with a hand hoe, weeding and thinning out some parsnips that I sowed in late April. Parsnips take ages to germinate, and the weeds have been growing steadily. It's only now that the parsnips are established (and clearly identifiable) that I can see the rows and weed safely. In addition to the weeding I am also thinning as I go, removing the excess parsnip seedlings.

As I worked my way down the bed, I noticed briefly how calm I felt and how I hadn't really been thinking for the 20 minutes I'd been there. With that brief period of 'no mind' comes a heightened awareness. I followed the path of a gleaming beetle as it scurried across the newly weeded soil. I heard birdsong and a pigeon flapping in the trees. I stopped working to notice a blue tit land on the gutter over the potting shed carrying a grub of some description in its beak. It looked around feverishly and then dropped it into the gutter. I then heard the urgent *cheep-cheep-cheep* of its chicks, obviously nesting out of view and getting an afternoon meal.

Once I'd finished, I stood up and stretched, feeling a dull ache in my back from all the stooping. I checked my watch and the little voice returned to remind me it was time to make dinner. Back to the world.

The purpose of companion planting is typically to reduce the impact of pests and diseases on your GIYing. In some cases, plants just like being planted next to each other and will fare better than they would do otherwise. Generally speaking, you meet two types of people in this world: those who think companion planting is brilliant, and those who think it's complete hooey.

7 june
companion
planting

Here are some examples:

- Plant dill with your brassicas, as the cabbage white butterfly apparently doesn't like the smell and will be less inclined to lay its eggs on the cabbage leaves. Happily, dill is a great herb to have growing in the garden – beautiful with fish and also great in salads.
- Marigolds and nasturtiums will deter whitefly and greenfly, so plant them around your tomato plants. Nasturtium flowers are also very good to eat. Marigolds are also useful near raspberries and strawberries to prevent greenfly.
- Sow summer savory among beans and peas to deter blackfly.

- Borage attracts pollinators and is therefore useful planted among courgettes, pumpkins and squashes.
- Sow chives around your apple trees to prevent scab and wallflowers to attract bumblebees.
- Grow carrots with spring onions or onions to deter carrot fly – but does this *really* work?!

9 june
commercial growing in Ireland

The situation in the commercial veg-growing world in Ireland is lamentable. A perfect storm of competition from imports, aggressive price discounting on veg by retailers and the low value placed on local veg has resulted in growers leaving the sector in their droves. The number of commercial veg growers has dropped 56 per cent in 15 years, down to just 140 or so growers left in the country. In some cases, there are vegetables (e.g. scallions) where we have just one commercial producer left, which says a lot about our food security as a nation.

The growers that are left have had to go big to compete. Most of them operate at extraordinary scale and tiny margins, which leaves them very vulnerable to external shocks. And the one thing we can be certain of with climate change is that external shocks are becoming the norm, including major weather events, such as high winds, snowstorms and summer droughts. While the general populace head to the beach to enjoy the heat and drought conditions, many field veg growers have to invest in hugely expensive irrigation systems just to keep their crops alive.

These unforeseen costs – you don't generally have to water outside in an Irish summer – are an existential threat for a low-margin business. Because of the power of the big supermarkets, and the fact that veg growers don't have a strong lobby voice the way beef or dairy farmers do, they have become price takers. They are literally given a price by supermarkets at which they must produce their crop. In recent years, fearing more producers going out of business and more jobs lost (and veg growing is labour-intensive), the growers had to go cap in hand to the supermarkets to plead for a temporary price increase. Bear that in mind the next time you see a picture of a smiling farmer in the middle of a field adorning the wall of your local supermarket.

Yet there are some reasons for optimism. First, the arc of health and sustainability is bending slowly and inexorably towards more local, seasonal veg consumption. Report after report highlights the importance to our health and the health of the planet of eating more local, in-season vegetables and less meat.

The more established generation of food growers fear for the future and wonder whether the next generation will want to take over the family business. They retain their passion for growing and have unrivalled growing expertise that risks being lost for ever. As consumers we must vote with our wallets, eating in season and buying Irish. Our national broccoli crop, for example, starts appearing on shelves this month and will be available (all going well with the weather) until November.

There are also newer entrants coming into the market who are disrupting the system and doing things their own way. Look at the innovation of Drummond House, growing garlic, garlic scapes and asparagus in County Louth. Look at Kenneth Keavey at Green Earth Organics, who is growing 40 acres of organic veg in Corandulla, County Galway (and employing over 20 people) selling direct to consumers in an at-scale box scheme. Look at Gavin Lynch of Hell's Kettle in Wicklow, who abandoned conventional mono-farming for a more varied life of organic dairying and growing 4 acres of hazelnuts. These are the stories that could inspire young growers into the industry. And if this is to be Irish horticulture's moment in the sun, it's that type of energy and innovation that's needed.

10 june
watering in dry weather

Which veg plants need a lot of watering in dry weather and which can withstand a bit of a drought? It's difficult to come up with a definitive list, but here are some guidelines. Leafy vegetables like brassicas, lettuce, spinach and celery need lots of water – 10–15 litres per square metre per week. Fruiting veg, like toms, peas, beans and cucumbers, need heavy watering when they are flowering and when the fruits are starting to swell.

Too much watering of root crops will only encourage lush foliage rather than good roots – in early stages, water only if the soil is drying out, but more is required when roots are swelling. The exception is when waiting for parsnips and carrots to germinate – keep the soil moist all the time.

With prolonged dry weather, it's important to get the most out of the water you use. Water early in the morning when it's cool and let the plants have a good drink before the water starts to evaporate in the heat.

11 june
abundance

I can see the veg patch out of the window as I write this, and I think it's fair to say that there's a real sense of abundant growth right now. May was quite a dry month, which didn't help the growth, so the substantial rain over the last few days has really driven things on. Though the weather continues to be somewhat unpredictable (still rather chilly and very windy), everything is growing like mad, including the weeds.

We've been eating new potatoes from the tunnel for a number of weeks now, and the crop outside in the veg patch is looking healthy at this stage. I am hoping that it will be ready just as the small polytunnel crop is finished (probably in a fortnight or so). The tops of the first sowing of pea plants are just visible behind the spuds and are doing well too. In the foreground I can see the garlic and onions. The former has developed rust, as it always does in our garden. It doesn't really affect the bulbs so it's more of an aesthetic problem than anything else. Beetroot, carrots, parsnips, celery, celeriac, courgettes and kale are all growing well but are still small.

There are quite a few crops that I've left in the soil from last year on the grounds that they either look very pretty or are useful in other ways. Considering how much of a neat freak I am generally, I am surprising myself with this laissez-faire attitude. The purple sprouting broccoli plants are long past their best, but they've a mass of yellow flowers on them and every time I go near them I can see the bees moving stealthily from flower to flower. It would be somewhat mean to deprive them of this valuable source of pollen. The remaining leeks from last winter, also past their best, have shot up and produced seed heads. Also very pretty and therefore getting a temporary reprieve.

Vika's new potatoes and egg salad

Last night we had our first meal of the year that came entirely from the garden. It was a simple enough affair – a new potato and egg salad. But still, it's an important milestone and hopefully the start of a self-sufficient and delicious eight- or nine-month spell. Vika Kelly is the queen of egg mayo sandwiches and egg salads in our house.

Serves 4
ingredients:
—   4 eggs
—   300g new potatoes
—   2 spring onions or green onions, chopped
—   salt and pepper

For the dressing:
— 6 tbsp rapeseed oil
— 4 tsp cider vinegar
— 1 tsp English mustard

directions:
Bring a pan of water to the boil and carefully lower the eggs into the water. Cook for 7 minutes. Take out the eggs and put them in a bowl of very cold water to stop them cooking. After 10 minutes or so, take the eggs out of the water, crack the shells and peel them. Chop the eggs roughly. Meanwhile, put the potatoes in a pan of cold water and add a little salt. Bring to the boil and then simmer for 15–20 minutes, until tender. Drain well and allow to cool. Chop them into bite-sized chunks.

Make the dressing: put all the ingredients in a jar, pop the lid on and shake well until it has all mixed. Finally, get a large bowl and add the eggs, potatoes and chopped spring onions. Season well with plenty of salt and pepper. Pour over the dressing and mix well.

13 june
grow
florence
fennel

Florence fennel is grown for its aniseed-flavoured swollen bulb – it's an acquired taste that doesn't suit everyone, and it's also a little difficult to grow well. On the other hand, it's an incredibly attractive plant that will look fantastic in your veg patch while growing. It's worth noting that Florence fennel is a different plant from herb fennel, though the leaves of Florence fennel can be eaten as a herb or in salads.

Florence fennel is frost-tender, so it makes sense to wait until now to sow it. Mark out lines and make a shallow drill 1cm (½ inch) deep. Water if the soil is dry and sow the seed thinly in rows 45cm (18 inches) apart. Thin to 30cm (12 inches) when the seedlings have established. You can also sow Florence fennel in module trays if you wish – sow two seeds per module and thin out the weaker ones when they germinate. Plant out after four to five weeks.

Keep well watered in dry weather (dry soil encourages bolting) and weed regularly. You can earth up the bulbs as they start to swell to make them whiter and sweeter. Harvest when the bulbs are 7cm (2¾ inches) across.

14 june
planting out

During the short but determined heatwave we've had these past few days, I made a rather rash executive decision to plant out pretty much everything that was left in the potting shed. For weeks I had been holding off on the grounds that it still felt like winter, and then suddenly we seemed to bounce straight into high summer, bypassing spring entirely. Briefly, gloriously, out came the shorts, white legs and sun cream.

Once I had decided to plant out the seedlings, the idea of hardening them off first seemed silly since it was almost as hot outside as it was in the potting shed. So today I decided to just go for it and spent almost the entire day in the veg patch, planting out seedling after seedling. At about 5pm I suddenly realised that the veg patch was pretty much full. Except for some space remaining in the brassica bed, which is reserved for the stalwarts of the winter garden – sprouts and sprouting broccoli – there isn't space to plant anything else. Even at that, I had to plant leeks between the rows of garlic, which should be okay, since the garlic will be coming out in the next few weeks.

During the hot, dry spell these past few days I was struck by just how time-consuming watering the veg patch can be. I am used to regular watering in the polytunnel (and filling drinkers for chickens and ducks) but watering the entire patch outside as well is another issue entirely. We GIYers are even more demanding about the weather than the rest of the populace – so yes, please, give us a dry spell by day so we can head for the beach, but we need rain at night so we don't have to take out the hose each day. We don't ask for much.

Aubergines are easy to grow but hard to grow well, if you know what I mean. I find the plants easy to raise, but it's a harder job to get good fruit. At this stage you should have plants ready for planting out (or you could buy them in a garden centre). You can either plant them out in a greenhouse or polytunnel (spacing is 40cm (16 inches) for standard varieties) or grow them in a 20cm (8-inch) pot in good potting compost.

Aubergines like some humidity, so you could put some buckets of water between plants so that there is some evaporation near them. Removing the growing point of the main stem when the plant is about 25cm (10 inches) high will help to encourage the plant to produce fruit on the side shoots. Once you have about five good fruits per plant developing, remove excess side shoots and new flowers. Water well and feed every two weeks with a liquid feed (tomato feed or comfrey tea). I grew aubergines quite successfully in a tomato grow bag one year, which speaks, I think, to the fact that they like a rich growing medium.

Things are progressing well in the veg patch. Today I sowed my maincrop carrots – it might seem a little late, but by waiting until now you get quick germination (within a few days, as opposed to the two or three weeks it can take when you sow them in April or May).

In the potting shed I am still nursing along the important winter/spring brassicas: purple sprouting broccoli and Brussels sprouts. These have been planted into larger pots to get them really big and hardy before exposing them to the various pests that love to munch them – pigeons, slugs, caterpillars and so on.

The tomatoes are progressing well in the tunnel, with side-shooting the main job at this stage. It's amazing how quickly the side shoots grow. Our neighbours John and Bridget, who help us out in return for some fresh veg, come once a week to do it. It's a small price to pay for having really productive plants. We've been harvesting broad beans for weeks now from outside, and beetroot and calabrese (broccoli) from the small tunnel. We've also an abundance of leaves (lettuce, oriental greens, kale, spinach and chard) and our first strawberries.

As we move into summer, it's important to keep sowing to make sure you extend your harvesting year. A lot of GIYers believe it's too late to sow seeds for this year. In fact, there are still loads of vegetables that you can sow from seed, including beans (French and runner), kale, peas, spinach, chard, summer broccoli, carrots, swedes, leeks, lettuce, Brussels sprouts, beetroot, chicory, endive, turnips, kohlrabi and fennel.

20 june
planting
out sprouts

Today I have been planting out my Brussels sprouts seedlings – it's strange to be working with the quintessential Christmas vegetable just as the vegetable patch is coming into its summer finery. That is the beauty of GIYing, I think – it's the opposite of our frenetic, immediate world where instant gratification is the norm. I love that some vegetables have such long growing seasons and that you have to think so far in advance.

I'm always super-careful when it comes to planting out Brussels sprouts. When you think about it, these are incredibly valuable plants since they will be providing food in leaner times. I was chatting to Richard, our head grower at GROW HQ, about this, and he said the tradition was to start these plants in seed beds and grow them up to at least 30cm (1ft) or more before moving them to their final growing position in later summer (often as late as August). This was to make sure they were hardy enough to withstand any slug attacks.

It's always a bit of a mind-bend for me to stick with the spacing rule on Brussels sprouts plants – you really do need to allow 75cm (30 inches) or more between plants. This seems ridiculous and enormously wasteful, but try to envisage how the plants will look by winter – they grow incredibly tall and stout, and are hungry feeders, so they need plenty of space between them. You can use the space in the short term by planting it up with annual spinach or lettuce, which will be out of the ground long before the sprouts need the space.

Net the crop against insects and pigeons and make sure the net is up off the leaves. I had my plants netted last year but the cabbage white butterfly managed to land on the leaves to deposit their caterpillar eggs – the plants were munched to pieces and had to be removed. If the plants are not growing well, sprinkle some chicken manure pellets around them. Support them with a stake to ensure they grow straight – otherwise you can end up with very strange-looking plants or, worse, they will topple over.

21 june
doing things with dad

Youngest Child has a little book called *Doing Things with Dad* that she pulls out occasionally when she feels the need to gently remind me to spend time with her. This Father's Day it was left on my setting at the breakfast table beside a card she made for me. The book is full of little projects that young girls can do with their father, so basically her Father's Day present to me was for me to spend time with her ... She's a smart one.

The project we settled on was making an insect hotel to encourage more wildlife and biodiversity into the garden, providing beneficial insects with a sheltered winter habitat. She's learning about the decline (collapse?) of our insect populations, but thankfully she's also learning about positive things she can do to help (rather than being petrified into complete inaction, which I guess is how most of society feels about the climate emergency). I love this sense of purpose in children, and I think adults are starting to listen and realise that it's not enough to be horrified – we must *do* something. Things are changing, albeit far too slowly, with people and local authorities starting to think more about rewilding spaces, knowing that we have starved insects of their food and habitats for far too long. There will always be sceptics who say these actions are a trifle in the grand scheme of the problem, but that is missing the broader point that individual actions can have immense power when done at scale.

From a food grower's perspective, encouraging insects into the garden is also a good plan since they play such an important role in the pollination of veg and fruit crops. They can also bring balance back to your veg patch in terms of natural predators. For example, when your broad beans get an attack of blackfly, instead of reaching for the spray you can hang tight and wait for the ladybirds to move in to deal with them.

An insect hotel provides an ideal habitat for all sorts of beneficial insects, particularly solitary bees and wasps that make individual nests for their larvae (as opposed to forming colonies). The wasps will use two of the great veg patch pests, caterpillars and aphids, to feed their larvae. Insect hotels should also attract ladybirds and lacewings, the latter also being a formidable natural predator of the aphid.

The result of our two hours together was an impressive contraption. Eldest Boy was dragged in to help for reconnaissance missions around the garden to gather materials. A more enjoyable time you simply could not have – activity with purpose, with those you love. Now we just need to wait for the hotel bookings to start rolling in.

22 june
strawberry
care
Strawberries will produce a good crop for three years and they should be replaced after that – a 'good crop' is about half a kilo (or about a pound) per plant. Bear in mind that you will pay €6–10 for a punnet of strawberries at the side of the road, which goes to show you how thrifty it is to GIY.

You can create your own new plants at this time of the year by potting up the 'runners' that the plants send out. To do this, anchor the runners in pots of potting compost and once they have taken root, snip them off from the mother plant. Plant these new plants in the autumn.

Strawberries will not ripen once removed from the plant, so pick only when they are fully ripe. Birds and slugs will also find the fruit irresistible. Net against birds if they become a problem, and if slug damage becomes an issue, check plants for slugs at night-time (and then remove them).

25 june
globe
artichokes

I like to consider myself somewhat of a food fanatic, but I have a confession to make that I think excludes me from ever being considered a proper foodie. So here goes … I think globe artichokes are a ridiculous vegetable to grow. Don't get me wrong, I'm not averse to putting enormous amounts of energy, care and attention into growing vegetables, often with very little return. And I like to eat artichoke hearts – I regularly get a tub of them from the cheese counter in my local supermarket. But as a veg to grow, in my opinion, they are a bit of a waste of time.

Globe artichokes grow to nearly 2m (6ft) tall and the plants must be spaced about 1m (3ft) apart. And despite taking up all this space, each plant yields a miserly four to six heads. To put that into context, I can grow about 40 delicious beetroot in a metre-long vegetable bed.

Whenever they are mentioned in cookbooks they are invariably described as (a) a delicacy and (b) fiddly. Fiddly doesn't even begin to describe how difficult it is to prepare them. The heart is buried deep inside the flowering head – first you must boil it up to get it tender. Then you pick the scaly little leaves off one by one. There's a tiny (almost non-existent) little bit of flesh on each leaf that you suck off – this is supposed to be the 'delicacy' bit, particularly if you dip it in melted butter. Let's be honest: week-old socks would taste good if you dipped them in

melted butter. After sucking and slurping your way through dozens of the leaves, your cholesterol going off the charts from all the butter, you still haven't actually eaten any food. Then finally you get to the centre and you're still not at the heart, but a rather ominous-looking 'choke' that you can't eat either and must be scraped off. And your reward after all that sowing, growing, cooking, de-leafing, dipping and scraping? A couple of measly mouthfuls of (admittedly yummy) artichoke heart.

I reckon a couple of artichoke plants in a flower border are a good plan – eat a few of the hearts for sure, but let the rest blossom into beautiful purple flowers (that your resident bees will love too).

kohlrabi, carrot and green onion slaw

This slaw recipe is something I made up to deal with some vegetables that I had just harvested or had in storage, some beautiful kohlrabi from the polytunnel (thriving this year) and some of last year's carrots from storage. I also added a baby green onion to it, which was delicious. A green onion is an immature onion, picked before it's ready – they pack an immense flavour punch and you can use them as you would a scallion, stalk and all. I suppose the combination of an over-ripe and under-ripe vegetable in the dish gives it some balance.

I love preparing food this way, experimenting with whatever the season and the garden has provided, rather than starting with a recipe and then going shopping. It's an altogether healthier and more delicious approach. This recipe will keep in the fridge for a few days. You could do it without the mayo or yoghurt to make it vegan, but I find that just a small amount brings it all together nicely.

Serves 3–4
ingredients:
— 1 medium kohlrabi
— 1 carrot

- — 1 green onion
- — a handful of walnuts, crushed or roughly chopped
- — a handful of raisins
- — juice of 1 lemon
- — 2 tbsp mayonnaise or natural yoghurt
- — salt and pepper
- — parsley (optional)

directions:

Peel and grate the kohlrabi and the carrot and put in a large bowl. Chop the green onion and add it to the bowl with the walnuts and the raisins. Add the lemon and the mayo and stir well to combine it all. Season to taste. You could also add a little handful of chopped parsley.

28 june
beetroot
bounty

We've been enjoying the first consistent supply of fresh beetroot from the veg patch over the last week. The ones from the garden are still a little small, but that's pretty much the perfect size for them. Just a little bigger than a golf ball is about right.

My favourite method of cooking beetroot is in a tinfoil parcel, with the skins on. This way you retain all the nutrition inside, rather than boiling it out of them as you do when cooking them in water. When beetroot are young and fresh, the skins will rub off under a cold tap after cooking. You can add some balsamic and olive oil to them (and maybe some goat's cheese or blue cheese), but they taste just as good 'naked', which allows you to really savour the earthy flavour. At this time of the year, they taste truly exquisite.

The beauty of beetroot is their versatility. In addition to cooking them, you can also eat them raw, grated in a slaw. Or you can make them into brownies or a ketchup like JB does at GROW HQ (when we don't have any tomatoes). Don't forget, the stems are also edible too. You can chop them up and sauté them slowly with some red onions for a quick and easy accompaniment to some good-quality sausages or steak. And I will always pick through the leaves before composting and take the smaller ones for a colourful addition to a salad.

I know it's something of a cliché to say 'I can't believe how quickly the year is going', but seriously – I literally cannot believe how quickly the year is going. How can it possibly be the end of June already? It feels like only yesterday that I was prepping beds for winter and sowing the first tentative tomato seeds back in February. And now it's nearly July! How did that happen?

Well, get on board, people, because we're into the second half of the year, with six full months behind us and the longest day of the year now in the rear-view mirror. That means, rather depressingly, that nature's grand pivot has happened again and it's now getting darker rather than brighter and the days are getting shorter rather than longer.

But never mind all that, there are multiple reasons for cheer. There is still (for now at least) up to 17 hours of daylight per day, which is just amazing – the day breaks around 5 a.m. and continues up to 10 p.m. That means there's lots of time for veg patch work (if you're willing to rise early or work late). And there's plenty to do.

July is the real start of a super-abundant period in the veg patch. Up to now our harvesting has been somewhat stuttering, but now it comes in waves – the copious quantities of salads and leaves are now joined by courgettes, cabbage, celery, kohlrabi, beetroot, new potatoes and, wait for it, tomatoes!

As the produce starts to flow in, don't forget to keep sowing too – no, it's not too late. A July sowing of beetroot, for example, can be harvested for storage in October, and of course we can continue sowing salads and salad herbs right into September and later for the polytunnel.

Abundance. The veg patch is churning out produce – every meal is homegrown now. Baskets full of tomatoes, courgettes, cucumbers, salad leaves and every other veg you could think of make their way to the table.

This month we're loving … tomatoes.

All the work pays off as we gorge on warm, just-picked toms.

1 july
seasonal
eating

A supermarket is a place where there are no seasons. You can buy any vegetable you want at any time of the year. Want a butternut squash in May? Your local supermarket probably has one for sale, though it may have been grown in Ghana and spent weeks in the back of a container lorry. For all its technological wizardry, there is a terrifying blandness about the modern food chain, with its continuous, year-round supply of mediocre, uniform produce.

The veg patch, on the other hand, is a place where, thankfully, the seasons still hold sway in all their riotous glory. Seasonality is not without its frustrations, of course (it involves a lot of waiting, for one thing), but at least it brings a narrative arc, diversity and variety in its wake. Vegetables were never designed to be available all year round – the wax and wane of the seasons is part of their nature. And, of course, nature knows best when it comes to deciding which foods we should eat at particular times of the year – the starchy root crops to warm the soul in winter and the water-filled luscious fruit to quench our thirst in the summer. Eating seasonally means eating nutritious, healthy food just when our bodies need it.

Summer is truly a time of plenty for GIYers – a time when we perhaps start to struggle to keep up with the output of the veg patch. Though the work is hard, we can also take time to enjoy the fruits of our labour. Savour the taste of produce that is organic, local and seasonal. Celebrate its diversity. If you grew a crazy-shaped carrot or a metre-long courgette, congratulate yourself on having produced something utterly unique that your supermarket wouldn't even let inside the door.

2 july
tomato
time!

It's tomato time, folks. I mean we've had salad crops like radish and lettuce and so on for weeks now, but the first tomatoes of the year is what really signals the arrival of summer. There are some vegetables that you grow yourself where you might find it hard to tell the difference between it and the shop-bought alternative. Tomatoes are not one of those veg.

Given the fact that most of the tomatoes in our supermarkets are the super-bland, all-year-round Dutch varieties and taste of, well, nothing at all, having a good crop of your own tomatoes is really one of the most rewarding things you can do. When the nerdy garden geek that I am sits down at the start of the year to write down the list of veggies to be grown for the year, tomatoes always go top of the list.

The reason is quite simply their taste. Tomatoes that you grow yourself taste a million times nicer than anything you will buy in the supermarket. Period. This is because most commercial tomatoes are grown for uniformity and durability rather than flavour. You are more likely to eat your own tomatoes as you would an apple rather than slicing them up and putting them in a sandwich. Given how useful they are in the kitchen, having your own tomatoes means you are starting many a recipe with a completely delicious core ingredient.

Today, walking around the big tunnel, I noticed that the recent fine weather's combination of heat and sun has brought the tomatoes along and I brought the first small bowl of fruit into the kitchen. They were a sweet, sumptuous treat, eaten while still warm from the tunnel. 'Tis the season, so enjoy 'em!

4 july
slug-o-war

Slugs are having an absolute field day in the big tunnel this year because of the cool, wet weather that we had to endure in May and June. For the first time ever, I am noticing considerable slug damage on tomato plants in the tunnel and on the tomatoes themselves, which is a nuisance.

Each night when I lock in the hens, I detour to the veg patch on the way back to the house to hunt slugs in the tunnel. Armed with either a miner's headlamp (good for hands-free slug hunting) or my iPhone (a surprisingly effective substitute torch, as it happens), I check the toms and my most vulnerable plants and seedlings for slugs – the most likely places to find them are on any of the brassicas, salad leaves, beans, courgettes, squashes, pumpkins, celery and celeriac.

Slug hunting is a grim task that brings out the worst in me. Every time I find one of the slimy little buggers climbing over a leaf, I find myself cursing – it's an instinctive response, one I am not particularly proud of, but there you go.

Sometimes I collect them in a container and then go about slicing each one with secateurs. Do I feel bad about dispatching them to the slug after-world like this? No, I do not. Other times, in a fit of annoyance and usually accompanied by another expletive, I throw them as far as I can into the field beside our house (apologies to Martin, the farmer who owns the field). No doubt they make their way back to the garden eventually, but I find the act of throwing them quite cathartic (even more so than killing them, in fact). I've started wearing gloves on this nightly reconnaissance now – slugs leave a surprisingly persistent slime on your hands as you collect them.

Slugs are formidable opponents at the best of times, but this year they seem to be in the ascendency. This week I have been hardening off a large module tray of celeriac seedlings. I put them on the gravel path beside my parsnip bed, believing

that slugs wouldn't travel over the gravel (they don't like abrasive surfaces, apparently). Clearly, the gravel isn't abrasive enough. Last night the light of my torch revealed a veritable army of slugs crawling all over the celeriac, stripping the little seedlings of their leaves. This morning I turned the tray over to find another battalion hiding out in the crevices under the tray. I even found slugs munching on heads of lettuce in my veg trug, which is a bed raised nearly 1m (3ft) off the ground on stilts! And GIYing is supposed to reduce stress levels?

You will hear lots of talk about effective slug remedies – copper tape, eggshells, coffee grounds, slug pellets (nasty, toxic) and more – but I find the most effective of all is physically picking them off plants, particularly the more vulnerable ones. A beer trap is a good way of killing slugs too. Slugs, it turns out, are big fans of beer and a saucer of the stuff left in the soil is something they simply can't pass. They will climb in to imbibe their fill and drown in the process. Presumably it's a happy enough ending for them. I find they are not particularly concerned with the quality of the beer (though they don't like non-alcoholic beer), and the craft beer revolution has passed them by completely. They are, however, concerned with freshness, so keep replacing the beer after a few days.

It's fair to say that laziness is never particularly rewarding or productive in the long term. This fact was brought home to me today when my decision not to put up supports for my broad bean plants was revealed as a serious mistake when a particularly nasty little wind felled most of the crop. I could regale you with a litany of other similar examples: say, walking past the sprouting broccoli plants, noticing the net had come off the plants and ignoring it, only for the plants to be massacred by pigeons a few days later … You know the kind of stuff.

Generally speaking, a fairly basic bamboo cane/twine frame is enough to support a double row of broad beans. I've seen

5 july
blowing in the wind

people supporting the individual plants with twiggy sticks, but I think that's overkill. I just put a bamboo cane on each corner of the bed and run a few lengths of twine around them to box in the plants and stop them falling over.

Having sown these particular broad beans pre-Christmas, allowing them to harden up over winter, I was lulled into a false sense of security by their all-round hardiness – the plants seemed tougher and sturdier than normal. Though there was part of me that knew it was folly, I decided I would try growing them without support. But then along came a gusty night, and the wind knocked down well over half of the plants. Most of the felled plants were killed off by this incident, so today I had to remove them and belatedly put a support in place for the remaining plants. Of course, by now they are too big and heavy to be supported by bamboo canes, so I had to use some fence posts and wire to do the job. Ultimately, a much bigger job than it would have been had I done it right in the first place. There's a lesson in there somewhere, which one would hope I will learn from (but there are no guarantees).

beet burgers

A good friend to GIY, Suzie Cahn, runs the remarkable Carraig Dúlra education centre in the wild hills of County Wicklow. On a recent visit, Suzie cooked us delicious beetroot burgers. When I asked her for the recipe she said, 'It's just grated raw beetroot, breadcrumbs and feta cheese.' I put together this recipe, which has a few more ingredients but is equally delicious. Dare I say it, it's almost meaty in texture. I serve these in a fresh blaa (Waterford's finest floury roll) with a yoghurt and dill dressing and a seasonal salad.

Makes 6–7 large burgers
ingredients:
— 500g beetroot
— 100g breadcrumbs

- 100g porridge oats
- 3 eggs, beaten
- 1 small red onion, very finely chopped
- a large handful of finely chopped dill, thyme and parsley
- salt and pepper

directions:

Peel and grate the beetroot and put it in a large bowl. Add the breadcrumbs, porridge oats, beaten eggs, onion and herbs and season well. Mix it all together well with your hands. Shape it into six or seven burger-sized patties and put them on a plate in the fridge for an hour or so. This will help ensure that the burgers don't fall apart in cooking.

Preheat the oven to 180°C.

Heat some oil in a pan and fry the burgers briefly on each side to seal them. Then put them on a baking tray and bake them in the oven for 20 minutes. Serve immediately. They are even better on day two if you have any left!

6 july
elderflower
foraging

There are great big blossoms of creamy-white elderflower in hedgerows at the moment, so it's a great time to get out there and start foraging. I always think elder is a great starter for novice foragers because it's so easy to identify. The biggest clue is that the flowers are cream, not white. They also have an unmistakably earthy, almost musty, aroma. The season for elderflower is short – about six weeks or so.

Remember when foraging for elderflower that you should not take more than a few heads from each bush – this ensures that there are enough flowers remaining to allow the bush to thrive (keep next year, birds and other foragers, in mind). Better to pick a few flowers from lots of different locations rather than stripping a bush in one location completely bare. Pick flowers that are at their best – you don't want to pick heads where the flowers aren't open; nor do you want ones that are obviously past their prime. You will need about 30 heads to make a decent batch of elderflower cordial or champagne (a quick Google search will yield loads of simple recipes). It's important to pick on a sunny day (chance would be a fine thing) as the heat will heighten the smell. Use them as soon as possible – collect them in a brown paper bag, rather than a plastic one, as this will allow them to breathe. As is always the case with foraging, avoid picking flowers on the roadside as they may be tainted with petrol fumes.

The ongoing warm, dry weather brings an increased workload for the GIYer, with extensive watering needed outside. Generally speaking, we don't need to water much, if at all, outside in the veg patch in a typical Irish summer. But in the current dry conditions (likely to happen more often with climate change), watering is necessary and conserving water becomes a significant challenge. Here are my top tips:

8 july

conserving water

- Water properly. Getting water down to the root zone takes much longer than you think. If you just water the top layer of soil, chances are it will evaporate off before it can benefit the plant. A good, heavy watering is better than an occasional light one. If in doubt, stick your finger down into the soil to check. A heavy watering is 20 litres per square metre (or about two standard watering cans per square yard).
- Water when it's cool – either first thing in the morning or last thing at night – to reduce evaporation and to get the most from your water.
- Having as much organic matter as possible in the soil will help to increase its water-holding capacity.
- Keep the surface of soil around plants mulched to prevent evaporation. Mulch after watering to retain the wet conditions for longer. Mulching can reduce a plant's water needs by up to 50 per cent. Straw and newspaper are both good mulches.

- Get rid of weeds – they compete with plants for water.
- It's too late in a dry period, but a rain butt to collect water from a shed or greenhouse roof will provide significant volumes of water for later use. They are a cinch to install, simply diverting water from a drainpipe into the butt. It's estimated that you could collect 24,000 litres of water a year from a standard roof. Whether you'd need that much water is another matter.
- Drip irrigation or seep hoses are efficient and can be buried under soil to reduce evaporation.
- Focus water *where* it's needed most – the leafy veg like brassicas, spinach, etc.; celery and celeriac; fruiting vegetables at flowering stage (but not too much when starting to fruit).
- Focus water *when* it's most needed – typically when seedlings are young and have not developed a mature root system, right after transplanting, during flowering and when they are starting to fruit.
- Reuse water used in cooking (when it's cooled down) and grey water from baths, showers, etc. for watering plants (but don't use water that has detergent or disinfectants in it).

9 july
in praise of
sunflowers

I met a guy who told me a story about the power of food growing to create an understanding in children about nutritious food and sustainable living. His children sowed sunflower seeds in planting cups in school and then brought them home, where they were planted down the end of the garden, against a south-facing wall.

In this high-tech age, he's been astonished by the interest the children have shown in their sunflowers – there are daily trips to the end of the garden to measure progress, which with sunflowers is a satisfying thing indeed since they grow so rapidly (and up to 3m (10ft) tall eventually).

Then a miraculous thing happens – the plants produce enormous, beautiful sunflowers. The sunflower is one of the most animated, optimistic and downright cheery flowers you can have in your garden – it literally follows the sun across the horizon by day, only to turn back and face east by sunrise.

This is a joy to behold, but it's also the starting point in the sunflower's demise – the flower eventually bows down and looks rather sad as it starts to die. But there's time for one more miracle in which the dying plant suddenly becomes useful from a food perspective – the seeds in the flower head can be harvested for food. So, from this strange plant, you get an unlikely abundance of seeds that can be nibbled on (wonderfully nutty) or sprinkled into yoghurt or on top of porridge.

If this direct connection between the act of sowing a seed and the act of food consumption wasn't eye-opening enough for this man's kids, consider what happened next. It occurred to them that the seeds they were about to eat looked the very same as the seeds sown in soil months back. And so a lightbulb moment occurred, and the full food life cycle – from seed to plant, plant to flower, flower to food, food to seed – was laid out before them. They had reached 'food empathy', a deeper understanding of seasonality and the life cycle of 'growth–decay–growth' that is so central to life on this planet.

We've been eating onions for the last month or so, even though they are not ready yet. The immature 'green' onions are a delight to eat and can be used in anything that asks for a scallion. At this stage, though, the onions are moving to the point where they are almost ready to harvest.

Onions have been revered through time, not only for their culinary uses but also for their therapeutic properties. The liberal use of the allium species, including garlic, leeks and different varieties of onions, has been associated with beneficial effects on cholesterol levels and heart disease (as long as it's not a cheesy, buttery French onion soup, I suppose). Onions are one of the few vegetables that are a source of biotin, a B vitamin that is important for healthy hair and nails. Biotin also helps your body to digest fatty foods (hence that steak and onions pairing).

Onions are also a phenomenally useful vegetable to grow for the kitchen. There are very few meals that don't involve peeling and chopping an onion. So it's a stroke of wonderful good fortune that one of the healthiest and most useful kitchen vegetables is also very easy to grow. A decent-sized raised bed will produce a couple of hundred onions (you get about 40 onions per metre in a 1.2m (4ft) wide bed), which would be enough for most families for up to a year.

So how do you know when your onions are ready to harvest? Thankfully onions are rather helpful on this matter, providing you with an indicator of sorts so you know when they are ready. The foliage on the onions will turn yellow and literally topple over (approximately 20 weeks after sowing). One of the most remarkable sights you will ever see in your vegetable plot is a bed of onions getting itself ready for harvest. In the last weeks of summer, a nutrient tug-of-war of sorts happens between the bulb and its foliage, which, of course, you are hoping the bulb will win. The bulb starts to suck all the vitamins and minerals from the foliage until finally, thoroughly beaten, the foliage turns yellow, withers and then topples over dramatically in a final act of surrender.

At this stage it's a good idea to gently loosen the soil around the onions (or turn the onion very carefully and very slightly in the soil – I've heard it described as turning it 'a half moon'). Loosening the soil like this allows the onion to expand in the soil. After this, leave them for another two weeks, and then your onions are ready to be harvested.

As documented earlier this year, there's a dark corner of my garage that's a graveyard for dead, decrepit and defunct garden tools. When I visit the garage to do stuff (cutting, sawing, sanding, hammering, etc.) I must avoid eye contact (figuratively speaking) with this Boulevard of Broken Tools because it is an embarrassment to me, a reminder of my appalling lack of DIY skills and questionable buying decisions. Some of the tools have bits falling off; others are broken in two; there are spades and shovels with handles missing; rakes rusted beyond redemption … In my defence I once turned a broken spade handle into a handy long-handled dibber using an approximation of the ancient skill of whittling, which felt pretty darn good – but I think it's broken now too.

13 july boulevard of broken tools

I've read in gardening books that you should finish each session in the veg patch by cleaning your tools. I've always thought this was the kind of ridiculous advice that no sensible person would ever really contemplate. But I must reluctantly agree that it has its merits. I now tend to line my tools up outside the potting shed and give them a good hard spray of water before putting them back inside. Even this old dog is still learning a few new tricks.

14 july
all hail the
legumes

It's been a great year so far for the legume family (peas and beans). Despite the storm damage, we had an abundance of broad beans in May and June from an over-winter sowing, though the dry weather finished them off earlier than normal. They were followed by the climbing French beans from the tunnel in early July and the peas around the same time.

French beans are, I think, one of the most underrated vegetables. Of all the legume family, they are my favourite to eat. I remember a sublime food experience at La Boqueria market in Barcelona, sitting up at a counter at lunchtime and eating French beans that had (I presume) been briefly blanched before being fried in oil and sprinkled with loads of rock salt. Perhaps that's where the love affair started.

You can grow two types of French beans: dwarf crops or the climbing variety. The beans from both types are pretty much the same. Dwarf beans grow just 45cm (18 inches) tall and are surprisingly prolific. Climbing French beans grow up to 4m (13ft) tall and produce a lot more beans on the same footprint. The seeds can be sown direct in the soil or in module trays ready for transplanting.

Though a row of climbing French beans is no doubt visually appealing (as is a tepee of them in the garden), I think dwarf French beans are somehow more impressive and surprisingly productive for such a neat little plant. Back in mid-March, I sowed a module tray of dwarf French beans in the potting shed. In early May, I planted these out in the polytunnel in two short rows in one of the side beds. There were 12 plants in total, and I planted them out 15cm (6 inches) apart in two rows 40cm (16 inches) apart.

Just two months or so later, aided by the sub-tropical climate in the polytunnel, the little plants are host to masses of slender, vibrant, delicious French beans. Cue repeats of my La Boqueria market experience. The good news is that once we've finished these, I've another three long rows (about 4m, or 13ft) of them outside in the veg patch, which are three to four weeks from harvesting.

The key, of course, with all the legumes (and this can be a challenge) is to keep picking them. The more you pick, the more they produce, whereas if you leave them on the plant to mature it reduces yields considerably. So it makes sense to get out there and pick every day if you can, whether or not you intend to eat them that day. All beans (broad, runner and French) and peas freeze incredibly well as long as you blanch them first. They will be very welcome in the freezer during the long winter and early spring months next year when there's little or no fresh produce left in the veg patch.

17 july
bolting

At this time of the year, as I wander around my own veg garden, I am keeping an eye out to see if any of the plants have bolted. It can be a common occurrence with the likes of onions, spinach and pak choi. 'Bolting' refers to vegetable crops that run to seed before their time. The plant is essentially rushing into procreation mode – trying to spread its seed (by producing flower or seed heads) before it dies. It is a perfectly natural part of the plant's life cycle, but unfortunately from a GIYer's perspective it usually renders them inedible. It is often caused by a cold spell, changes in day length or other stresses to the plant, such as lack of water. Some plants, such as lettuce, rocket and annual spinach, are particularly susceptible.

Although bolting occurs as the plant reaches maturity, it can be caused or initiated much earlier in the life cycle. In annual crops it is usually caused by changes in day length, but can be worsened by stressed conditions (lack of water, very dry soil, etc.). In biannual crops it is caused by unsettled weather conditions or a cold spell early in the propagation phase. Cold nights followed by hot days will also cause it, as will late frosts.

The three main methods of controlling bolting are: (1) ensuring you provide the veg in question with the right soil conditions; (2) paying attention to sowing times; and (3) using bolt-resistant varieties. I also find that succession sowings are the best way to beat bolting and provide a constant supply of produce.

18 july
a fresh look
at salads

The key to unlocking more diverse, delicious and flavoursome salads is to think beyond the traditional salad leaves of lettuce, lettuce and more lettuce. Throw in some oriental greens, baby chard and spinach, or go a step further and view almost every leaf in the veg patch as something that's potentially worth eating.

Many vegetables produce leaves that are worth eating in their own right. Beetroot leaf is delicious, particularly when the leaves are small and tender. We grow a beetroot variety called Bulls Blood, which has a beautiful dark red, almost purple leaf. The more standard green and red beetroot leaf is also a tasty and attractive addition to salads.

In a similar vein, pretty much the entire pea plant is edible. The leaves, shoots and flowers are all delicious, bringing a distinct pea flavour to a salad. The clinging tendrils that the pea plants use to hold on to supports is often used as a fancy garnish in restaurants. Removing the top shoot of a pea plant means hobbling the future growth of the plant – so it makes sense to grow some pea plants just for the purpose of harvesting the tops. But you can happily harvest the individual leaves of the plant without impacting growth – these are really tasty. The same applies to broad bean plants – both flowers and leaves are good to eat.

Don't neglect herbs, such as basil, coriander, parsley, mint, borage and lemon verbena, when it comes to salads. Use sparingly in a salad for a delicious and surprising treat. And, of course, edible flowers make a colourful and delicious addition to any salad – think borage, nasturtium and marigolds.

We've been harvesting tomatoes since early July, but in the last few days we've moved up to abundance territory, which is both incredibly welcome and a little earlier in the year than normal. That, of course, is down to the hot, sunny weather that the tomatoes are absolutely loving. You might recall that in an attempt to cut down the workload involved in growing 80 tomato plants, I made some changes and a bit of an investment in the big tunnel. I'm pleased to report these have paid off mightily.

First up, rather than having to water each plant directly (which took up to 45 minutes each time last year), I got myself a seep hose. The hose is laid along the ground, snaking along beside each plant. All I have to do is turn on the hose for about two hours a week and that's getting the plants the 13 litres (3 gallons) or so of water each that they need.

To reduce weeding I also basically carpeted the tunnel in Mypex, a weed-suppressing membrane that also acts like a mulch to minimise water loss due to evaporation. Happily, these two things combined have reduced the workload dramatically and with ongoing side-shooting help from my neighbour and friend Bridget, we've very little to do except enjoy the lovely tomatoes.

20 july
tomato
abundance

marinated beef tomato and cherry tomato salad with gazpacho, rocket and goat's cheese

With tomatoes in full flow now, this fine tomato salad recipe from JB puts them centre stage and particularly celebrates the first big fleshy beefsteaks.

Serves 4

ingredients:
— a small bunch of basil, plus a few leaves to garnish
— 2 cloves garlic
— 100ml Irish rapeseed oil
— 50ml red wine vinegar
— salt and pepper
— 2 large beef tomatoes
— 4–5 cucumber slices (the end of the cucumber would be perfect)
— 20 cherry tomatoes
— rocket leaves
— 50g fresh Irish goat's cheese, crumbled
— toasted sunflower seeds, to garnish

directions:
Blend the basil, garlic, oil and vinegar with a little salt and pepper. Cut two large slices (1–1.5cm thick) from the middle of each beef tomato, keeping the tops and bottoms for the gazpacho. Drizzle a third of the basil dressing over the tomato slices and refrigerate for a minimum of 4 hours. For the gazpacho, blend the beef tomato ends with the cucumber and a third of the basil dressing until smooth. Taste and adjust the seasoning if needed.

Halve the cherry tomatoes and toss them in most of the remaining basil dressing (keep a little aside for a final drizzle) with a few rocket leaves and the crumbled goat's cheese. Place the marinated beef tomato slices on a serving plate and top with the cherry tomato salad. Garnish with basil leaves, sunflower seeds and a drizzle of gazpacho.

22 july
a strange lull

Dare I say it? Things seem to have quietened down a little. I find myself standing in the vegetable patch and thinking, 'You know what? There's actually nothing more for me to do here. Go and do something else. Play with your kids or fix that gate that needs fixing.'

So what's going on? Well, ironically, even though the vegetable patch is resplendent and heaving with produce, there's actually very little to do. It's like we're in the eye of the storm – the worst has passed, or the worst is perhaps yet to come. But for now, well, everything's dandy.

Weeding duties are not as severe as they were earlier in the season. Sowing duties have slowed to a virtual stop – though they will ramp up again next month as we start sowing winter crops. I'm doing some harvesting alright, but it's an 'as you need it' type of harvesting rather than a major job like harvesting onions or spuds. We don't have massive gluts of produce that require processing (into jams, chutneys, pickles or preserves) yet.

July is, to my mind, one of only two months (the other one being December) in the entire year when I am freed from the delicious tyranny of the veggie patch. So I guess I should enjoy it. Shouldn't I?

23 july
bruschetta season

This morning I went down to the polytunnel to get a few fresh tomatoes to go with our breakfast eggs, and walked in on a group of birds conducting a daring raid. They had managed to pull a few ripe tomatoes off the plants and were busy gorging themselves on the fleshy fruit. Once disturbed they flew around in a panic, getting caught in plants here and up against plastic there. It took me some time to shoo all of them out.

We are in what I like to call 'bruschetta season' – it's a wonderful time of the year, when a simple lunch or dinner can easily be conjured up from nothing as long as you have some decent sourdough bread in the bread bin. Simply toast some of the bread, rub some cut garlic on it, add some slices of delicious ripe tomatoes (warm from the polytunnel) and some ripped basil leaves, sprinkle with lots of salt and pepper and drizzle with a good olive oil. Shake fists at the birds, and eat.

As we crop more and more vegetables, space is starting to become available again in what was, up to now, a very crowded vegetable garden. In particular, we have a good deal of space available where we lifted our new potatoes, and the onion bed will be free in a few weeks' time. The key to a productive veg patch is to use this space as it becomes available.

25 july
use all the
space

You can, even at this late stage of the year, grow some fast-growing crops such as lettuce, rocket, spinach, turnips and radishes. You could even chance a sowing of dwarf French beans and Florence fennel. Another option is if a few old tubers of seed size potatoes (the size of an egg) are on hand, these can be planted now and you will have new potatoes in September.

Another way to use available space in the veggie patch is to sow green manures such as mustard, buckwheat, radish, rye, alfalfa, clover and vetches. Green manures are plants that are grown specifically to improve soil fertility and structure and they are useful at times when beds are empty (as is often the case in summer). Grow directly in the bed and then cut down and dig into the soil, which will improve the soil structure and nutrient level and prevent the leaching of nutrients.

26 july
tedious
task

Today's veg patch activity was mainly characterised by shelling peas – a task that I am not particularly fond of. I am always somewhat conflicted in my views on homegrown peas. There is, of course, nothing quite like the flavour of a freshly picked pea and I love that our kids get to walk up and down the rows in summer grazing on peas. Increasingly, though, I'm of the view that while they are a wonderful thing to eat fresh, they are just not worth the hassle as a 'storage' veg, given the amount of labour that goes into processing them for the freezer.

This week I spent up to four hours working on peas – picking them, shelling them, blanching and freezing. At one stage all four of us were involved, with seemingly never-ending buckets of peas in front of us. The result of all that labour? Just under 2kg (less than 5lb) of peas, which would cost around €4 to buy from the supermarket freezer.

Still, there's a certain amount of satisfaction to be had from knowing that there are about 10 veg portions awaiting us (we froze them in individual 200g portions) for later in the winter, when they will be greatly appreciated. And besides, the process of shelling peas can be soothing at times – therapeutic, meditative even. Though I am not sure the kids would agree.

28 july
sow turnips

Turnips are very easy to grow and because they produce a crop so quickly, they are an ideal candidate for a late-summer sowing. You can even slot them into a bed that has been freed up by harvesting another vegetable (I generally sow them in the onion bed). Note that I'm talking about turnips here (with the white flesh) as opposed to swedes (yellow flesh), which take much longer to mature.

Though they can be sown direct, a foolproof way to grow healthy turnips is to sow them in module trays – sow one or two seeds 2cm (1 inch) deep in each module of the tray. They will germinate in about a week (thin out the weaker seedling) and will be ready for planting about a month later. Plant seedlings out, spacing them 30cm between rows and between each plant. Do not plant turnips where there have been brassicas in the last three to four years. For a cluster of small, golf ball-sized roots, sow three or four seeds in each module of a module tray. Then, rather than thinning out, plant them out in a group, allowing them to grow on together.

Sow turnips now and they will be ready to eat in six to eight weeks (end of September). Harvest when relatively small, if possible, and don't leave them in the ground too late in the winter, as they will be a target for mice and slugs. The green leaves that grow on top of the turnip can also be eaten. Water well in dry spells to prevent cracking.

Turnips will not store as well as swedes – hence it's not a good idea to sow too many of them. Harvest by simply pulling the root from the ground by the stem.

29 july
aubergine woes

Frankly, I am in two minds about aubergines. I have grown them for years, mainly because they are one of the first things you sow in the year – way back in February – and just because there's so little else to sow at that time of the year. They are a handsome plant, too, in the summer polytunnel and produce beautiful flowers.

We're spoiled rotten by the lovely shiny, smooth, jet-black supermarket aubergines. I'd like to say the ones you grow yourself are far nicer, but I can't say I've grown a decent enough one to be able to compare. Whatever about their flavour, the supermarket aubergine looks damn impressive. I have only grown decent aubergines once in all the years that I've grown them, and that year it was almost by accident. I ran out of space in the tunnel and planted them in a grow bag in the potting shed instead and they seemed to do well there. Every year, I tell myself that I won't bother with them, but then I am always hankering for things to sow in February and I enter another year of mediocrity with them. This year I have about five rather unhealthy-looking plants in the big tunnel, which I eye daily with barely disguised contempt.

On the other hand, I'm a big fan of chilli peppers. They also have a tremendously long growing season and were grown from seed sown way back in February. I find you are best off holding on to them in pots in the warmth of the house (or in the potting shed) as long as you can so they don't get caught by late frosts and cold nights.

Bell peppers are a little tougher to grow well, particularly if you prefer red peppers. All peppers start off green but go red as they ripen. The problem is that the ripening process takes up a lot of the plant's energy and so it can generally only support ripening a few peppers. You can get lots of small little green peppers if you keep picking them at that stage, but I don't much see the point of that when the red ones are so much nicer.

Ultimately, I think it's better to concentrate on chilli peppers, which are very prolific – a single healthy plant can produce 60–100 chillies. I've had good success with the mild variety Hungarian Hot Wax, which is almost like a hybrid pepper/chilli pepper and produces masses of fruit.

30 july
earth up
leeks

A good leek (from a culinary perspective) has a substantial amount of white flesh and a short green top. A bad leek has lots and lots of green top and only a short length of white flesh. The key to getting the former rather than the latter is to 'earth up' leeks at this time of the year to encourage blanching (or whitening) of the stems.

This is achieved by drawing soil up around the stem to exclude light. Be careful not to draw soil over the top of the leek (where the leaves turn into stem) – you will end up with soil down the inside of the leek, which will be a nightmare to remove when cooking. A leek 'stem' is not in fact a stem at all, but a series of tightly rolled leaves – it's almost impossible to get dirt out of there once it gets in! A cleaner method than using soil to earth them up is to pop the insert from a kitchen roll around the leek. This works well.

To encourage good growth in leeks, give them a feed in late summer; anything high in nitrogen, e.g. chicken manure pellets or a general-purpose organic fertiliser.

saturday morning eggs

A Saturday morning routine for me is to spend a little more time over breakfast, cooking up what we call in our house (not terribly imaginatively) 'Saturday Morning Eggs'. It is basically a one-pan spicy Mexican-style tomato, chilli and pepper sauce with eggs cracked into it at the end to poach. It's sort of like huevos rancheros, I guess, but without the beans (though you could add them if you wanted). With a combination of six different types of veg (chard, tomatoes, garlic, onions, pepper, chilli pepper) and the goodness of eggs, this must be one of the most nutritious breakfasts you could eat. It's also utterly delicious and filling enough that you might not even need lunch.

It's a particular treat at this time of the year when the veg you need are available in the veg patch. You could, of course, use good-quality shop-bought Irish tomatoes, or even an organic passata, but I think the flavour is best if you've got your own tomatoes in it. This week we also found a rather large and decidedly ready green pepper in the tunnel, which was an early surprise. I don't think I've ever had peppers ready this early in the summer and I can't exactly explain why that is – though I think I just got lucky and had healthy plants started early in the year.

A good chilli pepper is vital to give the recipe some zing. Though I don't have any ripe chillies from the garden yet, I do still have some nice red ones in the freezer from last year. Chillies freeze well, so if you have a glut, it's a great way to store them. To defrost, just bung them in the oven for a few minutes before chopping. Any leafy green will work, but I like chard the best because of the extra bit of colour you get on the plate. Don't forget to use the stalks as well.

Give yourself the time to prep and cook, then enjoy it all on a slice of sourdough toast, with a pot of coffee and the weekend newspapers.

Serves 4
ingredients:
— 1 tbsp oil
— 1 onion, chopped
— 2 large garlic cloves, chopped
— 1 large green or red pepper, deseeded and chopped
— 1 mild chilli pepper (like Hungarian Hot Wax), chopped
— 1 tsp cumin seeds, ground
— 6–8 large tomatoes (about 450g), roughly chopped
— 200g rainbow chard, stalks finely chopped and leaves sliced into ribbons
— 1 tsp balsamic vinegar
— salt and pepper
— 4 eggs
— parsley, chopped
— a dollop of yoghurt
— a pinch of cayenne pepper

directions:
Heat the oil in a large frying pan and gently fry the onion for 5 minutes. Add the garlic, green or red pepper, chilli and cumin and cook for a few minutes. Add the chopped tomatoes, chard stems, balsamic vinegar and 250ml water, stir and bring to a simmer. Pop the lid on and let everything cook down for 10 minutes to make a chunky sauce. Stir in the chard leaves and cover the pan for 5 minutes to allow them to wilt. Take the lid off, season to taste and, if needed, cook a little longer with the lid off to thicken the sauce.

Use a spatula to make a small indentation in the sauce and crack in an egg. Repeat with the other three eggs. If you pop the lid back on, the eggs should be ready (whites set and yolks runny) in 3–4 minutes. Scatter over some fresh parsley, a dollop of yoghurt and finish with a sprinkling of cayenne pepper.

august

High summer and there's a gentle pause in the growing year. We're poised between the intense growing activity of June and July and the intense harvesting/ processing of the autumn months. For now, just enjoy it.

This month we're loving … courgettes.

Later in the year I might come to resent just how prolific they are, but for now they are playing a role in almost every meal.

It's felt like allium central at home recently, with the harvest being done on all the onions and garlic. As I write I am looking at the garlic braid hanging up in the kitchen and it's insane how much pleasure I get from this simple thing. It was garlic that started me on my growing journey nearly two decades ago, so I suppose I retain an extra fondness for it. I lifted the garlic about two weeks ago and it's been drying outside on a wire rack since – it's been ideal drying weather, with very little rain. (I have dried garlic in the potting shed in particularly wet weather but it does better outside, where it's exposed to air and wind.) Properly dried out now, the garlic in the braid should last us until well into late summer next year, and I also have about 20 other bulbs that weren't in good enough condition to include in the braid. They will be used up first.

We also lifted the onions today – well, the kids did it and it's a job they enjoy. I get them to use a trowel to harvest them, easing it in underneath the onion while gently pulling the stem. It's easy to break the neck of the onion so it's a job that needs to be done with care. The onions can be left on the soil to dry out for a few weeks, which will help to cure the skin and remove some of the moisture from the neck. Again, this helps with storage. I've a decent crop of onions this year, nothing award-winning, you understand, but perfectly adequate. Quite a few of the red onions have gone soft on me, which seems to happen with the spring-sown varieties. Far better, I think, if you are trying to grow red onions to sow the previous autumn (October) – they seem to fare better when grown like that.

Incidentally, summer onions can be used as required (fresh) straight out of the ground while you wait on the rest of the crop to ripen. In other words, you don't have to dry them out before using – the drying process is only to enable storage.

How to dry and store onions:
The ideal way to dry onions is to leave them out in the sun and wind, but, of course, the Irish climate's fondness for precipitation can wreak havoc with this plan. So, if I have to, I resort to laying

them out on a wire rack in my potting shed for two to three weeks and then hanging them in a twine braid.

Having braided them, I will leave them in the shed for another month or so and then move them into the kitchen. Braiding onions is a time-consuming process, but if there's a more impressive kitchen decoration than a homegrown onion braid, I've yet to see it. If you don't have time to braid, you can always just grab a big bunch and tie them together around the necks with a strong piece of string. Hanging the onions is more effective than sitting them somewhere as they will go soft where they come into contact with the surface.

Make sure to hang your hard-earned onions somewhere very dry – if there is any moisture at all in the air, the onions may rot. I stored them in our porch one year and lost several braids because the air was too damp there. These days I generally hang them in the polytunnel and then bring in one or two bunches to the kitchen as needed. Check the braid frequently and use/remove any onions that are showing any signs of softening.

One of the great lessons I've learned in my 'apprenticeship' as a GIYer is that the sowing season doesn't stop at the end of spring. In fact, if you want a consistent supply of vegetables over the winter, and particularly in the difficult 'hungry gap' months of March, April and May, this is a crucially important time of the year to be sowing seeds. Rather than seeing this as a chore, I actually love this shift in emphasis so late in the season. The last two months have been all about harvesting and lately I've been getting this feeling that the GIY year was about to start its inexorable decline towards autumn and winter. (What can I say? I'm clearly a 'glass-half-empty' kinda guy.)

But before we start feeling all autumnal, we have a reprieve and we're back to the wonderful world of potting compost, seed trays, germination and the like. If, for whatever reason, you didn't get a chance to sow much this year, then here's your

3 august

august sowing

chance for redemption. When it comes to August sowing, I am thinking about three main categories of vegetables:

- Winter 'salad' greens to supply us with green leaves right through the winter. In this category you can include winter lettuce, lamb's lettuce, claytonia, rocket, mizuna, mibuna, French sorrel, chard, endive, parsley, coriander, mustard greens, pak choi and spinach. We eat spinach or chard every other day in our house through the winter, so a decent supply of both in the tunnel is a must-have.
- Quick-growing vegetables that will, if sown now, churn out a crop before winter, such as peas, Florence fennel, Chinese cabbage, dwarf French beans, radishes, turnips, baby carrots, baby beetroot and 'quick-heading' calabrese. Try to source quick-maturing or late-season varieties of these.
- Vegetables that you get in the ground now to provide a crop next spring, like spring cabbage, kale and salad onions. Incidentally, also in this category, I will be sowing garlic and broad beans later in the winter. Though it's too late now to start purple sprouting broccoli and Brussels sprouts from seed, if you can source a couple of plants from your garden centre you could chance planting two or three plants of each in your veggie patch.

6 august
the
spiraliser

It's time to add one more piece of kitchen equipment to your arsenal: a spiraliser. It's a nifty and relatively inexpensive little machine that turns fruit and vegetables into noodle-/spaghetti-shaped lengths. Mrs Kelly and I have recently taken delivery of a spiraliser, not because we feel particularly guilty about eating pasta or because we've gone gluten free (we haven't), but because the spiraliser is a brilliant way to eat veg raw and make it look prettier or just a little more interesting. It also helps us make light work of two of the most glut-prone vegetables, which can be a struggle to keep up with at this time of the year: courgettes and cucumbers.

We've tried all the recipes dealing with courgettes that you could imagine – throwing them into stews, soups, breads, cakes and more – hell, even throwing them at the neighbours. None of these is as quick or delicious as converting them to courgetti. If you have trouble getting your kids to eat vegetables, they might well be more inclined to eat them if they've been involved in the fun of spiralising them. Incidentally, I don't think one would ever necessarily confuse courgetti with actual spaghetti, but that's hardly the point. It's delicious in its own right.

I checked in on the pepper and chilli pepper plants in the tunnel today and they are doing well, but some were starting to lean and sag with the weight of the fruit on them. You can either support the whole plant with bamboo canes or support individual fruit-bearing branches. There's a lot to be said for treating them the same way as I do tomato plants – with a string placed underneath the plant at planting time and tied to a bar at the top of the polytunnel – but I don't have that option at this stage and am using bamboo instead.

7 august
pepper
plants

Once the fruit sets you also need to give them plenty of water and mulch around them to conserve moisture. Give them a good feed every 10–14 days using tomato or comfrey feed if fruit development is poor, but not otherwise. Pick fruit young to encourage cropping. Peppers will go from green to red eventually as part of the natural ripening process, but you have a balancing act to do – do you want lots of green peppers or a small number of red ones? The plant probably won't have energy to do both. If there is still unripe fruit at the end of the season, lift the plants whole and hang them upside down in a greenhouse or porch – they will continue to ripen. (This works for tom plants too.)

8 august
pickle stuff

With increasing gluts of produce arriving in from the garden, thoughts turn to preservation. It's the great August pivot when we move from eating all the harvest to finding ways to preserve it. I love how ancient it all feels – stocking up the larder with the fat of the land and an eye to leaner times. Of course, pickling is one of the oldest methods of preserving food and it's an invaluable tool for the GIYer to prolong the life of produce, particularly when you have gluts that you can't eat straightaway.

I always use the following recipes:

- **Piccalilli:** A delicious way to preserve cauliflower. I don't grow much cauliflower but if I have three or four decent heads I will make piccalilli as a way to get the most out of that harvest for the longest possible time.
- **The cucumber pickle below:** Over a long cucumber harvest period, I could make three or four batches. It has a brilliant flavour and is mostly used for the kids' school sandwiches.
- **Green tomato sour:** Despite the fancy name, it's basically a chutney and a brilliant way to use green tomatoes at the end of the season. Absolutely delicious.

- **Pickled jalapeños:** I keep two or three big Kilner jars of pickled jalapeños in the fridge and use them in lots of recipes, but especially for Friday night pizza.
- **Pickled pears:** A Christmas favourite in our house, this is a delicious way to preserve pears (which are a very perishable fruit).
- **Sauerkraut:** It isn't a pickle, but I also make sauerkraut (see pages 213–214) to make the most of cabbage.

zingy cucumber pickle

I've been using this recipe for about 15 years and at this stage have no idea where it came from. The addition of turmeric and mustard seeds gives it a real kick and as a result this was one of the most coveted jars of preserved veggies we had in the cupboard over the winter.

ingredients:
— 4 large cucumbers
— 3 medium onions
— 50g salt

For the syrup:
— 570ml white wine vinegar
— 450g soft brown sugar
— 1 tbsp black mustard seeds
— ½ level tsp ground turmeric
— ½ level tsp ground cloves

directions:
Wash the cucumbers and slice very thinly. Peel the onions and slice very thinly. In a large bowl, layer the cucumbers and onions with a sprinkling of salt between the layers. Weigh down with a plate. Leave to stand for 3 hours, then pour away the liquid and rinse the cucumbers and onions under running water twice. Put your jars in the oven to sterilise them.

Put the vinegar, sugar and spices in a stainless steel or non-stick saucepan and stir over a medium heat until the sugar has dissolved. Add the cucumbers and onions to the saucepan and bring to the boil. Boil for a couple of minutes. Remove the vegetables with a slotted spoon and set aside. After 10 minutes or so, gently fill the warm, sterilised jars with the vegetables. Don't press them down. Meanwhile, reduce the remaining syrup for 15–20 minutes. When the syrup has reduced, pour it over the vegetables in the jars. Cover immediately with plastic-lined, sterilised metal lids.

When cold, label and store in a cool, dark place, away from damp.

11 august
pimp up the composting system

I decided recently that it was time to pimp up my composting system. For the last five years or so I've been composting in a three-bay composting system down the end of the garden that was hastily constructed using some old timber pallets and lots of rope. A decidedly ramshackle affair, it did the job for me for a few years but it had started to fall apart of late. In the end, I think the pallets were composting quicker than the material I was trying to compost in them.

I considered buying timber and building something sturdier myself, but thankfully common sense prevailed and with a nod to my DIY limitations, I decided to buy a kit instead. Technically, these three-bay systems are known as a New Zealand Box (no, I don't know why) and the benefit of this one over my DIY version is that the timber boards at the side and front can be removed to make it easier to get in and turn the compost.

All plants and animals (including ourselves) will decompose and turn into compost eventually. A good compost system is simply about making that happen quickly – in three to four months, ideally. It's somewhat counter-intuitive, but the key to good composting is to turn the heap regularly. One might have thought that leaving it alone to rot would be the quickest way but,

in fact, by turning the heap you introduce oxygen, which helps the decomposition process.

In a three-bay system the idea is that you move the compost from one bay to the next about once a month or so. When the first bay is filled to the top (in layers of green and brown materials), you tip all the material from it into the second bay, which allows you to start using the first one again for new material. When the first bay fills a second time, the compost from bay two is tipped into bay three, allowing you to tip the material in the first bay into bay two. By the time the first bay is filled a third time, the compost in bay three should be ready to shovel out and use.

A veg garden produces large quantities of green materials at this time of the year. It's important to balance that with a brown material such as cardboard or newspaper. I have a bin beside the compost heap where I store these brown materials so they can be added to the heap when I've put in a new layer of green. One final point – my old pallet assembly was down the end of the garden beside the ditch, and it was a constant battle to stop the hedgerow from encroaching on the compost heaps. This time around I've built the system in a more open area out in the field with enough space all round it to enable me to mow the grass behind it to keep it clear.

13 august
brassica
war

I try to be magnanimous towards all the creatures that live in the veg patch, but at this time of year the job of growing brassicas (kale, cabbage, cauliflower, sprouts, etc.) feels like a war between me and all the creatures that want to eat my plants. The primary enemy is the cabbage white butterfly, a butterfly that dances prettily around the veg patch from spring until autumn. It lays eggs on the leaves of the plants and those eggs turn into larvae (caterpillars) that feast on the leaves. An infestation of caterpillars can completely strip a brassica plant of leaves if given the chance. That's not so pretty.

As an organic grower there is a limited but thankfully effective array of weapons at your disposal to deal with the cabbage white. A physical cover to prevent the butterfly from landing on the leaves is the most effective of all. I use a net called Bionet, which I drape over the plants and pin down with bricks or stones at the edges. But be careful – it needs to be well secured, for the cabbage white is a crafty opponent and has literally nothing else to be doing with its time than trying to find gaps so it can flutter in to lay eggs on the leaves. I looked out the window of the house one day last week, casting an adoring eye on my beloved veg patch, listening to the birds and feeling peaceful and at one with nature's majesty – and then I saw a butterfly flying around, trapped inside the netting. The zen mood wasn't long departing.

The second and altogether less attractive option is to inspect the underside of the leaves for the eggs (little clusters of skittle-shaped yellow eggs) or, later in the season, to pick off (or wash off with a hose) the caterpillars themselves. The caterpillars of the small cabbage white butterfly are green, while those of the large white are yellow and black. Clearing caterpillars off plants can be an increasingly futile effort if they've got really established. I find I start the season with great intentions to keep checking the leaves, but I become less careful later (ironically, since this is when vigilance is most needed).

Here's an important little tip, which for some reason I had forgotten about and which has had an impact on the success of my lettuce growing this summer: lettuce seeds go dormant and will not germinate over 25°C. I had noticed this spring and summer that germination rates were low in the lettuce I sowed in module trays in the potting shed. At first, I wondered whether it was the seed that was perhaps poor quality or old. Then I realised that the temperature in the potting shed is obviously breaking 25°C some days and that some of the seed is going dormant. For the most recent sowing I put the module tray in the garage, where it's nice and cool, for a few days and hey presto, 100 per cent germination. Once the seeds have germinated the seed tray can

**14 august
lettuce
germin-
ation**

be moved back into the warmth of the potting shed, polytunnel or greenhouse for the next few weeks before being planted out.

No other vegetable better exemplifies the problems of blandness in the commercial food chain than the tomato. It has suffered more than most, I think, from the rigours of mass food production. Where once tomatoes were a delicious, sweet treat, they have now become little more than a mind-blowingly bland sandwich filler. But how did this happen?

The journal *Science* reported on a study that revealed a genetic reason for tomato tastelessness. A common problem for commercial growers in the USA in the 1930s was that (quite naturally) the 'shoulder' of the tomato used to stay greener for longer than the rest of the fruit. Consumers didn't like the look of tomatoes that were even a little green, so the growers embarked on a quest for the holy grail: a tomato that would ripen in a uniform way.

One commercial grower managed to breed a tomato plant that produced fruit that ripened from an even shade of green to an even shade of red – this new mutation was called the 'uniform ripening' trait and because of its appeal to consumers it was quickly bred into other varieties. Unfortunately, this wasn't the end of the story. Scientists have since discovered that the same trait that made those green shoulders on the tomatoes was also making them sweeter and creating more flavour. The uniform ripening trait they produced disabled this gene, resulting in fruit that had less sugar (and therefore less sweetness) and fewer carotenoids (less antioxidant potential). Quite literally, commercial growers had unwittingly sacrificed flavour and nutrition for uniformity of appearance.

Heirloom varieties fell further out of favour because they had the annoying habit of coming in all shapes and sizes – this made them difficult to pack. And since they had softer skin, they were more likely to spoil in transit. Growers have therefore bred firmer skins into the tomatoes – ideal if you want to inflict some damage at the La Tomatina food fight festival, but not so good to eat.

Thankfully, as home growers we can celebrate the diversity, variety, flavour and lack of uniformity in our tomatoes. We can grow tomatoes that taste how tomatoes should taste – divine little balls of sweetness. In fact, if there is a downside to growing your own tomatoes it is that once you've tasted the homegrown varieties, it's very hard indeed to go back to shop-bought ones when your tomato season ends. That makes tomatoes a July–October delicacy. But oh, what a delicacy.

18 august
fleece covers for kale

If caterpillars are making a misery of your brassica growing, a physical cover over the plants is really the most effective way to keep them out. In addition to the Bionet mentioned earlier, a covering of fleece will also do a very effective job of keeping the cabbage root flies and cabbage white butterflies away. It's also cheaper than Bionet. The fleece is draped over the plants and buried beneath the soil at the edges of the beds – an edging tool that you use for edging your lawn is the ideal tool for burying the fleece quickly. Any covering on a bed makes weeding and harvesting a little more cumbersome, of course, but at least you've got perfect plants beneath.

The veg patch feels like a hard taskmaster right about now, churning out seemingly never-ending gluts of produce. On one level I feel grateful for this abundance, particularly when it's all laid out in big, beautiful trays, buckets or bowls. But there's another level at which I feel *enough already!*, particularly when said trays, buckets or bowls of produce have been hanging around the kitchen for three days and I know I must do something with them.

Specifically, it's the tomatoes, cucumbers, courgettes and French beans that are unwaveringly relentless at the moment and no amount of chutneying, spiralising, saucing or freezing seems to get to the bottom of them. The porch (a cool place that's ideal for storing veg) is full of produce at the moment and I know that after I finish writing this, I should really saucify another six or seven baking trays of tomatoes for the freezer. And after *that*, I should really go out and harvest another massive batch of tomatoes that need picking too. (By the way, if saucify is not a word, it totally should be.)

There's a simple way to reduce the incessant flow of vegetables, and that's to sow less of them. But sowing less of things is not something that I would ever really consider. I know if I did that, I would just be annoyed with myself sometime after Christmas when I go hunting in the freezer for a lovely homegrown tomato sauce for a pizza and see that we've run out. But I reserve the right to moan a little at this time of the year.

Anyway, there are obvious upsides to all the work, albeit that the gratification is somewhat delayed. At last count, there are now 40 tubs of passata in the freezer, which by my nerdish reckoning should take us well into the late spring of next year (using one a week). Mrs Kelly's just finished making a batch of cucumber pickle, which is one of the handiest sandwich fillers known to humanity, and if there is a better accompaniment to a pair of good-quality sausages and a decent Waterford blaa, I've yet to find it.

We're spiralising the divil out of courgettes. Tonight's dinner of courgetti with (you've guessed it) tomato sauce will see our family of four munch through two marrow-esque courgettes. We're also freezing French beans like there's a flood, war or some other class of pestilence coming down the tracks. Thirty-odd bags of them in the freezer will join many a quiche, stir-fry or Sunday roast during the hungry gap next year.

my go-to tomato sauce

We're in full-on tom glut territory at the moment, so it's time to pull out the old tomato sauce/passata recipe. We get tubs of this sauce into the freezer, from where they can be plucked in the dreary winter months to form the base for soups, stews and casseroles, pizzas and pastas. It's designed to be quick and straightforward and I don't pay particularly close attention to how much of each ingredient goes in. Just bung them in a baking tray, season and add some oil. Bake in the oven, then blitz, cool and freeze. Simple.

ingredients:
Per baking tray:
— enough tomatoes to fill the base of the tray
— 1 small courgette, roughly chopped (no need to peel)
— 3–4 cloves garlic, peeled
— some fresh herbs – sprigs of rosemary, thyme, parsley, etc.
— salt and pepper
— olive oil

directions:
Preheat the oven to 180°C.

Halve the tomatoes (or quarter them if they're very large) and put them in an appropriately sized baking tray. Use several trays if you have a large quantity. You are aiming to fill the base of the tray but leaving enough room to add the other veg. Roughly chop the courgette and add to the tray. Roughly bash the garlic cloves and add them to the tray with the herbs. Season well and add a good lug of oil. Mix it all together with your hands to coat the veg in seasoning and oil. Put in the oven and bake for 45 minutes to 1 hour. Allow to cool completely.

Blitz with a hand blender to a smooth, saucy consistency (or leave it a little chunkier if you prefer). Decant into Tupperware tubs and put in the freezer. (It will keep for 3–4 days in the fridge.)

22 august
weed
therapy

If you can get out of your head and into your hands for an hour or so in the veg patch, you will feel remarkably calm and at peace. But I find that in the veg patch, as with most places, it's often a challenge at first to stay mindful and focused on the job in hand. I am hand weeding a bed of leeks, which, like everywhere else, has become weed-ridden almost overnight. My weeding muscles have grown lazy after a glorious summer when weeds, like all plants, struggled in the heat. But with a return to more normal temperatures and rainfall, weeds are popping up in abundance (as are other pests in the garden – welcome back, slugs).

My mind is distracted at first. Agitated. Impatient. Petulant.

I have resolved to weed just this one bed this evening to make the bigger task more manageable. A single bed about 4m (13ft) long and 1.2m (4ft) wide should take about 45 minutes. A bite-size chunk from the larger ordeal. I reason if I do a bit like this each day, the whole patch should be done in a week or so. It's like a bit of bargaining you would do with a small child. 'Let's just do this job little by little and we'll get through it in no time,' I assure my mind.

But my mind is having none of it. As I start weeding, working through the weeds one by one with a trowel, it gets busy. It constantly goes back to reminding me how big the veg patch is, and how many weeds there are, and how I deserve this

208

for not staying on top of things. I yank a dock from the soil and curse when it snaps off, leaving the root in situ. 'Bloody docks! That always happens.' My mind directs my hands outside the bed we've agreed we're focusing on and into an adjoining one. I focus it back gently. 'Why focus here when it's just as bad over there?' it says petulantly. 'Why did you let things get this bad? Why isn't anyone else out to help?' I suddenly become acutely aware of a sense of remove, of detachment. There's the moany, whiney me and then the other me, watching, slightly bemused, as I sometimes do with my own kids when they are moany or whiney.

After 10 minutes or so, the moany me gradually seems to give up complaining (perhaps disappointed that it doesn't seem to be getting anywhere) and I become more mindful and at peace. I focus attention on my body. Knees resting heavily on the kneeling mat. A stretch in my spine as I reach to another weed relieves the slight ache. The feel of the sun on my face. A prick from a bramble seedling. Sounds. A bird. A passing car. Windchimes. Sights. I tune in to how alive the soil looks. A ladybird scampers over a weed. ('We're ruining its habitat by pulling out all these weeds, you know,' my mind reminds me.) Among the tender annual weeds I spot what looks like a tiny bulb fennel seedling that must have self-seeded from last year. ('How on earth did that get there?') A bee buzzes around over my shoulder, flitting between borage flowers. Another ladybird. 'Is it the same one?' And then, I notice there's a gap. There were no thoughts at all for a time there. Just my senses. Just the trowel in my hand going from weed to weed. I stand up and run the rake up and down the path and the soil beneath turns crumbly – I notice my footsteps in the newly prepared soil and rake it again to get rid of them.

I am finished. More to do tomorrow. But a sense of satisfaction and calm for now. I walk back up to the house. Turn around to look back at my work. 'Sure, that wasn't too bad,' my mind says.

panzanella

This is my version of the classic Italian peasant's lunch of stale bread and tomatoes. Though purists might sniff at the presence of courgettes, I think they work well if sliced very finely. I use 300ml of passata to soak the bread instead of fresh tomatoes, but if you have a glut of tomatoes you could of course use them instead (rubbed through a sieve). All in all, it's not too shabby being a peasant.

Serves 6

ingredients:

— 300g slightly stale sourdough bread
— 300ml organic passata
— 4 tbsp olive oil
— 2 tbsp apple cider vinegar
— salt and pepper
— 20 black olives
— 1 tbsp capers
— 1 small yellow courgette, thinly sliced
— 1 small cucumber, peeled, deseeded and chopped
— 1 small red onion, halved and thinly sliced
— 10–15 cherry tomatoes, halved
— 200g red or green pepper, deseeded and sliced
— a handful of basil leaves, roughly chopped

directions:

Tear the bread into large chunks and put it in a large bowl. In a separate bowl mix the passata, olive oil and vinegar and season well. Add it to the bread, stirring well to mix it all together. Add the olives, capers, courgette, cucumber, onion, tomatoes, sliced pepper and basil. Toss everything together. Leave it to stand for half an hour to let all the flavours mingle.

There's an ancient ritual associated with making sauerkraut that appeals to me greatly. I love the idea of putting away cabbages for the winter in the form of a kraut. Sauerkraut has had a resurgence of popularity in recent times as a gut-health miracle food, but I think the GIYer's use of it to preserve a cabbage glut is more consistent with its origins.

We often assume that sauerkraut is German (and of course the name comes from the German words for 'sour' and 'cabbage'), but in fact the Chinese were making it over two thousand years ago using rice wine to start the ferment. It *was* the Germans who first dry-cured cabbage using just salt; that was in the 1600s. The salt draws the water out of the cabbage, creating the brine that the cabbage is submerged in. In the days prior to refrigeration, sauerkraut was a method of preserving large quantities of cabbage, saving up its valuable nutrients for the lean winter months.

Some European families might have put away as many as three hundred cabbages using the sauerkraut method, with the cabbages shredded by hand using a knife – little wonder that peddlers often went door to door to offer their services to do this chore. My own haul today was more modest – around 10 Hispi cabbages – and I threw them in a food processor, which makes light work of the shredding task. I don't feel bad about taking that shortcut.

The 'sour' taste alluded to by the name is a result of fermentation. The sugars in the cabbage turn into lactic acid, which acts as a preservative. The fermentation process actually increases the nutritional strength of the cabbage, making it more digestible and creating a probiotic effect in the gut. Its superfood status is deserved – it is packed with vitamins (particularly vitamin C – one-third of your daily intake), gives the immune system a boost and balances the bacteria in the gastrointestinal tract. I can't prove it, but I feel strongly that the more sauerkraut I eat, the more I seem to crave it.

An old Polish proverb says, 'Where there is beet soup and sauerkraut, there is plenty.' I don't have any beet soup yet, but at least the sauerkraut is under way.

26 august
second
harvest

Unless you have a plan for your cabbage bed and need to remove the plants after harvesting the cabbages, there's a neat little trick to encourage a second harvest. After cutting a head of cabbage, cut a cross into the stalk left behind in the ground and it will eventually produce four mini heads of cabbage (one from each quadrant of the cross). These little cabbages will be like an enormous Brussels sprout, smaller than a regular head of cabbage. The regrowth can also be used as cabbage greens.

If you are removing the stalks and roots of the cabbage from the soil, bash them up before adding to the compost heap so that they will rot down quicker.

28 august
radishes

I've always been impressed by radishes, mainly for the speed at which they grow, but have never been particularly delighted about eating them. I've seen the TV shows and read the books that evangelise about how they need nothing but a dip in some butter and salt to make them a special delicacy. I've even tried it. And not once have I thought to myself, 'Wow, that's an amazing culinary experience.'

I've chopped them into salads and thought to myself, 'Meh.' I've munched on the odd one raw out in the veg patch. I've sort of enjoyed the moxy and fire of the French Breakfast variety. But when compared to the homegrown carrot, or beetroot, or sweetcorn or tomato or courgette or cucumber or, well, pretty much any veg, actually, they just seem a little inconsequential.

Quite by accident I came across a recipe that recommended baking them for 20 minutes – it promised that by doing so the humble radish would be transformed from salad afterthought to a brand-new baked root crop discovery. And you know what? I've tried it and that's exactly what happens.

Take a bunch of radishes and twist the leaves off, leaving a little nubbin of stems (handy for picking them up), then wash them and throw them in a baking tray. Sprinkle with oil, season well with freshly ground pepper and salt and bake for 20 minutes in an oven at 180°C. Turn them once while cooking and at the end add a generous knob of butter. And then eat. And now we have something really interesting. An earthy, on-the-turnip-spectrum root crop delight that's utterly delicious. A crop that tastes great, that can be grown pretty much all year round and takes just six weeks to grow? Sign me up.

How to grow radishes:
- Radishes can be sown pretty much anywhere – often thrown in among other veg and even in partial shade. Always sow directly in the soil – they don't fare well when transplanted. Sow a small number of seeds regularly (every two to three weeks) from April on.
- Sow thinly in a shallow drill 1cm (½ inch) deep and thin to 3cm (1½ inches) apart as they grow. Water regularly in dry weather but don't over-water as it will encourage too much leafy growth. They will be ready to eat within four to five weeks, which makes them one of the fastest of all vegetables. Don't let them get too big as they become

overly peppery and tend towards tasting 'woody' when too large.

- Fast-growing radishes are often sown between rows of slower-growing vegetables as they can be harvested without upsetting the other veg. They are a brassica, however, so ideally you should keep them in the brassica group in your rotation plan. Tiny radish tops can be used as a salad leaf and, when slightly bigger, in soups.

29 august
eat more
plants

I'm absolutely loving the harvest this year and seem to be spending almost all my free time with a knife in hand in the kitchen – peeling, cutting, dicing or chopping some fresh vegetable from the garden. It can be hard to keep up with the produce coming from the veg patch at this time of the year, but it's made a lot easier if you approach the task with a grateful mind, rather than feeling the time is somehow wasted.

I'm mindful of the need to change our diet and eating habits to allow for the fact that there's this mountain of fresh vegetables and fruit coming in from the vegetable patch every other day. Primarily this has meant eating far less meat than we used to – this is no hardship, since the GIYer in me wants to make the vegetables the star attraction rather than forcing them to play second fiddle to the meat on the plate.

In fact, lately I've found myself imagining something that would have been almost unthinkable to me in the past – giving up meat entirely. I must be honest and confess that it has more to do with taste than it does with animal welfare or environmental concerns. Everything is just so damn tasty from the veg patch right now. I think there are also health benefits – eating less meat and more vegetables just seems good for my energy levels. Bottom line: I feel good when I eat vegetables.

Meat-free meals require more thought, undoubtedly, but that's mainly about convention. We feel something's missing when there is no meat on the plate and feel the need to make up for that somehow by tarting the whole dish up. For some strange reason, a plate with, say, a lamb chop with some new potatoes and a portion of peas is considered a complete meal. But replace the lamb chop with another portion of a different vegetable and convention tells us this is not a complete meal. What's wrong with just eating a plate of vegetables, I wonder?

Anyway, it's a good plan to arm yourself with some really good vegetarian cookbooks and plan ahead. I find *River Cottage Veg Every Day!* the most useful companion – somehow, I take comfort in the fact that it's written by Hugh Fearnley-Whittingstall, a committed carnivore. Denis Cotter's *For the Love of Food*, Yotam Ottolenghi's *Plenty* and *Vegetarian Cooking for Everyone* by Deborah Madison also come highly recommended.

september

Gluts. And more gluts.
The veg patch becomes a
harder taskmaster as we
spend hours in the kitchen
processing kilo after kilo
to store up for the winter
months. The last sowings
of the year are done to
make the most of the
growing year.

This month we're loving …
onions.

The onion crop is lifted
for storage and the first
steaming pots of French
onion soup are served.

1 september
summer
into
autumn

There's been a sudden drop in night-time temperatures, which, it has to be said, can't be unexpected given the time of year. Still, with the kids back to school as well, it's a fairly dramatic switch in season from summertime to autumnal.

After a summer of leaving the tunnels and potting shed open on balmy nights, it's back to a routine of closing them up at night to preserve as much of the daytime heat as possible. It is getting down below 7°C at night now, a temperature that could cause problems for tender salad leaves and tomatoes. I'm also doing some night-time slug hunting using the light on my phone to find them. They are a particular problem in the smaller tunnel, where they are to be found after dark on the spinach (both on a new sowing of annual spinach and on the hardier perpetual spinach) and on salad seedlings. They can also occasionally be found in the potting shed, where they can wreak havoc on a tray of emerging seedlings. Recently they munched through an entire just-germinated tray of lettuce that was destined for the salad tunnel. Grrr.

There's a definite sense of the growth disappearing gradually from the year. Though the winter greens that I sowed a few weeks back in the potting shed are growing, it's a slower growth than earlier in the year. The trick, I think, is to ignore that sense of impending winter as much as possible and keep on sowing.

Thankfully there's still a feeling of abundance to counteract the gathering gloom, particularly in terms of courgettes, tomatoes and cucumbers, which are still churning out their fruit at levels that are hard to cope with. I've a new outlet for some of this abundance now, given that our chef at GROW HQ will take whatever excess I have, and it's far easier to pop a few courgettes and cucumbers into the laptop bag to bring to him than process them myself in the kitchen. I worry that this will mean I won't have quite as large a stash of chutneys, pickles and the like – but in the grand scheme of things that's only a minor worry.

If you grew sunflowers this year, you will most likely have been enjoying the beauty of the flowers in the last few weeks. Don't forget, they also provide a wonderful, protein-rich food bounty – the flowers are hiding hundreds of sunflower seeds that you can harvest and store to sprinkle on your porridge. The key to successfully harvesting the seeds is to get the flower head dry – this can be done outside (if the weather's fine and sunny) or else by removing the head and drying it indoors.

Wait until about half the yellow petals have dropped and the flower is wilting. Have a look at the seeds – you will see them lurking in behind the black florets. Remove the head, leaving 30cm (1ft) of stem attached to the head. Tie a paper bag over the head and fasten it loosely with some string or twine. Don't use plastic – you want air to circulate inside the bag. Hang the head upside down indoors somewhere dry and bright for about a week. I hang them in the greenhouse. The bag captures any seeds that fall off. The seeds should come away easily when dry, simply by rubbing them. Wash the seeds, then dry them well and store in an airtight container. If you can, be generous and leave some of the sunflowers in situ for birds and other wildlife to share the spoils.

3 september
sunflower
seeds

Successful food growing is as much about time spent in the kitchen as in the veg patch and at this time of the year that point is usually in sharp focus. The garden is at its most productive in September and you're unlikely to be able to use all of its bounty straightaway. So storing the produce or finding some way of processing it is as important as growing the food in the first place.

Sometimes, processing jobs can be mercifully straightforward – for example, in about 15 minutes a crop of garlic can be turned into a garlic braid that will hang happily in the kitchen for about five months. Squashes and pumpkins make their way from the veg patch to the top of the dresser in the kitchen where, thanks to their thick skins, they will store until next spring. A

5 september
in the
kitchen

221

colander full of French beans just needs a dunk in some boiling water to blanch them before you bag them up for the freezer.

Other processing jobs require more of a time investment. Today I literally spent an entire day in the kitchen surrounded by boiling pans, bubbling pots and chopping boards laden down with vegetables. There are times when I find this somewhat of a chore, but today I had cleared the decks and so was in the right frame of mind. We're still in glut territory with the tomatoes, so they were the main priority. I 'sun-dried' one batch of the much-coveted Sungold variety in a very low oven overnight and then put them in a sterilised Kilner jar and covered them with olive oil. Another batch went on a tray into a hot oven with some garlic, seasoning and rosemary, cooked for 30 minutes, then blitzed to turn them into passata (which will emerge from the freezer later in the year for a pizza or a pasta sauce). And finally, I used 1.5kg (3lb) of bigger tomatoes to make a big batch of tomato ketchup, which is a great way to make a relatively small amount of tomatoes go a very long way indeed.

I am a glutton for punishment, so while I was at it, I also made a big batch of gut-friendly kimchi (fermented cabbage, carrot and beetroot). I could have put the filled jars straight in the cupboard, but I left them on the counter so I could enjoy looking at them for a little while first. It's hard work, but these are some of the growing year's most satisfying moments.

Pea shoots make a great addition to salads – the leaves and tendrils have a wonderful delicate pea flavour and are high in vitamins B1 and C. You can grow peas specifically to eat the shoots and because you are harvesting the little shoots at just 12cm (5 inches) or so high, it's a brilliant fast-growing crop that doesn't need much space and is perfect for container growing. You can grow them pretty much all year round, indoors if you wish, and a single seed tray will yield about a hundred shoots. Simply fill a seed tray with seed compost, water well and then sprinkle peas generously on top. Arrange them on the surface of the compost so that they are about 2cm (1 inch) apart – then push them down into the compost to a depth of about 2cm (1 inch) and backfill the little holes with more compost. Place in a bright spot, but not direct sunlight. In about three to four weeks, harvest with a pair of scissors – you might even get a second harvest from the regrowth.

carrot and turnip soup with fresh thyme

We're into soup season now as the days grow a little colder. This is a delicious soup from JB that uses the quick-growing Milan Purple Top turnips that we grow at GROW HQ.

ingredients:
— 300g carrots
— 200g Milan Purple Top turnips
— ½ leek
— 1 stick of celery
— ½ onion
— 2–3 garlic cloves, peeled

- — 50g butter
- — 2 pinches of salt
- — a small pinch of white pepper
- — 1 sprig of thyme, leaves separated

directions:
Wash the carrots, turnip, leek and celery. Peel the carrots, turnip and the onion. Chop the vegetables into chunks. On a low heat melt the butter in a saucepan and add the chopped vegetables and the salt and pepper. Stir for 3–4 minutes. Cover with cold water (about 1 litre) and turn up the heat to medium.

Let it cook for 15–20 minutes, until the carrots are soft. Roughly chop the thyme and add it to the pot, then use a hand-held blender to blend the soup. Serve with crusty bread or savoury scones.

You can adapt this recipe and use different vegetables from your garden at different times of the year.

9 september
bye-bye
beans

After a long season, I took out the climbing French beans in the big tunnel this week. They performed well again this year. It always amazes me how well they do in the tunnel, and just how prolific they are. I cut back the amount I sowed this year because we had way too many beans last year. But even with two relatively short rows (maybe 2m/6ft long in total), we still had more beans than we could cope with. That was despite eating lots of them fresh ourselves, getting about 20 bags of them into the freezer (blanched first) and encouraging our French bean-loving neighbours John and Bridget to help themselves.

At this time of the year, the plants start to go over; the leaves begin to go yellow and the remaining beans are getting a little big and stringy. They are not as nice to eat at this stage as they were back in early summer.

Taking down the plants can be a laborious affair given they've wrapped themselves around twine on their way to growing

up to 3–4m (10–13ft) tall. Once I've managed to untangle them, I chop up the plants before putting them on the compost heap. Any straggler beans are rerouted to the kitchen. Incidentally, you can also let them alone for another month if you want them to turn into 'haricot' beans for storage – the unused pods start to swell up with beans and when the papery pod is opened up there are lots of lovely beans inside. JB took a big batch of these off me one year and they showed up on the HQ menu about five months later.

Today I also harvested red cabbages for the first time this year. I like growing red cabbages – the densely packed heads are more resistant to slug damage, I think. They make a lovely slaw, too, and I put two of them into a red sauerkraut. Red sauerkraut is called rotkraut in Germany, which doesn't sound like the most appetising dish, it has to be said, but with its proper pronunci-ation (*rot* to rhyme with boat), it starts to make sense, *rot* being the German word for red. I'm a little obsessed with making sau-erkraut this year and there are various Kilner jars bubbling away in the corner of the kitchen.

10 september
sweetcorn
harvest

Though the sweetcorn harvest is never vast in the way that, say, tomatoes or courgettes are, it's still one of my favourite harvest-ing moments of the growing year. This year I sowed six plants and planted them out in the big tunnel. I think the combina-tion of warmth, humidity and good soil fertility there caused the plants to grow taller than normal (up to around 2.5m/8ft), but all that plant growth seemed to be at the expense of fruiting. I had just one or two cobs per plant. Still, there's something so elemen-tally enjoyable about peeling back the skin to find the beautiful shiny yellow kernels underneath.

As always, timing is everything when it comes to har-vesting and eating sweetcorn – you are trying to catch the cobs when they are ripe and before the sugars start to turn to starch. The classic test is to pierce some of the little kernels and judge the liquid that comes out. If it's too watery, the corn is not quite ripe; too viscous and it's gone too far. With regular checking you should be able to harvest the cobs at peak freshness. I've always said (half-joking) that you should have a pot of water on the boil and run from the veg patch to the kitchen with your corn to make sure you cook it immediately and get that absolute peak freshness experience. You will never taste anything quite like it.

Years ago, when giving talks on growing, I used to bring a pack of two vacuum-packed sweetcorn with me to show the contrast with the immediacy of fresh, homegrown sweetcorn. The vac-packed corn, entombed as it was in plastic, simply refused to die as I went from talk to talk, for months on end. The best-before date was about six months away when I started bringing it to talks and it had passed by another six months when I finally had to throw it out. It goes without saying that it wouldn't have tasted great at that stage.

Even though sweetcorn is a slightly incidental crop for me, it's worth reminding yourself that it is one of the top three crops grown in the world – with wheat and rice, it accounts for 60 per cent of all calories consumed by humans globally. For all that, only about 1 per cent of the corn produced around the world is eaten as the whole grain – the rest is used as animal feed, as fuel (ethanol) or as a starch food additive or sweetener. It's strange that something so fundamentally healthful (whole-grain corn is a rich source of vitamins and minerals) has played such a large role in creating ill health globally in the form of corn syrups.

12 september
order garlic

Garlic can be sown twice each year – a winter sowing at some stage before Christmas and another in the spring. Different GIYers have different opinions about which approach is more fruitful. Garlic benefits from a good cold spell (it needs at least a month or two at temperatures below 5°C in order for the cloves to split), so I think the winter-sown garlic is a safer bet.

The general consensus is that you should sow winter garlic before the shortest day of the year (21 December). I'm inclined to think it's a good idea to get the garlic to a point where it's a little bit hardy before the real inclement weather sets in later in the winter. I always sow mine in October, so now is a good time of the year to start thinking about ordering your winter garlic.

If you have good drainage in your soil, you can sow cloves direct. If not, it's a good idea to add a little peat-free compost to the soil where you are sowing, or sow them in module trays and plant out when they have produced 4–5cm (1½–2 inches) of growth. It's not a good idea to use supermarket garlic, as it could introduce diseases to your garden that can be impossible to shift. Certified disease-free garlic from your garden centre is a better option. Or, even better, keep back some of your own garlic bulbs for sowing.

13 september
two-track
harvesting

There's two-track harvesting taking place in the veg patch these days. First, you have the veg that are harvested once, in their entirety, like squashes, pumpkins, garlic and onions. Then there are the ongoing, 'rolling' harvests – these are the veg that you either harvest as you need them (like salads, beetroot, potatoes and carrots) or the ones that need regular harvesting to keep them going (like tomatoes, courgettes and beans).

Into this mix, and with a slight shift to more autumnal weather, we've also started to harvest kale. My father-in-law still dismisses kale as cattle feed when he sees it growing in my garden, but the NutriBullet generation has given it a hipster image make-over and it's rightly valued now as a nutritional powerhouse. I see it as a relatively low-maintenance crop that tolerates even the harshest of winters and I absolutely love the look and taste of the luxuriant dark green leaves of the cavolo nero variety. Kale is, happily, less prone to (though not entirely immune from) some of the great brassica pests. A Bionet or fleece cover is generally enough to keep pigeons and the doughty cabbage white butterfly away. I sow kale in June to ensure I have good hardy plants heading into the winter, and with a bit of luck we get to harvest right through the winter and into March or even April of next year.

On the advice of our head grower, Richard, I sowed kale direct in the soil this year rather than in module trays as I've done previously. I then used the tender thinnings in the row as salad leaves (as quickly as 25 days after sowing), eventually getting to a spacing of just one plant every 60cm (20 inches), with these plants being left to grow on for winter. Now these plants are about 1m (3ft) tall and are ready for more serious cropping. We harvest the leaves when they are 10–15cm (4–5 inches) long, starting at the bottom of the plant and working our way up. If you continue to take leaves from the lower part of the plant, it will continue to grow, producing new leaves as it does so.

fermented hot chilli sauce

I have my eye on the polytunnel chillies and we've started using some of the unripened fruit in the kitchen. Later in the month and into October, I'll be processing them to make sure I use every last one. I will always do a jar of pickled jalapeños for the fridge (used every week for Friday night pizzas in our house) and will freeze some for 'fresh' use through the year. JB's recipe for a hot chilli sauce has a great additional layer, where you ferment the chillies in the jar. Hot hot hot! (Note his mild admonishment to grow your own coriander seeds – and he's right, of course; it's a cinch to let a few coriander plants go to seed and collect them.)

Makes approx. 500g
ingredients:
— 500g red chillies
— ½ tsp smoked paprika
— ½ tsp roasted coriander seeds (very easy to grow yourself)
— 10g granulated sugar
— ⅓ tsp salt

directions:
Take the stems off the chillies and deseed them. Blend all the ingredients together in a food processor until it turns into a paste. Pour into a clean 750ml Kilner jar. Close the lid without the rubber seal to avoid a build-up of gas. Place in a cool, dark place (a kitchen cupboard would be perfect) for five to seven days, stirring thoroughly every day. Place the rubber seal on the jar and refrigerate.

This fermented hot chilli sauce will last three to six months in the fridge.

**15 september
tend to
your celery**

Celery was traditionally considered a 'difficult' veg to grow because it had to be grown in trenches and required regular blanching (making the stems less bitter by forcing them to go from green to white by depriving them of light). Thankfully, self-blanching varieties have been developed that make life a lot easier for the celery grower.

If you sowed celery earlier in the year, it should be ready now and will do fine in the ground until the first frost. The main thing to bear in mind in terms of tending celery is that it needs a

consistent supply of water to produce good yields and it doesn't like weeds. Harvest celery by cutting at ground level – make sure that you do so in such a way as to keep the stems together. Celery will keep for a week or so in the fridge and will in fact continue to blanch once picked. Wash in cold water and dry carefully before putting it in the fridge. You can also harvest individual stems (rather than the whole plant) if you wish.

16 september
how long do seeds last?

There's nothing more irritating than poor seed germination, particularly if you don't know *why* the seeds didn't germinate. Did you plant them too deep or not deep enough? Was it too cold, too hot, too moist, too dry? Sometimes, however, it can be because the seeds are past their use-by date. Parsnips are a classic example of a seed where you really should be buying new seed every year, because the seeds are very perishable. Here's a rough guide to how long you can keep different veg seeds:

- **1 year approx.:** parsnips, beetroot, leeks, sweetcorn, peppers (sweet and chilli), spinach, onions, parsley
- **2–4 years:** squash and pumpkin, courgette and marrow, beans and peas, carrots
- **4+ years:** Brussels sprouts, cabbage, cucumber, kale, lettuces, radish, tomato, turnips.

17 september
last hurrah for legumes

Bean and pea plants are on their last legs at this stage, so we can go ahead and strip them of pods, compost the plants (chop them up first, which will help decomposition) and deconstruct wigwams and other supports. Blanch and freeze beans and peas that you can't eat immediately. Beans that can be dried, such as borlotti, can be left on the plant if the weather is dry. If not, cut the plants and hang them somewhere dry and warm. Once dried you can shell the beans and put them in airtight containers – they store well like that and make a great addition to stews and soups.

Don't forget that legumes are nitrogen fixers – they take the nitrogen from the air and put it in the soil during the growing season, which improves the soil for next year, particularly for nitrogen-hungry crops like brassicas. So, instead of removing the roots when pulling out the plant, cut the plant at soil level with a knife and leave the roots behind in the soil to rot down over the winter (and return their nitrogen to the soil). If you're curious, you can even dig up the roots carefully to see the little nitrogen-producing nodules (tiny white clumps) hiding among the roots.

pickle-athon

I was about five hours into my monster eight-hour 'pickle-athon' and up to my neck in diced fruit, veg and vinegar syrups. I had just peeled, cored and chopped 2kg (4½lb) of pears (I didn't count how many pears that is, but it's a lot) and a pan of boiling, sugary stickiness had just overflowed on the stove. The kitchen looked like a bomb had hit it. The kids were still in their school uniforms, homework was undone and dinner was chronically late. I was tired, cranky, sweaty and (ironically) hungry. It was at that moment that Mrs Kelly chose to arrive in from the garden with another enormous bucket of windfall pears and a big smile on her face. 'Look what I found,' she said, beaming at what was surely an entire winter's supply of over-ripe fruit. 'That's great,' I deadpanned, without much conviction, before turning away and muttering something unprintable.

I was focused on two vegetables in particular last evening: beetroot and pears. Both are in serious glut territory at the moment and suspended in that no man's land between abundance and waste. So you must move fast – do something with them or lose them for ever to the compost heap. That means making the conscious decision to make it a priority to roll up the sleeves and dedicate the time required to make a jam, pickle or chutney or whatever other recipes you have in your arsenal. Five large beetroot became a sweet beetroot marmalade and the pears morphed into a sweet pear pickle.

When it comes to getting produce into 'storage' for the winter, we need to put aside any romantic notions about how the hours spent peeling, podding, dicing and chopping will make you a better person. Let's be honest – it's just hard work, particularly if it's a serious attempt at winter larder-filling. You don't even get the benefit of instant gratification from eating a crop that's just being picked – most pickles, for example, need to be left for a couple of months before eating.

This morning, the vinegar fumes having dissipated, I had that wonderful, unique smug/satisfied feeling that arises the day after a mammoth session of food processing. I gazed along the rows of different sized jam jars and Kilner jars and congratulated myself on a job well done. It's an annoying habit of mine that I leave jars out on the counter for a few days so I can remind myself repeatedly how amazing I am.

In January or February next year, when fresh produce is starting to wear thin, I can pop open a jar and taste this year's harvest all over again. 'Do not store up for yourselves treasures on earth, where moths and vermin destroy', the Bible tells us, but surely that line should have read: *Do* store up for yourselves the treasures of the earth, use copious quantities of vinegar and store somewhere cool and dark.

20 september
apple
harvest

The summer harvesting of salads and tomatoes might be easing off a little, but it's replaced by an abundance of apples. The joy of having your own fruit trees is that September brings gluts of fruit, but on the flipside the challenge of having your own fruit trees is that you have do something with those gluts! This week I have been grappling with buckets and trugs full of apples.

We just have four or five apple trees in the front garden, but as they mature (they were planted maybe five years ago) the amount of fruit they produce is growing dramatically. We've been eating apples for a few weeks now – grabbing a handful as we head out in the morning – but it's time to get serious about the harvest while it's at its ripest. Birds and dogs are our most persistent apple pests now. The former sit on the branches and peck at the fruit, while the latter develop a serious seasonal interest, grabbing whole apples straight from the tree and munching them contentedly on the deck.

Getting serious about the harvest means getting up on a ladder (or putting a child on your shoulders!) and taking all the apples from the tree. There's a certain hunter-gatherer pleasure in stripping an entire tree of ripe apples rather than picking one or two here and there, but then of course the challenge becomes what to do with them. How can we store hundreds of apples to make them last into the winter?

Here are some ways you can store a glut of homegrown apples:

1. **Store them:** Wrap each apple in a little newspaper and lay them carefully in a clean plastic bin with thick sheets of cardboard in between layers. Try to make sure the apples are not touching each other. Only store the perfect

specimens – direct any fruit with bruising or other imperfections to the kitchen. Put a tight-fitting lid on the bin and store somewhere cool – a cool but frost-free shed is ideal. Check the apples once a month or so and remove any that are starting to rot.

2. **Dry them:** A brilliant way to store apples is to slice them thinly (with a knife or mandolin) and dry them. Dip the slices in a bowl of water with a tablespoon of lemon juice added – this will stop the slices going brown. Dry them and lay the slices on parchment paper on a wire rack, making sure they are not touching each other. Place either over a wood-burning stove or in a low oven. I find it takes 4–6 hours in an oven on the lowest setting (70°C), turning them from time to time. If you place them on top of a lit stove before you go to bed, they should be dry the next morning.

3. **Stew them:** Peel and core five apples, cut into chunks and then stew them in a tablespoon of water in a saucepan with a lid for 3–4 minutes. At this time of the year you could add a handful of blackberries too, or you could sweeten a little to your taste with honey. Stewed apple will keep in the fridge for a week or you can freeze it. We make enormous batches for the freezer and it's a brilliant thing to have to brighten up your morning porridge over the winter.

apple traybake

I like baking that has no faffing, and this is a really simple traybake that you can whip up in minutes. You could certainly fire in some blackberries when layering it up and it would only add to the overall marvellousness.

Serves 8

ingredients:
— 450g cooking apples
— juice of ½ lemon
— 280g golden caster sugar
— 225g butter, softened
— 4 eggs
— 2 tsp vanilla extract
— 350g self-raising flour
— 2 tsp baking powder
— 100g blackberries, washed and dried
— demerara sugar, to sprinkle

directions:
Preheat the oven to 180°C.

Butter and line a baking tin with parchment paper. Peel, core and thinly slice the apples, ideally with a mandolin. Put the slices in a bowl and pour the lemon juice over them. Mix the sugar, butter, eggs, vanilla, flour and baking powder in another bowl.

Pour half the mixture into the tin. Arrange half the apples and half the blackberries over the top of the mixture, then repeat the layers. Sprinkle over the demerara sugar.

Bake for 50 minutes, until golden. Leave to cool for 10 minutes, then turn out of the tin and remove the paper.

22 september
an apple a
day

The 'apple a day keeps the doctor away' lessons of youth have stayed with me all my life. I've often thought it strange, however, that such a traditional saying must surely have originated at a time when it would have been difficult to follow the advice and eat an apple each day all year round. The apple season here runs from late August until Christmas, but since apples store quite well (kept somewhere cool and dark), you could eat Irish apples until March or April. After that, traditionally, it was time to move to the great summer fruits such as currants and berries and then wait until August for the new-season apples to appear again.

These days, of course, one can eat an apple a day all year round with no problem whatsoever, thanks to the abundance of imported apples available in our supermarkets. In a strange way, the apple-lover in me would be glad about this if we were only eating imported apples when the Irish ones were all finished. But, sadly, that's not the case.

In fact, well over 90 per cent of the apples consumed in Ireland annually are imported. Even in peak apple season in Ireland, the apples on our supermarket shelves are more likely to have been grown in France, New Zealand and South America.

So how has it come to this? Part of the problem is that Irish growers just can't compete with the big European and South American producers (and particularly their low labour costs). But we've also been brainwashed into thinking that apples should all be the same size, shape, colour and flavour. Almost all the apples consumed worldwide now come from just a handful of varieties, such as Pink Lady, Golden Delicious and Granny Smith. Such homogenisation suits the food chain, but it deprives us of the opportunity to sample the incredible diversity of apple varieties. We have hundreds of native varieties in Ireland alone and because of our cooler climate, Irish apples are sweeter and crisper than the warm-climate equivalent. The Irish Seed Savers Association has a collection of over 140 native apple trees, cultivated to do well here and to be grown without the use of pesticides and other chemicals.

As consumers we have tremendous power to lower the import levels, support Irish apple growers and get our hands on better-tasting apples at the same time. It's simple – between now and spring of next year, simply do not buy imported apples. Ask for local apples in your supermarket or go direct to growers. If you find an apple you really like, buy them in bulk and store them.

Growing your own apples is a good way to access a superb seasonal product with zero food miles. In addition, you can also try lots of different varieties and flavours. But even if you can't or don't want to grow all your own apples, growing even a small number of trees is a great way to expose yourself to those new varieties and flavours. Once you experience the joys of an Elstar, Katy, Discovery or Jonagold apple, it's hard to go back. It will also give you a new-found appreciation for the work done by our commercial apple producers. As the apple season kicks in, make sure to vote with your wallet and buy in-season local apples.

24 september
a virtuous
cycle

Today I spent some time at each end of the food-growing cycle: at one end, up to my neck in compost, turning the heaps at the end of the garden; at the other, once again up to my neck in a mountain of fruit in the kitchen, turning them into a pickle for the winter larder. When it comes down to it, you have to be willing to invest time at both ends of the cycle if your food growing is to thrive.

Turning compost heaps is unsung, hard bloody work and not particularly glamorous, it has to be said. But it's a vital beginning and end to everything that happens in the veg patch. Spent vegetable plants and the rich manure-covered straw from the hen house are barrowed to the compost corner, and with the help of some time (and some back-breaking labour) magically turn into crumbly black gold, which is given back to the veg patch soil. I find it immensely comforting to be part of this virtuous circle.

At the other end of the cycle, there are food gluts to deal with. Every day as I wander down to the end of the garden to feed hens or collect eggs, I'm conscious that the fruit trees (apple, pear and plum) are still creaking under the weight of fruit (a mature pear tree, for example, can yield 50–100kg (110–220lb) of pears). If they are not to be wasted, another marathon of peeling, chopping and general sweating over a hot stove is required. There is, however, a quiet satisfaction to be had in surveying a row of Kilner jars and knowing that nature's great bounty has been harnessed yet again for the winter.

I harvested the last of the peppers from the polytunnel today, mainly to free up some bed space for autumn/winter salad greens (claytonia, chervil, chard and the like) that have been hanging out in the potting shed and are more than ready to be planted out. It's been a long and finicky growing season for peppers, which were sown over seven months ago in chilly February.

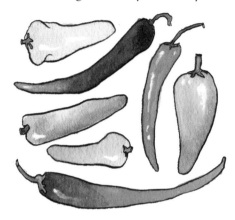

They are not all ripe at this stage, with a mix of green and red on most plants, but I'm always relatively happy to pull out the plants since it's kind of nice to have a mix of green and red in the kitchen. We tend to forget that a green pepper (chilli or bell) is effectively not ripe yet. Though the green ones are fine to eat, I reckon they are tastier and sweeter when allowed to go red. Isn't it odd that we happily eat a green, unripe pepper but wouldn't consider eating an unripe apple, banana or other fruit and veg?

Chilli peppers also generally get hotter as they mature from green to red. This year I grew the chilli varieties Ring of Fire and Hungarian Hot Wax. The two varieties give us a nice range of heat – from relatively hot to 'blow your head off'. As always, the chilli peppers are far more prolific and reliable than the bell peppers, and less prone to slug damage. They also grow really well in a pot or container.

The Hungarian Hot Wax variety is generally harvested when still yellowy-green, though it will mature to orange and then red if left on the plant long enough. It is mild and big enough when green to be used as a bell pepper in cooking. In fact, I've been known to munch on them raw in the polytunnel earlier in the year (though they are a little hotter now).

They have a Scoville scale (a scale for measuring the hotness of chillies – the higher the number, the hotter the chilli) rating of about 15,000 units. To put that into context, the Ring of Fire chilli has a Scoville rating of 70,000 units, while the Naga Jolokia (the world's hottest chilli) measures an eye-watering 1 million units. Ring of Fire produces masses of long, tapered chillies that start dark green and get hotter as they turn red. So, from that perspective, harvesting at least some of them green is not a bad plan.

26 september
storing
chilli
peppers

With so many chillies coming into the kitchen in one go, thoughts turn to how to store them. As with many things, I use lots of different methods, from the relatively simple drying and freezing to slightly more elaborate approaches like making oils and salts.

- **Dried:** Get out a needle and thread and 'sew' a string of whole chillies together by threading the cotton through the stalks of the chillies. This is the traditional Mexican way of storing them, known as a *ristra*. Hang them somewhere warm and dry (but not too warm or they will get brittle). Only ever store perfect fruit, as any little hole or blemish will get worse in storage.
- **Fridge:** Chillies will keep in a freezer bag or Tupperware container in the fridge for two to three weeks. Removing the stalk first will prolong their storability even more. I also make a jar of 'jalapeño' peppers by chopping/pickling them and then storing in the fridge.
- **Freezer:** Chilli peppers freeze remarkably well, and they are very handy to have in the freezer. Because they get a little mushy when thawed out, I usually grate them from frozen to use them. I generally freeze them on a tray first

and then pop them in a freezer bag so they don't clump together when they're frozen. You can also chop chillies into an ice-cube tray, cover with water, freeze and then bag up the cubes. Then you can add ice cubes of chilli to soups, stews, etc. when needed.

- **Oil:** A chilli oil is a very fine condiment to have. I won't eat a pizza without it. Warm a tablespoon of oil in a saucepan and add two to three whole chillies and a teaspoon of chilli flakes. As soon as they start to sizzle a little, add another cup of olive oil and let the whole lot warm up. Do not let it get too hot – you should still be able to put your finger in it. When it's warm, turn off the heat and allow to cool down completely. Put into a sterilised jar or bottle. After a few weeks you can strain the oil (discard the chilli and flakes) into a new bottle, and this will prolong the life of the chilli oil (the chillies themselves will be the first thing to rot).
- **Chilli salt:** JB, our chef in GROW HQ, makes a chilli salt by blitzing whole chillies with some coarse sea salt. Then he spreads the mixture on a tray and puts it somewhere warm (e.g. the hot press) for a few days to dry out before transferring it to a jar.

Claytonia (also called winter purslane or miner's lettuce) is a really useful, hardy, heart-shaped winter salad green that can be used to bulk up winter salads and stir-fries, and can still be sown even at this late time of the year. It was called miner's lettuce after the Gold Rush miners, who valued its high vitamin C content, which warded off scurvy. A hundred grams of claytonia contains a third of your daily requirement of vitamin C, 22 per cent of your vitamin A and 10 per cent of your iron. So this little leaf packs a nutritional punch.

Claytonia is succulent and almost meaty to eat. It will also withstand cooking (so is excellent as an alternative to spinach)

27 september
claytonia

and is very easy to grow. Though claytonia will grow in the spring/ summer, its real value is in providing us with winter greens from October or November right up until April of the following year.

We sow claytonia in module trays (four to five seeds per module) in August and September, though you can keep sowing until the end of October if you have a greenhouse or polytunnel. After sowing, keep it well watered. The seeds will germinate rapidly. After two to three weeks, carefully plant out each little clump of seedlings into soil either in the polytunnel or outside, allowing 7–10cm (2½–4 inches) between plants.

Claytonia prefers cooler temperatures, which is why it is ideal for autumn sowing, and it will tolerate cold winter temperatures (although it might need to be covered with a fleece or cloche during very frosty weather if grown outside). Make sure to keep it well watered if you are growing it under cover or if you get a very dry spell outside (unlikely in the winter).

To harvest, cut it with scissors, leaving a few centimetres of the base of the plant in place – you will get at least four or five cuts off each plant over the winter. Claytonia deteriorates quickly once picked, which is why you almost never see it available to buy commercially – it will, however, keep in the fridge for a few days. The leaves are at their tastiest when young and tender. The smaller leaves are great in salads, while larger ones can be cooked (throw into a stir-fry at the last minute or boil briefly, like spinach).

In the 24/7 supermarket food culture we live in, storing food has become somewhat of a defunct skill. Our immediate forebears were expert at it (and, of course, they had to be) – by necessity they developed and used cutting-edge, yet ancient, techniques for storing and preserving food. In Ireland entire crops of spuds and carrots could be stored for months on end in an open field with a covering of straw and soil in a process known as 'clamping'. In Germany they preserved cabbage by making sauerkraut, while in Austria whole cabbages were stored in 4m (13ft) pits and the fermented end product, known as grubenkraut, could last for up to three years.

In theory, many crops, such as potatoes, beetroot and carrots, can be left in the soil and used as needed over the winter. In practice, if I leave crops in the ground, I find that they simply get damaged by my wet soil or by pests (worms, slugs, mice, etc.). So instead I lift the crops and store them. With the exception of some kale, leeks and the hardy parsnips and celeriac, my veg patch is more or less in lockdown from November until April. Though there are some additional veg like oriental greens and other leaves available in the polytunnel, it is from stores that the majority of our food will come.

There are all sorts of methods to store vegetables and we use pretty much all of them at home. Some methods suit some vegetables better than others. Berries, celery, tomatoes, courgettes, chilli peppers, peas and beans are freezer-bound. Onions and garlic will be hung in braids. Cucumbers and pears will be pickled. Apples will be juiced or stewed and frozen. Pumpkins and squash will take pride of place above the dresser where, thanks to their thick skins, they will survive for months. There will be chutney. Lots of chutney. Potatoes will be stored in sacks, beetroot and carrots in sand. Parsnips and celeriac are tough enough to survive life outside in the cold soil.

As the winter draws in, nothing brings out my inner hunter-gatherer quite like having a full larder.

october

The days get shorter and darker, and the growth is gone from the year. But the veg patch is still heaving with produce and every hour spent there is matched with one in the kitchen to make the most of the lovely homegrown fruit and veg.

This month we're loving … beetroot.

A July-sown crop is harvested now and stored in a box of sand for the winter. Delicious and easy to raise, it's one of our favourite things to grow.

As we head into October, the turnover of the big tunnel into winter mode continues. In September I removed the climbing French beans and replaced them with the final crop of beetroot for this year. I was a little concerned that I had left the beetroot too late to transplant, but in fact they've flown along and are starting to turn recognisably into tiny beetroot. Hopefully with a month left of growing, they will give us a crop of roots for winter storage.

Today I started to take out some of the tomato plants. There's still at least three to four weeks of harvesting left to do (particularly on the Sungold variety that always crops latest), but I am removing some plants at this stage to make a start. I've had fresh tomatoes right up to December some years. The tomatoes have been abundant this year – we've more than enough tomato sauces made for the freezer, so we're on the wind-down – eating fresh whatever tomatoes are left. Incidentally, if you can't be bothered making something with the unripened green tomatoes and if they don't appear to be ripening outside, here's a good hack to get them to turn red: put them on a baking tray with a banana and cover the baking tray with parchment paper. Tie some string around the edge to make sure the paper stays put and leave the tray in a sunny spot in the house. The tomatoes should turn red within a week to 10 days, due to the ethylene gas that the banana gives off as it ripens. It really is like magic.

I aim to cover my soil with *something* over the winter to protect it and feed it, replacing the nutrients that we've taken from it by growing food in it during the year. Generally, that's either a covering of seaweed (gathered from the beach), home-made compost or a green manure (that is, a plant that is grown to feed the soil). It would be simplest, of course, just to use one of the three, but I don't tend to have enough of any of them, so I generally use a combination.

In the space made available by clearing some of my tomato plants, I sowed rows of the oriental green mizuna, which will have the benefit of providing some salad leaves for the house in the coming months while also improving the soil. As Richard

Mee, our head grower at GROW HQ, is always telling me, grow-ing something in the soil over the winter is better than nothing. Bare soil is bad. So from that perspective sowing a late crop of mizuna in the tunnel is better than leaving the soil bare. It's not a green manure in the sense of feeding the soil while it grows in the way that a legume (like clover or beans) would, but it will improve the soil biologically and if chopped up and dug into the soil in the early spring, it is organic matter that will improve the soil. As I clear more tomato plants in the weeks ahead, I will be sowing the Landsberger Mix green manure from Fruithill Farm, which is a brilliant groundcover containing vetch, crimson clover and ryegrass. Some years, I chop the tomato plants up with a pair of secateurs in situ as I remove them and dig them into the soil before I sow a green manure. This is a big job and I only do it every few years. The decaying tomato plants will both feed the soil and increase the amount of organic matter in it.

Even if you don't do this, there are still opportunities with the spent tomato plants. They are a valuable source of nitrogen, so they get chopped up and form a nice thick green layer in the compost heap.

3 october
storing
beetroot

I love beetroot – actually, I don't think there's much you can say against it. You can grow large quantities in a small space, it's easy to grow and relatively trouble-free, stores exceptionally well and is incredibly good for you. So what's not to love? From three timely sowings a year, we have our own supply of beetroot almost all year round. We had our first fresh beetroot of the year from the polytunnel in mid-May this year; more from the veg patch outside about a month later; and the winter storage crop will last right up until next April if we're lucky.

Unlike hardier roots like parsnips, I don't leave my beet-root in the soil for the winter – today I lifted the whole lot of them for storage in a box of sand. I harvested 60 or so in all, which were from the third sowing I did, in July. Before putting the roots into sand, they need a little cleaning up. Having twisted off the foliage on the beetroot (leaving a 5cm (2-inch) crown of stalks), I give the roots a good rub to remove most of the dirt. It's not a good plan to wash them as they might go soft. Then I grade them. Only the best ones should be stored, so any that have holes in them go straight to the kitchen to be used now.

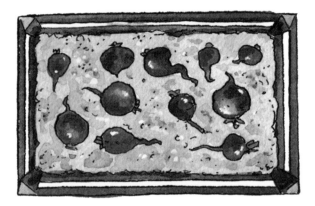

I use horticultural sand, which you can buy (cheaply) in garden centres, but be mindful that you may need to dry it out before use (particularly if it has been stored outside). Mine felt wet when I got it home, so I simply emptied the bags out on the bench in the potting shed to let it dry out for a few days. When it's ready, place the roots between layers of sand in a box, making sure they are not touching each other. Store the box in a dark, frost-free shed. If we use three roots a week, this stash should last us about five months.

4 october
dis-
connected

Well over a century ago, Karl Marx believed that workers of the world would eventually rebel against their oppressors because the industrialised age was dividing their work into meaningless, repetitive tasks. The factory owner assumed that the most efficient and productive factory system resulted from forcing employee A to stick widget B into product C repeatedly, all day long. But because employee A never gets to see product C to its completion, he/she quickly becomes disengaged and doesn't really care about the quality of the end result. Marx called this 'alienated labour' and argued that the separation from the completed products served to disconnect the workers from the meaning of their work and, therefore, from themselves.

I'm re-reading Barbara Kingsolver's *Animal, Vegetable, Miracle* at the moment, in which she argues that something very similar has happened to us as food consumers over the last two or three decades. From a point where most people would have had a decent knowledge of how and where food was produced (or had a direct hand in producing it themselves), we've become completely disconnected from the process of food production – milk comes from cartons, peas from the freezer, and beyond that we care not. Rather like the automaton factory worker, we're highly specialised at just one small task in the food process: eating it. Beyond that, we are pretty much in the dark. The result is a disengaged consumer disconnected from the significance of food and lacking any real appreciation for the rest of the process.

This, I think, partly explains why growing your own food is so satisfying – you get to pop the bonnet and take a look under it to see how the thing really works. You get to be curious and see how the different stages are interwoven and interdependent. You can try out each one of them, taking the process all the way from sowing a seed to raising a seedling and plant, harvesting food and finally turning it into the end product (either direct to plate or by processing into a preserve, pickle, chutney, etc.) – hell, if you want to complete the cycle you can even compost the waste to return nutrients to the soil or save seed for sowing next year. Marx would no doubt identify with the tremendous sense of freedom and satisfaction we gain from the individuality of our efforts.

It hardly seems possible but it's the first week of October already. Appropriately enough, today I was out in the veg patch harvesting our pumpkins and squashes. I managed to grow about 40 fruits

5 october
squash
harvest

this year, ranging from the petite Delicata to the pale blue Crown Prince squashes to the stunning red pumpkin Rouge Vif d'Etamps. Forty fruits is a good result and (using one a week from November on) they should see us through to April next year.

As with my tomatoes, and pretty much everything else in the veg patch this year, I reckon we're three to four weeks ahead of schedule harvesting these. This is good and bad – it's good to have them harvested and safely in out of the veg patch where they would be vulnerable to night-time frosts (when they arrive). But on the downside, they looked absolutely stunning in the veg patch, which suddenly seems rather dull without them.

The potting shed, where the fruits are spending some time curing on shelves, is now a glorious place to be – there's a stunning array of fruits of all shapes, colours and sizes. I know we should leave them be, since by virtue of their tough skins they can survive for months in storage, providing food at a time of the year when there's a scarcity elsewhere, but I couldn't resist making a squash meal for dinner from a little Delicata squash. And how delicious it was.

Remember that when you're harvesting you should leave 10–12cm (4–5 inches) of the stalk attached to the fruit. If you snap it off the fruit, the hole left behind is more likely to invite rot.

french onion soup with garlic and smoked cheddar toasts

With shorter, colder days closing in I'm in the mood for warming soups now, and what better warming soup is there than French onion? Thankfully, JB is a Frenchman so you know he's all over it with his recipe for French onion soup.

ingredients:
For the stock:
— leftover chicken bones/carcass
— a handful of garden herbs , such as sprig parsley and thyme

- — 1 carrot
- — 2 tomatoes, chopped
- — 1 celery stick

For the soup:
- — 250g onions
- — 4 tbsp rapeseed oil
- — 25g plain flour
- — 1 glass of dry white wine
- — 1 bay leaf
- — salt and pepper

For the toasted cheese:
- — 4 slices of yeast bread
- — 1 garlic clove
- — 100g grated smoked cheddar
- — sea salt and crack black pepper

directions:

For the chicken stock, put the chicken bones left over from your Sunday roast in a large saucepan. Add the herbs, carrot, tomatoes and celery and cover with cold water. Simmer for 2 hours. Pass through a sieve and allow to cool. Refrigerate overnight and discard the top layer of fat.

For the soup, peel and slice the onions and fry them in a stockpot with the rapeseed oil until light brown. Add the flour and stir for 2–3 minutes. Add the white wine (don't drink it all) and cook on a low heat for 2–3 minutes. Add 1 litre of the chicken stock, the bay leaf and seasoning. Leave to simmer for 20 minutes.

Meanwhile, lightly toast the bread. Rub both sides of each slice of toast with the garlic clove. Sprinkle the grated cheese over the toasted bread. Place under a hot grill for a few minutes. Serve the soup piping hot in warm bowls and put the slices of cheesy toast on top.

Lots of people ask, 'What can I sow at this time of the year? Is the growing season over?' No, not yet. Here are 10 things you can sow this week.

1. **Broad beans:** Autumn-sown broad beans are ready a good month before spring-sown beans and they don't get black-fly. These will be ready in May. Try the variety Aquadulce.
2. **Peas:** Ditto for autumn-sown peas – try Meteor.
3. **Sugarsnap peas:** If you can get your hands on early varieties such as Snow Pea Gigante Svizzero, it's worth a try – growth will be slow but you will get small pods early next year.
4. **Garlic:** Plant cloves 2cm (1 inch) below the surface. Try the Provence variety.
5. **Onions:** Try the varieties Electric, Radar or Shakespeare.
6. **Spring cabbage:** If you can get your hands on some cabbage plants from your local garden centre, plant them 30cm (12 inches) apart and earth up the soil around the base of the stem.
7. **Winter lettuce:** You can still sow some really hardy varieties of winter lettuce outside – cover with fleece in cold weather. Try Winter Gem.
8. **Lamb's lettuce:** Easy to grow and undemanding.
9. **Spinach:** The beauty of sowing spinach at this time of the year is that it won't bolt (which is the great blight of growing spinach earlier in the year).
10. **Asparagus:** Sow autumn-planting varieties.

There's an old saying about winter seed sowing: 'One for the mouse, one for the crow, one to rot and one to grow.' It hints at the fact that sowing seeds at this time of the year can be a hit-and-miss affair, so you should sow some extra ones in case of mishaps.

Back in late summer when the broad beans, early peas and early spuds had finished cropping, I cleaned up the beds and sowed a green manure called phacelia in the beds (the seeds were broadcast liberally in the soil and then raked in). The seeds germinated within a few days, and within weeks we had a lovely carpet of light green plants covering the beds. Today, the phacelia was ready to be cut down and dug into the soil.

A green manure is a fast-growing 'cover' crop grown specifically to add nutrients and organic matter to the soil. While it is growing the green manure protects the soil (its roots hold the soil together) and because it grows so quickly, it also suppresses weeds.

Green manures are dug into the soil when the plants are still young and typically before they flower (the phacelia was just starting to produce pretty little blue flowers). The green leafy material is very high in nutrients, so as it decomposes, it improves and protects the soil. The upside of digging in when the plants are young is that they are still quite tender and easy to work with. They also break down in the soil quite quickly. If they're allowed to get too old and tough, it becomes a more difficult job.

To dig in the manure, I simply used shears to chop down the manure at ground level. I also chopped at the plants to break them down into smaller bits as I went. I have heard of people using a strimmer where there are larger areas of ground covered in green manure, but the shears were fine for me and it didn't take long. Rather than digging it in, it's even better at this time of the year if you just leave it on the surface of the soil and cover it with a light-excluding cover – it could be black silage plastic or cardboard. By the spring of next year, the material will most likely have disappeared, with the worms doing the work of incorporating it into the soil.

Homegrown herbs can make every meal feel like it was produced in your garden – this can be important in winter months when you may not have so much fresh produce available (if any at all).

Potting up herbs and growing them indoors is a great way to maintain a consistent supply of fresh herbs such as thyme, rosemary and sage through the winter months and save yourself money.

As long as they get some sunlight, water and air, they will do well indoors, and this is a great time of the year to start them – they will have time to get settled and established before winter. They should show signs of growth about three to four weeks after potting up and continuous harvesting will encourage growth. They will grow slowly over the winter, but they *will* grow – and they should keep you in herbs for the winter months. They can be planted out again in the spring.

Use relatively small plants (about 15cm/6 inches) that will grow happily in 15cm pots. Dedicate a pot to each herb if you can. Getting the balance right with drainage is important. Herbs don't like to sit in wet soil, but potted herb plants always dry out quicker than they would in open ground. So keep a close eye on them. Make sure there are drainage holes in the pots and don't use garden soil – potting compost is better aerated.

To pot them up, fill the pot with compost about two-thirds of the way up. Create a well in the middle and gently put the plant in it. Fill in the well with the remainder of the compost and firm it in gently.

Keep the herbs in a sunny location. Water every two weeks or so and be careful not to over-water. The soil should be dry but not dried out. Mist them every now and then if the air is dry in your home.

12 october
sowing broad beans

After the dry, warm Indian summer, the weather has suddenly turned cold and wet and it's feeling properly autumnal (or, dare I say it, even wintry). Fires and stoves are being lit, heating turned on and the Great Coat is being brought down from the wardrobe. Everyone you talk to about the weather says, 'Well, we can't complain,' and it's true that it was a brilliant and extended summer. But I still reckon I could find cause to complain a little if we jumped straight from summer to winter, skipping autumn altogether.

Anyway, before we hibernate for the winter, there is still much to be done in the veg patch: beds to be cleared, compost/manure to be spread on idle beds, etc. But today I decided to neglect the general clean-up that needs doing and focus instead on sowing broad beans. It felt unseasonal, and yet immensely satisfying. One could say this is the first official sowing of next year's growing season – you just have to love how utterly relentless food growing is.

Broad beans can be sown in either the winter or spring (or both). Sowing in winter gives an earlier crop the following year, with the beans harvestable from May onwards. I find it interesting that sowing the seeds four or even five months early only really buys you a month at the harvesting end. This is because the plants grow slowly for most of the winter, waiting to burst into life in the spring.

For next year, my legumes (peas and beans) are being sown where the spuds grew this year. As a result the soil is in good nick and needed just a gentle raking to get the bed ready for sowing (spuds have that kind of effect on soil). I sowed the super-hardy variety Purple Guatemalan from Brown Envelope Seeds, but you can use any over-wintering variety, such as Aquadulce Claudia.

kale and pinto bean soup

This feels more like a broth than a soup, but it's delicious and makes a virtue of kale, which is still in season. This soup makes a great healthy lunch, or if you want to turn it in to a hearty supper, add 100g of cooked pasta (something small like macaroni) and serve with crusty bread.

Serves 6

ingredients:
— 2 tbsp olive oil
— 1 small onion, diced
— 2 stalks celery
— 6 large carrots, chopped
— 2 cloves garlic, minced
— 1 tsp each finely chopped rosemary and sage
— 1 tsp cumin
— 1 chilli, finely chopped
— salt and pepper
— 1.8 litres vegetable stock
— 400g tin of pinto beans
— 225g kale, chopped

directions:
Put the oil and onion in a large saucepan on a medium heat and sweat until softened. Add the celery, carrots and garlic and cook until the mixture is caramelised and cooked through. Add the herbs, cumin and chilli with a good sprinkling of salt and pepper and stir well. Pour in the vegetable stock, beans and kale. Cook for 1 hour on a medium heat, until the beans and carrots are tender.

14 october
plant a fruit tree

October to March is the time to plant a new fruit tree, as the trees are dormant. Here is how to do it:

1. Dig a hole deep enough to comfortably accommodate the root system of the tree. When the tree is placed in the hole,

the grafting point (the small bulge at the base of the tree that indicates where the tree was grafted onto the root-stock) should be just above ground level.

2.   Add some garden compost or well-rotted farmyard manure to the base of the hole and mix it in with the soil.

3.   Sit the tree in the hole and knock in a sturdy post about 8cm (3 inches) from the tree. Backfill the hole with a mixture of the soil you dug out and compost. Firm in the soil with your boot.

4.   Use a tree-tie (or a pair of tights) to attach the tree to the stake. Do not use a cable tie as it will cut the bark on the tree as the tree grows. The tie will need to be slackened off as the tree grows, and the support can generally be removed a year or two later.

5.   Give the tree a good drenching to encourage root growth. In dry weather, keep it well watered for a few weeks while it's getting established.

6.   What to grow? Well, I think it's a good plan to have at a minimum a mix of apple, plum and pear.

15 october
the pivot

There's always a moment in every GIYer's year when things pivot from a focus on the current year to preparing for the next. It amazes me how suddenly it happens. Today I was clearing a bed in which I had grown squashes, pumpkins, sweetcorn and beans this year, harvesting the last of the produce, getting the dead or dying plants on the compost heap and turning over the soil with a fork to clean up the beds.

It struck me that for the end of the growing season, the soil was in pretty good nick – dark and crumbly. I'm not sure whether that's a result of the amount of compost I added to it last winter (and the winter before, and the winter before that) or because of the nitrogen-fixing qualities of the bean plants that grew there this year. Or perhaps a little bit of both.

Either way, I was thinking that the bed probably doesn't need a big covering of compost this winter. I try to cover most of the beds with a decent layer of the black stuff or seaweed each year, except the root crop bed, which generally doesn't need to be too nutrient-rich. Think about it – you really want your carrots and other roots to be going in search of nutrients (and therefore getting longer) rather than finding them too easily. Not surprisingly, then, carrots tend to fork when grown in a heavily manured/composted soil.

So anyway, I immediately started to think about what would be growing in that bed next year. In the potting shed I have a notebook in which I plan my crop rotation – that sounds more organised than it really is. My 'planning' involves no more than a basic sketch of the veg patch so I can map out a five-year rotation with the patch divided into five areas, one for each major veg family (based on the easy-to-remember mnemonic People Love Bunches Of Roses: Potatoes, Legumes, Brassicas, Onions, Roots). So everything simply swings around for next year, with the brassicas going where the legumes were this year and so on. It's pretty straightforward.

Having worked out broadly what's going to go where next year, I found myself standing in the veg patch imagining what will be in each location and thinking about the soil requirements and the work to be done on each area over the winter. As you can imagine, I had long since lost sight of the job I was there to do. The focus had moved on again and another year of growing suddenly beckoned.

We have a pretty fixed view of what makes up the human body: cells, blood, tissues, bone and so on. But did you know that inside your gut you carry around a whopping 2kg (4½lb) of microbes, which comprise over a thousand different species of bacteria that outnumber our cells 10 to 1? Most of us are aware that these bacteria play a hugely important role in the digestion process (breaking down food, absorbing nutrients, etc.), but science is increasingly viewing the microbiome as a new, unexplored and possibly intelligent organ in its own right. Scientists are now asking: what's the connection between the health of our micro-biome and our overall health? What role does the microbiome play in mood, depression, diabetes, autoimmune disease, inflammation, food allergies and cancer?

It's an emerging field, but scientists seem to agree that a diversity of gut bacteria is good for our health and that (not surprisingly) what we put into our bodies has a huge impact on our microbiome. Diets high in processed foods are thought to have a huge impact on our gut micro-organism levels. Dietary sugar and fat encourage bad bacteria and reduce the level of the virtuous ones. Excessive antibiotic use is also a concern – a study co-led by researchers at the University of Valencia found that antibiotic treatment causes significant and sometimes irreversible changes in our gut community. Specifically, the study found that the gut microbiome shows less capacity to absorb iron and digest certain foods during antibiotic treatment (but it can recover afterwards).

There are major health claims being made about fermented foods in relation to gut heath, some of which we should probably treat with caution. They are purported to improve intestinal tract health, enhance the immune system, improve absorption of nutrients and reduce the risk of certain cancers. Scientists seem to agree that the bacteria in fermented foods help to pre-digest food components, making it easier for your gut to handle them and for nutrients to be absorbed.

When I first started fermenting food at home, I was just as interested in how it could help me to store food as I was in its potential health benefits. Kimchi and sauerkraut, for example, are centuries-old methods (from Korea and Germany, respectively) of preserving cabbage. To start with I was sort of afraid of fermenting, but over time you learn to trust your eyes, nose and palate, and to recognise the sour taste that is the hallmark of a kraut that is ready to be eaten and also the smell when it eventually goes off.

From a culinary perspective, kimchi is the more elaborate of the two. In Korea there are thought to be literally thousands of kimchi recipes and it was traditionally stored in clay pots buried underground to keep them cool and slow the fermentation process. I have got into the habit of eating a small serving of kimchi or kraut every day. Potential gut health benefits aside, it's a delicious way to deal with a glut of homegrown veg.

19 october
soil

Soil. Well, it's just dirt really, isn't it? It's something to be cleaned off our boots and scrubbed off our hands, right? When I started growing my own food, I didn't have any respect for the soil that the veg was growing in. My focus was on the seed, the plants, the vegetables. In fact, the soil was a source of annoyance to me – it had to be dug, raked, hoed, rotavated, coaxed and cajoled. It had to be bent to my will.

If we brought in a big digger and scraped the thin layer (about 15–20cm, or 6–8 inches) of rich topsoil off the surface of our planet, all life as we know it would cease to exist. Plant matter would not grow, and without plant matter there would be no animals (including humans). Given its importance to our survival, it's strange that we treat it with such contempt. Centuries of commercial agriculture has assumed that we can continue to rob the soil of its nutrients by growing intensively from it and that all we need to do is replace the three core nutrients of nitrogen, phosphorus and potassium (the key ingredients of commercial NPK fertiliser).

In fact, what soil needs to support life is far more complex than that. Composts and manures (which are the organic alternative to chemical fertilisers) also return dozens of trace minerals and other nutrients to the soil. As a result, the vegetables that grow in this soil have more nutrients in them – and healthier veg leads to healthier people. Then, having served their purpose in the kitchen, the vegetable trimmings and waste are returned to the compost, releasing the nutrients that are left back to the compost heap and then eventually back to the soil. Even a cursory understanding of this never-ending cycle of growth–maturity–decay leads you to one conclusion: growing your own food is *all about the soil.*

From that perspective, my most significant achievement as a GIYer has been to learn how to make proper compost. Each winter I put wheelbarrow loads of the crumbly stuff on my vegetable beds. And each year my soil starts to look less like a potter's clay and becomes a little darker, a little crumblier and a lot more lovable. I've stopped treating my soil like dirt and learned to love it.

roast squash with caramelised red onions, cashel blue and hazelnuts

It's squash season and this roast squash recipe from JB will create a great centrepiece for a mezze platter.

ingredients:
— 1 whole squash (butternut or Crown Prince)
— 1 tsp salt
— 3 tbsp olive oil
— 2 large red onions

- — 1 tbsp organic golden granulated sugar
- — 100g Cashel Blue cheese
- — 100g crushed hazelnuts

directions:
Preheat the oven to 150°C.

Halve and deseed the squash (keep the skin on). Place the squash, skin down, on a roasting tray. Sprinkle with the salt and drizzle with the oil. Cover with tinfoil and bake for 30 minutes to 1 hour. Use the point of a knife to check that the squash is completely cooked.

Peel and chop the onions. Fry them for a few minutes on a high heat with the remaining tablespoon of olive oil and add the sugar. Allow the onions to caramelise, then take off the heat.

Take the tinfoil off the roast squash and cover the squash with the caramelised onions. Crumble the cheese over the onions and sprinkle over the crushed hazelnuts. Turn up the oven to 180°C and bake for a further 15–20 minutes.

21 october
seaweed
mulch

I had a particularly weedy time of it in the vegetable patch this year – even regular hoeing barely seemed to keep them in check. Apart from how maddeningly persistent the weeds were, I was also struck by the fact that many of them seemed to be making their inaugural appearance in my garden. The most likely reason for these new visitors is the fact that I brought in about 20 bags of farmyard manure from a local farmer last winter. He kindly let me help myself to a large pile of rotted manure at the back of his cowsheds, which was like discovering the lost treasure of Machu Picchu. Alas, these glorious finds can also bring with them all manner of strange weed seeds, waiting to burst into life among your veggies the following season.

Of course, I would much prefer to use only homemade compost to return nutrients to my beds each year, but I generally can't make enough to cover all the beds. So I have to go beyond

the garden gate, supplementing my compost with blagged farm-yard manure. Stung by the weedy time I've had this year, I am also going to use seaweed on my beds in the winter ahead.

So today we spent a few hours on Woodstown Strand in Waterford gathering seaweed into sacks. It's a pleasant way to spend a morning, and it gets the children (and dogs) some exercise and fresh air at the same time. I filled 10 old fertiliser bags with seaweed and can vouch for the fact that it's a more civilised process than filling bags with stinky farmyard manure. Once ferried home in the boot of the car, the 10 bags covered four of my raised beds. It will take several more trips to the beach to get enough to cover the remaining beds, but that's okay – as long as I get them covered down pre-Christmas, it will be time enough.

There is often confusion about whether it's legal to take seaweed from a beach. The bottom line is that 'sustainable use' is permitted, which means it's perfectly fine to collect seaweed that's been washed up on the beach, but not cool to pull living seaweed from rocks. For ease of collection, the drier seaweed up the beach is lighter than the wet stuff beside the surf – you don't want to be lugging litres of heavy seawater home in addition to your bags of seaweed.

Convention has it that you should wash your seaweed before putting it on top of veg beds, but our friend Joy Larkcom reckons this is nonsense and that there's no evidence that salt in the seaweed will cause you problems. A decent covering of seaweed (as thick as you can manage) will suppress weeds and improve your soil immensely. First-time growers are generally surprised to hear that a thick layer – say, 20cm (8 inches) of seaweed on top of the soil – will completely rot down over the winter months.

22 october world food day It's World Food Day today and, as I always do with these vast global events, I tried to think about it at the only level that makes any sense to me – my vegetable patch. One of my main motivations for growing my own food is that supermarkets just don't provide any real variety when it comes to fruit and vegetables. I mean, on the face of it, they seem to be stacked high with produce, but when you really look at it, you realise that mostly they play it very, very safe. There is an assumption that because our world is so small now, we have access to a vast array of new and exotic vegetables from all over the globe. In fact, ever more powerful transnational supermarkets are forcing food producers into the straitjacket of monoculture – producing higher yields of ever-decreasing varieties of vegetables. Typically, these varieties are chosen not for their taste, but for their ability to survive very long journeys from farm to plate.

What does this really mean? Whereas a decade or two ago you could find 10–15 varieties of apples or tomatoes in a supermarket, now there are just a couple. And in all likelihood, they will be the same two or three varieties available in a supermarket in Spain or America or Asia. In fact, 75 per cent of the world's agricultural diversity has been lost in the last century, according to the UN Food and Agriculture Organisation.

This tragic blandness suits retailers (and producers to a certain extent) who are only interested in bulk selling, but it's terrible for biodiversity, taste and variety. Given the vulnerability of monocrops to attack from pests and diseases, it's also downright dangerous from a food security perspective. And, of course, when farmers in the developing world are forced to grow crops for export to developed countries, it leaves local populations vulnerable to food poverty.

The beauty of the veg patch is the diversity it offers us. We have at our fingertips a smorgasbord of varieties of each veg that we can dip into each season. We can grow purple carrots or giant parsnips. We can grow vegetables that you rarely get at all in a supermarket, like kohlrabi, artichokes or Florence fennel. We can grow a variety of tomato that we know to be particularly tasty. We can save seed from varieties we like. In short, we are empowered.

Today I harvested the first of our Florence fennel and I have to say I'm delighted with the results, and already thinking I should have sown more than 12 plants (my GIYing always seems to contain an element of 'should have'). Florence fennel, which is different from herb fennel, is grown for its aniseed-flavoured bulb. Though it takes up quite a lot of space (45cm (18-inch) spacing per plant), it's repays your investment by being entirely edible – the bulb, the celery-like stalks and the feathery leaves can all be eaten.

It's a satisfyingly quick crop to grow too – it's just 14 weeks since I sowed the seeds back in June. I was late getting them in to the ground (as I often am), but although I didn't know it at the time, this is actually a good thing, since fluctuating temperatures (a feature earlier in the year) can cause fennel to bolt. I also ignored the advice to sow it direct, and instead sowed the seeds in module trays in the potting shed and then planted them out a few weeks later.

Isn't it wonderful that even after years of our GIYing adventure, a vegetable can still come along and surprise us? We ate our first batch tonight, cooked simply with a herb crust on top, and it blew us away. It tastes of liquorice, for one thing. Or Pernod. Fabulously succulent and fresh tasting, Mediterranean, a little exotic, even – a wonderful foil to the earthy root crops that are such a feature of the autumn veg patch.

Few vegetables divide opinions as much as Brussels sprouts. But, love 'em or loathe 'em, what is beyond doubt is that they can provide the GIYer with a very valuable crop in the winter months (usually September to February). They freeze well and are very good for you – high in vitamins D and C and dietary fibre. There's also an incredible amount of goodness packed into a neat little package – take a single sprout and remove all the leaves and spread them out on a chopping board and you will see what I am talking about.

27 october
**love 'em or
loathe 'em**

At this time of the year, it's important to earth up and stake the plants as they can blow over in heavy winds. Wind rock causes the roots of the plant to unsettle, which results in lower yields and causes the sprouts to open prematurely. If sprouts start to open up, give the plant a good nitrogen feed (like comfrey or nettle tea) and remove any open sprouts. A good mulch at this time of the year is always a good idea to feed the plants – they need lots of nitrogen to develop those leafy sprouts.

If you have an aversion to sprouts, which I did for years, know this: the key to a tasty dish is to lightly blanch and then fry them in some butter or oil and rock salt. I suspect that many an Irish mammy (though not mine, of course) unwittingly created a lifetime hatred of sprouts by putting them on to boil at the same time as the Christmas turkey went in the oven.

I've had two incidents in the last week where tomatoes I brought in from the tunnel tasted like they had gone off. Probably because they had gone off, I suppose. The tomato plants are looking pretty bedraggled now and there are only a few dozen toms left, but they aren't in great nick, to be honest. I think I pretty much must accept that the cold October we've had this year means the tomato season is over. It's not bad to have made it to the end of October. I might leave one or two plants where they are for a few more days, just so I can say that I had tomatoes right up to November. This is the kind of thing that matters to me.

28 october
**end of the
toms**

Thankfully, my tomato obsession was satiated by a bumper crop this year. At times, we literally struggled to cope with the volumes of tomatoes coming in from the veg patch. I put pretty much every recipe I could think of to work, making sauces, salsas and ketchups. I pickled them, sun-dried them and put them in chutneys. Our bigger tunnel was all about the premise that you could 'never have too many tomatoes' – this year I had to admit you come to a point where you actually can.

So anyway, we've enough tomato sauce in bags in the freezer to keep us going right up until the new tomato season next summer. But for now, the joy of freshly picked tomatoes has passed, and it feels like it was a fairly short season overall.

We live in a post-seasonal world, where every vegetable is in season somewhere around the world and there's a transport system to facilitate its speedy movement from point A to point B. That's all fine and dandy, but there are two problems with this as far as I can see. First, the veg shipped in from The Other Side of the World can't compete flavour-wise with something that's just been picked. Second, and perhaps this is more important, the lack of seasonality means we've become tone deaf to our body's needs at different times of the year. There's a reason we're less interested in salads and more in soups as the winter comes in, and by eating seasonally you tune in to that wisdom.

When a staple veg like the tomato goes out of season, a question is asked of you: do you want to forget about tomatoes until next year or start eating an imported version until next summer? Somewhere in the world (usually Spain or the Netherlands), they will be able to grow tomatoes all through the winter and supermarkets will import vast quantities of them. The question is, will they taste as nice? Does your body need them? Personally, I'll be signing off fresh tomatoes until next summer. I'll miss them, particularly at breakfast time, but abstinence will make next summer's new crop all the sweeter.

Even though we've only used a small amount of this year's garlic crop so far, today it was time to plant next year's crop. Though the tradition is that garlic is sown before the shortest day of the year in December (and harvested by the longest day in June), getting them into the ground earlier than that gives them the best chance of getting the cold weather they need to thrive.

Though sowing garlic is easy, it generally necessitates some bed clearing and a bit of forward thinking about next year. More specifically, I have to consult my gardening diary to see where the crop rotation that I follow is dictating things are to be grown next year. So next year, the onion family (garlic, leeks, onions) will be going where the brassicas are this year, alongside the small tunnel at the back of the veg patch.

Once a bed is cleared, sowing the garlic only takes a few minutes, with Eldest Child tasked with measuring out the rows and placing the cloves on the ground. I sowed around a hundred cloves in total, which is probably way too many, but I am allowing for some of them not to grow and others to be on the small side. Around 50–60 decent bulbs would be a great result, and the balance could be eaten green about a month before the rest.

november

Though there's still plenty to eat and enjoy from this year's season, thoughts turn to next year's growing as we start to prepare the ground and make the last sowings of over-wintering veg like onions, broad beans and garlic.

This month we're loving … garlic.

As I sow the crop for next year (ideally before the shortest day of the year), we're also admiring a braid of this year's garlic in the kitchen.

Things feel like they are winding down a little in the veg garden now, to the extent that today I felt (for the first time since January) that I really had no pressing task to do in the veg patch and could probably do something else instead. That's an odd feeling. The veg garden is a hard taskmaster for much of the year, but it's becoming a little more chilled out now as we move into November. Unusually for me, I feel I am well ahead in terms of getting the veg patch ready for next year.

In the big polytunnel there are still a small number of tomato plants left, but only a few. I've been steadily removing them (and chopping them up for the compost heap) for the last month, so there are only a couple of plants left now still carrying tomatoes. During the summer, I was bringing large crates of tomatoes into the house to be processed, but today it was just a small bowl. How sad. I put some in the fridge for eating fresh (I refrigerate tomatoes at this time of the year so that they will keep a few days longer than they would at room temperature), while the rest got made into a passata, which can be used as the base sauce for a veg stew or soup later this week.

Back out in the tunnel, I was a little worried that it was too late for the green manure I sowed a few weeks back to establish, but it's flying. I sowed some outside too in the courgette bed on the same day, but that has only just germinated and with colder temperatures arriving I don't know that it will amount to much. I am delighted with it in the tunnel and the carpet of green in the beds looks fantastic. The fruit on the chilli pepper plants, which I hung upside down in the tunnel so I could clear the beds, were starting to soften, so I stripped them and brought them to the kitchen to pickle.

pickled chillies

Pickled chillies are my new favourite thing and they are a brilliant way to store chilli peppers, which can be super-abundant at this time of the year. They are really easy to make.

Slice the chillies into small rounds and stuff them into sterilised jars (jam jars or Kilner jars). In a saucepan, heat equal parts vinegar and water (how much depends on how many chillies you have to pickle, but let's say 200ml (⅓ pint) of each) with a teaspoon of salt, a tablespoon of sugar, a bay leaf and a teaspoon each of coriander seeds and mustard seeds.

When the liquid comes to the boil, pour it over the chillies in the jar (making sure they are covered with the liquid) and then pop on the lid to seal the jars. They will keep for three to four months (I keep them in the drawer in the bottom of the fridge).

4 november
the value of
irish veg

I recently went on a sobering visit to a couple of our biggest field veg growers: Paul Brophy in Kildare, the largest grower of broccoli in the state; and the Weldon brothers (Martin and Enda) in Swords, who supply the majority of the Brussels sprout crop. Their operations are truly massive and impressive, and, like most veg growers, they have had to specialise and go large in order to compete. In the 15 years between 1999 and 2015 there was a huge drop in the number of field veg growers in Ireland – from 377 down to 165. Either way, that's a pretty tiny number of growers who are responsible for our entire veg output. Interestingly, the output levels in edible horticulture haven't dropped in that same time period. In other words, the remaining growers have ramped up their production big time.

Commercial veg growing was always a tough game, but growers seem to be facing particular pressures now. The effects of climate change, and its accompanying extreme weather events, have a huge impact on them. Climate change is creating additional uncertainty and cost for growers and with our veg output concentrated in the hands of ever fewer growers, it makes our indigenous food chain very vulnerable indeed in the years ahead.

The extreme weather alone doesn't explain why so many growers are leaving the market. That, alas, is largely down to the fact that there is so little margin in selling the veg. Competition from cheaper imports plays a part, as does below-cost selling and discounting in supermarkets. In recent years, we've all seen the aggressive pre-Christmas price promotions on fresh-from-the-field veg like sprouts and carrots for sale for as little as five cents a kilo. It's typically the supermarket that takes the hit on this (though some have been known to lean on growers to share the burden), using it as a loss leader to draw us in, and of course consumer groups will say it's great for the consumer to have access to cheap, healthy vegetables. But these are short-term benefits. In the long term, these promotions set ever lower benchmarks for the value of veg, which will drive more growers from the industry. Ultimately, we will be left with less choice as consumers and more and more imported veg. That's bad for jobs here at home and it reduces our access to healthy, seasonal, fresh food and the kind of taste that can only come from just-picked veg.

Most important, the Brophys, the Weldons and the like are producing food that is everything food should be – incredibly good for us, nutritious, seasonal, fresh and local – and they create jobs. We should be paying a fair price for that instead of discounting it. As always, we have power as consumers. When buying your veg, always seek out local vegetables and try to avoid the price promotions. Remember, there is always a cost to cheap food somewhere down the line.

It's always an exciting experience to grow something you've never grown before. I grew the South American tuber yacon for the first time this year, thanks to some donated plants from a neighbouring grower. He gave me the plants in July, and I planted them in the big polytunnel where they grew rather slowly through the summer. In our climate, yacon will do best in a polytunnel or greenhouse, but they can be grown outside if you have a very sheltered, sunny spot for them. I sort of assumed I had planted them out too late (around May or early June is the typical planting-out time). It was only as autumn approached that they really took off, and they are now well

5 november
a new tuber in town

over 1.5m (5ft) tall. Unlike the potato, the yacon is a problem-free plant to grow – blight doesn't affect it, and the tubers seem to be immune to slug and worm interest. Bonus!

Today I harvested some from under one of the plants. It's a surreal experience. The process of harvesting them is very similar to that of harvesting potatoes – digging up a big leafy plant to find large tubers hiding beneath. But when you get them to the kitchen, their path quickly diverges from the humble spud. First, you can (and should) eat yacon raw. It has a surprisingly sweet, apple- or melon-like taste and a juicy texture, rather like a water chestnut. The juiciness is in fact what gives it its name – yacon means 'water root' and it was valued by the Incas for its thirst-quenching properties.

Yacon is creating quite a buzz among nutritionists because of the unusual way it stores its carbs, as indigestible sugar (inulin) rather than starch. It is therefore highly promising as a way to introduce sweetness into the diet of diabetics, and converted into a syrup it's a way for the rest of us to introduce sweetness without the calories of honey or maple syrup. Yacon is also thought to be a digestive aid, improving the health of the bacteria in the intestinal tract and colon. The formidable leaves are also nutritious and edible if cooked like chard or spinach.

Unfortunately, although it's being grown a bit in the USA, it's not a vegetable that's readily available to buy here. Given the excitement about it and how easy it is to grow, that might change. For now, though, if you want to eat it, you have to grow it yourself. The tubers from which you grow the plants can be hard to source, but the good news is that it's a perennial, so if you can get your hands on some tubers or plants you will never need to buy them again.

7 november
converting a lawn

A question we're often asked in GIY is this: if you are starting out with a lawn and want to grow your own food next year, where do you start? Let me start by saying this – now is a great time of year to be thinking about this issue because if you do some preparatory work now, you can have the soil ready to grow on by the spring of next year. But if you leave it until next spring to think about it, it will be too late to get the soil right for growing.

The traditional way to convert a lawn into usable ground for growing vegetables was to double-dig it – this is back-breaking stuff, and entirely unnecessary. Here's a way to do it that involves no digging or rotavating. How does it work? Well, instead of breaking your back, you get soil microbes and earthworms to do the hard work for you, breaking down the organic matter and leaving you with beds that will be rich and fertile. All you will need is some good compost or well-rotted manure, plenty of organic matter (straw, kitchen and garden waste) and some cardboard.

The first step is to mark out the area that you want to convert into a vegetable bed. This can be as big or as small as you want or need. Spread a 5cm (2-inch) layer of compost or well-rotted manure on the grass and give it a water to moisten it. Next, cover the compost with a layer of cardboard – this prevents light getting to the grass, therefore killing it (and any weeds). Spread another 5cm (2-inch) layer of compost on the cardboard and then a big 45cm (18-inch) layer of mixed organic matter. The best option is a mix of grass cuttings, leaves, straw, seaweed (if you can get it), kitchen and garden waste. Moisten this layer too. This is a lot of organic matter, so you will probably need to stockpile it for a few weeks before you start. Finish with a 5cm (2-inch) layer of straw. Then wait.

Ground prepared like this now should be ready to grow on in April or May of next year. It will simply require a forking over.

9 november
divide and conquer

A stroll around the veg patch today made me think about rhubarb plants and how hard they worked this year. You can and should divide rhubarb plants every four or five years to give the plants more room and reinvigorate them. The best time to do this is when the plant is dormant, so between November and February.

Dig the rhubarb using a fork to lever the crown carefully from the soil, trying to avoid, as much as possible, damaging the roots. Once you have it out of the ground, remove any rotting sections from the plant and give it a general clean-up. Then, using a sharp spade, press down heavily and divide the crown in three. Ideally you want each section to have a crown, a large amount of root and at least four or five pink buds.

Then dig a hole for the divided crowns and place one crown in each, roots downwards, with the top of the crown roughly 2cm (1 inch) below the soil surface. You can pop some well-rotted manure or compost in the hole first if you want to add some nutrients. Backfill with soil, firming in gently. But remember, new plants shouldn't be harvested too heavily in the first year.

11 november
carrots

There is simply nothing nicer than harvesting carrots – it's a delight for the senses. The beautiful vibrant orange colour emerging from the brown earth; the crunching sound as you pull them; and that lovely earthy smell. Harvesting all the carrots at once is actually a lot of fun, because I get to line them all up on the soil to have a satisfying look at the entire crop. Any damaged ones are put in a 'use-first' pile and stored in a hessian sack in the garage. Next up, a pile of baby carrots – these went straight to the kitchen, where they were blanched and frozen.

I buried the main bulk of 130 or so carrots in the veg trug in the garden – it's basically a raised bed on stilts, filled with a soil/compost mix that is empty of crops at this time of the year. I dug a large trench in the centre, buried the carrots and then covered it with fleece. It's a sort of modern equivalent of a clamp. I will be keeping a close eye on it for signs of tampering and checking the carrots frequently.

The main principles of storing carrots are to store only those that are in sound condition; remove excess stalks and leaves that could rot in storage; keep them slightly moist so that they do not dry out, while keeping out the wet, which would make them rot; and prevent frost and light getting to them. I have stored carrots successfully in a box of sand in the garage, although two years ago during a really bad winter the frost got to them even there.

The vitamin A content in carrots will actually increase in their first month in storage, and they will retain their nutritional value and flavour for several months if kept away from heat and light. We have roughly two hundred carrots in total, which at a rate of 10 a week should last us five months.

12 november feeeeeel your soil

Okay, so your neighbours will think you're nuts if they catch you, but getting to know your soil by feeling it is an important first step to knowing what type of soil you are dealing with. And if you know what soil you are dealing with – clay, sandy, silty, loamy (they sound like characters in a Disney movie) – you will know whether it's rich in nutrients (or not) and free-draining (or not). Pick up a handful of soil, roll it between your hands and concentrate on how it *feels*.

If it's a clay soil it will feel lumpy and sticky when very wet. Clay soil drains poorly and has few air spaces, which makes it difficult to grow in. On the plus side it usually has plenty of nutrients in it, so if you can improve the drainage by adding lots of organic matter, it will serve you well and produce lots of nice veggies. If it feels gritty to the touch, it's a sandy soil. Sandy soil will drain easily in winter, which is good, and it also warms up quickly in spring, which is also good (you can sow earlier). On the other hand, sandy soils don't hold nutrients as well and can be a struggle to keep watered in summer.

A silty soil feels smooth and soapy. It is very well drained and richer in nutrients than sandy soil. It tends to get damaged in winter because it has a weak soil structure and consequently is tough to manage. Loamy soil is the GIYer's utopia – it is the perfect soil to grow in and easy to cultivate. It lies somewhere between clay and sand. It has perfect structure and drains well but retains enough moisture for plants and therefore won't dry out in summer. It is also full of nutrients.

There is always a point around mid-November when I am suddenly not terribly interested in eating salads any more. I am
always surprised at how quickly this transformation happens.
One day I'm enjoying the last of the summer salad crops and
thinking of ways to use them up. The next I have an inexplicable
desire for something more warming – a good bowl of soup or a
homely one-pot stew. Suddenly, the remaining salad crops in the
veg patch seem to have outstayed their welcome.

Growing your own food and eating seasonally is a way of
reconnecting with the nutrition cycle that nature intended for us.
When our bodies are leading us towards eating one type of food
over another at particular times of the year, we would do well
to listen to its wisdom for physiological reasons. In the spring
we should consume lots of tender, leafy vegetables that represent fresh new growth and cleanse and lighten our systems. In
the summer, foods that are light and full of water, such as tomatoes, will help keep the body cool, hydrated and balanced. In the
autumn and winter, nature is in transition. Our ancestors would
have faced some very lean months now. Perhaps this explains
the intuitive need to store nourishment by eating richer, heartier
foods.

Even in modern times, the winter body needs food to keep
it warm and to help it conserve energy – so we need a different
type of fuel. Tomatoes and cucumbers just won't cut it. In general,
foods that take longer to grow are more warming than foods that
grow quickly – so think classic stockpot veg like carrots, onions,
garlic and potatoes.

In this context, think about how utterly lacking in seasonality the modern food chain really is. Glossy strawberries,
plump tomatoes and other out-of-season vegetables grace supermarket shelves throughout the winter. At first this might seem
exciting, but just because modern food chain logistics allows for
these marvels doesn't mean that our bodies wouldn't be better off
with more seasonal fare. Traditional Chinese medicine suggests
that we should eat different foods for different seasons, and that

eating seasonal foods that are similar in nature to the external environment will help us to adapt better to seasonal changes and remain healthy.

The Danes have a word that I really like in the context of the transition to more homely winter meals. That word is *hygge* – there is no direct English translation, but it hints at a cosy state of wellbeing where one is feeling homely, warm, comforted and in the company of good friends. There are as little as five hours of daylight in the winter in Denmark, but they fight back with warming food, open fires and good company. Most surveys place Denmark as among the happiest nations on earth, despite their cold, dark winters. Perhaps their embrace of *hygge* food explains it.

16 november
happy
hour in the
tunnel

It's tempting to avoid the veg patch when the weather is this grim and the ground is so wet, and I'm inclined to give myself a pass on the basis that I'm more or less on top of things. There are still beds that need a cover of seaweed or compost before the year is out (to return the nutrients we took from the soil with this year's growing), but there's still time for that.

Today, I did spend a happy hour in the big polytunnel, where it was nice and dry even though the rain was pelting down on the plastic outside. It does feel like it's the last of the harvesting in there finally – remarkably, there were still some cucumbers to gather, but the plants are on their last legs. I harvested six or seven cucumbers. From six plants, we've been eating cucumbers pretty much consistently since early July, which is an impressive five-month streak. Though I'm not minded to eat salads at this time of the year, cucumbers are still a great lunchbox filler to have in the bottom of the fridge (and of course they can be cooked too, in stir-fries and the like).

The over-wintering onions have pushed themselves out of the soil – a cheery sight. The green manure I sowed in October has flown along, and the intense mat of green makes my heart glad in the dreary weather. I like the idea that these lovely green plants are feeding the soil as they grow. We still have parsnips, leeks, celeriac, sprouts and kale in the ground outside, as well as squashes, pumpkins, onions and garlic in the house and a larder full of pickles, chutneys, sauces and krauts. Despite the onset of cold weather and short days, I feel blessed to have so much delicious, nutritious food to hand.

warm bulgur wheat salad with squash

Thanks to this year's growing, we have an abundance of squashes left. And thanks to their hard skins, some varieties will store for five months or so. Any variety of squash will do for this recipe.

This is a delicious winter salad – the flavour of the squash really is superb, bringing an incredible sweetness to any dish it graces, and I love the crunchy nuttiness of bulgur wheat.

Serves 4
ingredients:
— 300g squash
— 4 tbsp olive oil
— 500ml stock (chicken or veg)
— 150g bulgur wheat
— 1 tbsp balsamic vinegar
— 1 clove garlic, minced
— 50g walnuts, roughly chopped
— 60g goat's cheese, crumbled
— 50g mixed oriental greens (such as rocket, mustard, mizuna)

directions:
Preheat the oven to 200°C.

Peel the squash, chop it into small chunks and put them on a baking tray. Add 1 tablespoon of the olive oil, give it a good mix and roast for 20–30 minutes, until it is soft and starting to char at the edges.

Meanwhile, make your stock in a measuring jug, add the bulgur wheat and cover with a plate. Leave to soak for around 20 minutes, until soft. Drain off any remaining liquid.

In a small bowl, combine the balsamic vinegar, the remaining 3 tablespoons of olive oil and the garlic, then stir this dressing through the bulgur. Serve the warm bulgur wheat with the roasted squash, the chopped walnuts, the crumbled goat's cheese and the salad greens.

17 november
freeze your celery

We've been lifting our celery as we've needed it for the last two months, but now it's time to get the crop out of the ground before the worst of the winter weather arrives. Celery won't fare well if left in the soil to face frosts, ice or snow. Use a fork to gently lift the plant, roots and all. A head of celery will keep in the fridge for up to three days. If you have more than you can eat in the coming weeks, you can freeze celery (it will last up to a year in the freezer).

Here's how. Wash the celery thoroughly under running water. Trim and cut the stalks into 2cm (1-inch) lengths. Blanch it by immersing it in a large pot of boiling water for 3 minutes, then drain and quickly immerse it in iced water (this will immediately stop the cooking process). Allow it to cool for about 5 minutes, then drain and dry it. Pack it in a freezer bag, excluding as much air as you can, then pop it in the freezer.

19 november
sort your seeds

It's a great time of the year to address those tasks that we often put on the long finger, like sorting out your seeds. Having a good seed storage regime (if that doesn't sound too nerdy) will make your seeds last longer, save you money and ensure better germination rates. Bear in mind that the storage lives for seeds listed on packets are generally for unopened seeds – the viability of seeds is cut drastically once you open the packet.

Here are three tips with that in mind:

1. Tightly close opened seed packets – if they are in a foil or paper wrapper inside the packet, make sure to fold this over tightly.
2. Store the seed packets in a sealed container (e.g. a Tupperware container with a tight-fitting lid). If you're feeling super organised, you could 'file' them alphabetically or by veg family type – that really is super nerdy. Store the container in a cool, dry, dark place.
3. Discard seeds that are out of date – they will only lead to lost time in the veggie patch next year.

20 november
covering
beds

It's been a dodgy few weeks of weather and I have to admit that I've been spending very little time in the veg patch so far this November. The days are too short now for pre- or post-work GIYing, and recent weekends have been too busy. So the only visits to the veg patch of late have been rain-soaked hit and runs to grab some grub for the dinner.

As I've looked glumly from the house at the sodden garden, it's been playing on my mind that it's high time I got the beds in the veg patch covered for the winter. That's primarily about returning nutrients to the soil that we took from it in a year's growing. But it's also about putting a physical barrier on top of the beds to protect them from winter weather.

The nutrients come in the form of one of four things (or sometimes a mix of some or all of them, depending on what I have to hand). It could be seaweed (foraged from the local strand), compost (from the compost heap), farmyard manure (if you have a stables nearby – if not, you can buy bags in a garden centre) or a green manure (a crop grown specifically to feed the soil).

The physical barrier can also take the form of cardboard or black plastic, which serves a number of purposes: keeping the inclement weather off the beds, keeping them warm and dry and killing off any weeds (which will return their nutrients to the soil as they die off). It also helps ensure that the nutrients in the seaweed, compost or manure aren't washed away in heavy winter rain. Though I am not a fan of plastic per se, if you have a big sheet of black plastic, it is useful and reusable year on year.

The process of covering bare beds will continue right through the winter as more and more bed space gets cleared of veg. Generally I aim to have it done before Christmas.

22 november
cats in the veg patch

Is your moggie (or the neighbour's moggie) causing you stress in the veg patch? Try these common deterrents:

- Stretch rows of chicken wire over seedling beds to prevent cats rooting them up or spraying on them.
- Sticking twigs into the soil in newly sown beds will prevent digging.
- Cats like dry soil to do their business – they don't like wet soil so much – so keep the soil moist.
- They dislike the scent of citrus fruits – orange and lemon peels scattered around the soil in your veg patch may discourage them. We've also heard of people using rags soaked in vinegar (and left on the soil) to deter them. They also dislike the scent of rosemary and lavender.

- A spray of a hose if you catch them in the act will make them scarper.

23 november
food miles

For Science Week, we had schools visiting us at GROW HQ and we did a range of food-related activities with them. One of my favourites is our food miles exercise where we take five vegetables that are 'in season' and available at HQ currently, then show them an imported equivalent from the supermarket. We lay the two veg (the HQ-grown one and the supermarket equivalent) side by side on a table and get the children to guess how far the veg have travelled (clue: it's always more than you think). It's a fantastic way to get children thinking about where their food comes from and the health and environmental impact of the choices they will make as consumers.

So, here's the thing. I have no issue with anyone buying imported food when it's something we can't grow or produce here in Ireland. And I have no issue with supermarkets selling it. Yes, if you were to follow me around the supermarket (don't do that, it's creepy), you would certainly find many an imported item in the trolley – bananas, the odd pineapple or satsuma, certainly some coffee and the like. At certain times of the year, you might even find things that grow in Ireland but which are (a) out of season and (b) something I just can't do without.

Where it gets completely nonsensical is when it's food that we can grow here in Ireland, and which is currently in season. I've spotted strawberries from Israel in a supermarket during strawberry season. It's a great example of a completely needless import that's bad for our planet (all the energy required to get it here), bad for Irish growers and their livelihoods and, most likely, bad for our wellbeing too (because the food is not as nutritious having travelled all that way). That's before you get to the unnecessary packaging required to transport it.

For the record, the veg we used for the Science Week food miles exercise were onions (from the Netherlands, 779km), salads (three different salad leaves from three different countries in one 'superfood' salad bag – UK, France and Spain – a total of 2,973km), squash (from Portugal, 1,742km), garlic (from China, 5,160km) and finally (wait for it, it's a classic), carrots – yes, carrots (from South Africa, 9,083km). That's a collective journey of a whopping 20,000km for five very standard, very staple vegetables, all of which are available from Irish growers right now.

This being food, there are always exceptions, outliers and other things to consider. What's better, an imported organic carrot or a non-organic carrot from down the road? That's a real head-scratcher. What about a consumer in Donegal considering two options, one from the Isle of Man and the other from Kerry – the former being closer to Donegal than the latter? The point is that these consumer decisions we make are important and have consequences – for our health and the health of our planet. There's not always an easy or a right answer, but we should deliberate and take our time. As consumers, we have tremendous power in our wallets – buy local and seasonal, or better still, grow it yourself.

25 november
lovin' leeks

Now that my vegetable patch is really starting to wind down for the winter months, there are just five fresh vegetables left in the ground holding the fort: parsnips, sprouts, celeriac, kale and leeks. There's a fine crop of leeks this year. While there are still so many other wonderful vegetables to eat from the veg patch and from the store, we try to hold off until post-Christmas to start delving into the leeks. In fact, the St Stephen's Day dish of turkey and leek pie is normally the first outing (for a whopping 2kg (4½lb) of them).

Leeks often don't get the health headlines enjoyed by their allium cousins, garlic and onions, but they contain most of the same flavonoids and sulphur-containing nutrients. A hundred grams (3½ oz) of leeks contain over half of your daily vitamin K requirements, 30 per cent of your vitamin A and high levels of vitamins C and B, iron and folate. They are also high in polyphenols, and therefore useful as support for any health issues related to oxidative stress or low-level inflammation.

There is a traditional, and rather unlikely, link between a strong voice and the consumption of leeks – the Roman emperor Nero supposedly ate them daily to make his voice stronger. It was the Romans, in fact, who are credited with introducing leeks to Britain. From there leeks eventually made their way to Ireland, and they did well here since they are unaffected by winter cold.

They were so popular across the Irish Sea that they became the national emblem of Wales and the national soup of Scotland. It's not immediately clear whether the Welsh national emblem thing arose because of the custom of Welsh soldiers wearing the leeks in their caps to differentiate themselves from their opponents or because the vegetable could withstand the cold Welsh winter. Perhaps it was a little of both. The leek remains an important vegetable in many northern European cuisines and is the core ingredient in the famous French vichyssoise and Scotland's national soup, cock-a-leekie. When the Scottish speak about a dish that will chase away the winter chills, we should really listen to them – the men wear kilts and no undies in the winter, for God's sake. Cock-a-leekie soup is a wondrously healing, warming affair and well worth adding to your winter recipe arsenal.

The wonderful name apparently derives from a mispronunciation. When Mary Queen of Scots left France to claim the Scottish throne in 1561, she brought her chefs along with her and one of her favourite dishes was coq au leek (rooster with leek). It's hard not to smile when imagining how quickly that morphed into cock-a-leekie in Scotland.

I had a bit of a panic when it occurred to me that I hadn't sown anywhere near enough spinach when I did my 'winter sowing' back in October. I'm a big fan of spinach, particularly in the winter months when there are few other sources of leafy greens **26 november panic sowing**

in the vegetable patch. I love using tiny little spinach leaves in salads and larger ones in stir-fries, soups and the like. But the problem is, I reckon I only have enough left in the veg patch to see me up to Christmas, which would leave me with at least two or three spinach-free months in the new year.

Spinach is a nutritional powerhouse – calorie for calorie, it provides more nutrients than any other food. It is rich in vitamins, minerals and concentrated antioxidant phytonutrients, such as carotenoids and flavonoids. It is thought to be anti-inflammatory and anti-cancer and provides more than you could ever need of vitamins A, C and K (over 1,000 per cent of your recommended intake). It's no wonder that it made Popeye so strong – and incidentally, the stuff you pick fresh from your veg patch is even better for you than the stuff he ate from a can. (Come to think of it, can you really buy spinach in can?) Nutritionists recommend a one-cup serving of spinach at least twice a week.

Anyway, I sowed a small tray of spinach back in October but, given the slow rate of growth at this time of year, I didn't sow anywhere near enough. So last week I decided to sow another tray of spinach – along with some more chard and some peas – more in hope than expectation, given that we're well into November. I put the module tray on a warming mat in the potting shed and lo and behold, within three or four days it germinated and is already showing very promising signs of life. I assume the constant 'heat from beneath' provided by the mat was instrumental in helping it to germinate, but either way it gave me such a buzz to see *anything* germinate at this time of the year. I will be planting it out in the polytunnel in a few weeks, where I assume it may need a fleece covering in very cold weather. Here's hoping for a healthy crop by January.

28 november
generational
growing

Pretty much every taxi journey I've ever taken has involved the driver telling me how his dad or granddad grew all their own food. It's a common theme whenever I tell people what I work at.

It always strikes me how many people in my generation remember their fathers (usually) toiling away in the garden and that we're only just that one generation removed from the soil. I find that comforting.

So I wasn't surprised when Declan, a consultant we're working with in HQ, told me how his father, Patrick Finn, grew loads of his own food in a house he bought in Walkinstown in Dublin in 1949. Working as a civil engineer at the time, he also worked hard to transform the back garden into a veg plot, enjoying the fruits of his labour for around six years. Sadly, he contracted TB shortly after, which cut his veg-growing exploits short.

A few days after we first spoke, Declan brought in a real treasure to show us – an old journal belonging to his father in which he catalogued his growing adventures, dating back to 1955. Though it's nearly 65 years old, it all looked so familiar. I can't comment on Patrick's growing abilities, but his need to get organised is something I can both admire and empathise with.

In my first years of growing I was so daunted by the extent of things I had to learn that I put together a spreadsheet with all the veg I wanted to grow down one side, and the months across the top. I then looked up the growing info for each vegetable in books, trying to make sense of all the differing advice, and put it all into the spreadsheet so I would know when to sow, grow and harvest each vegetable. To figure out what I had to do in any given month, all I had to do was scan down the column for that month and I would have a list of growing tasks for all the veg. That was the theory anyway. It took a few years before I realised how the weather and other factors could wreak havoc on even the best-laid plans.

That spreadsheet served me well for the first years of my growing until my experience caught up with my enthusiasm. The technology may have been different from Patrick's time, but the idea was the same – trying to condense the complicated and nigh-on unfathomable into an at-a-glance guide. In college I used to do the same, condensing 12 weeks of lecture notes (usually someone else's, I hasten to add) into one page of micro-notes.

Anyway, there was a surprise to be had in scanning down through the list of veg that Patrick grew in 1955. I wasn't surprised to see that he was growing way more traditional veg like turnips and cabbage than I do, but I also came across three more hipster veg that I assumed our generation of GIYers were leading the charge on: kale, kohlrabi and celeriac. Okay, so kale is common enough, but who knew people were growing kohlrabi and celeriac 65 years ago? We can't learn from his journal how well everything grew that year, but it does tell us he sowed the celeriac in March, transplanted them in May and spaced them 15cm (6 inches) apart. The kohlrabi he succession sowed every month from March to July. Let's hope his organisational skills paid off and he had a good year.

29 november
discretionary
chores

If there's a shortcut I can take in the veg patch, then I will generally take it. It's not that I am particularly lazy, it's just that sometimes it's hard to find time for all the jobs I should be doing in the garden with so many other things to do. So, as with most people, my GIYing, although life-affirmingly important to me, always has to find its place amidst a crowded schedule of 'things to do'.

I am pretty good at sticking to the broad outline of the growing year schedule and getting the 'must-do' things done each season: among other things, returning fertility to the soil in the winter, sowing in the spring, watering and weeding in the summer and harvesting in the autumn. But beyond that, when things get a little more ... ahem ... discretionary, things get tricky.

I can comfort myself to a degree with the thought that there's nothing madly urgent to be done at this time of year. There's nothing major being missed, no major milestones being ignored. Most of the work that needs doing could be broadly grouped under the phrase 'clean up', and that's a discretionary category if ever there was one. Still, it means that when I take a trip down to the patch these days to grab some carrots or pick some salad leaves, I have to avert my eyes from the jobs that need doing.

Over here, a green manure seems to have self-seeded rather alarmingly on the gravel path. Over there, a courgette plant is looking bedraggled and should be removed. The fact that there are a couple of small courgettes still on the plant provides a handy excuse for leaving it there until next weekend – just to see what will happen to them in a heavy frost, you understand (so it's practically a science experiment). I don't even have to go into the polytunnel to know that the last of the tomato plants should have been removed and composted weeks ago. Never mind.

Jerusalem artichoke and fennel seed hummus

We start harvesting the tubers from Jerusalem artichoke plants at this time of the year in GROW HQ. They are most commonly used in soups, so this hummus recipe from JB is unusual – but delicious.

ingredients:
— 250g Jerusalem artichokes
— salt
— 50ml extra virgin rapeseed oil
— 2 tbsp raw cider vinegar
— a pinch of chopped chilli
— ½ tsp fennel seeds
— 1 tbsp flax seeds

directions:
Scrub and wash the artichokes. Chop them roughly and place them in a saucepan. Cover them with cold water, 1 teaspoon of salt and 1 tablespoon of the cider vinegar. Simmer for 15–25

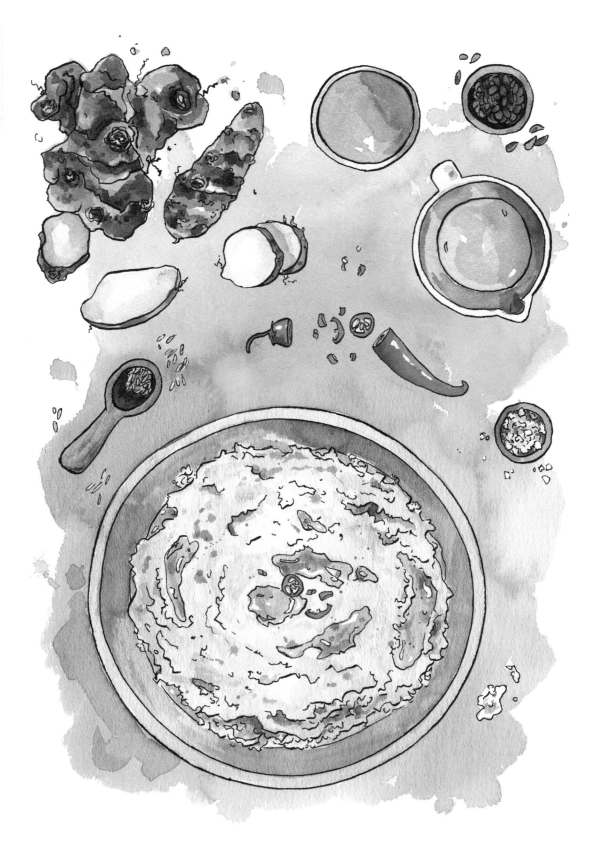

minutes, until the artichokes are cooked through. Strain the artichokes and keep a few tablespoons of cooking liquid.

In a small saucepan, roast the fennel seeds for 1–2 minutes on a medium heat. Add the oil and chilli and leave to cool off the heat for 5–10 minutes.

Put the cooked artichokes and the spiced oil in a food processor and blend slightly. Add the remaining tablespoon of vinegar and a few tablespoons of the cooking liquid. Blend for 1–2 minutes and adjust the seasoning.

december

The end of the growing year arrives and the veg patch is in its winter slumber. We enjoy a break from the veg garden to reflect and enjoy many a gluttonous feast to mark the shortest days of the year.

This month we're loving … Brussels sprouts (of course).

A surprisingly divisive little veg that has much to recommend it and is delicious when homegrown.

december
salad
leaves

Here we are with just 31 days left of the growing year. Things are relatively quiet in the vegetable patch – apart from preparing beds for next year, there's very little to be done. I'm glad to report that the oriental greens I sowed in the polytunnel back in September are doing well, though I have a sense that if I had sown them three or four weeks earlier we would be a little further along.

I sowed mizuna, mibuna, red mustard, komatsuna, salad rocket, texel greens and tatsoi in two separate sowings: one broadcast, or spread liberally in thick bands direct into the soil in the tunnel; and the other in module trays in the potting shed. The latter are much further along now, since presumably the potting shed is heating up quicker by day than the tunnel is, and they haven't had to contend with the colder soil in the tunnel.

I transplanted the greens from the trays about two weeks ago, and they are doing well despite some very harsh night-time temperatures. One could start harvesting a little from them at this stage, but only a little. That's okay, because amazingly we still have some lettuce outside in the veg patch that we can harvest – particularly the super-hardy red variety Matador, which seems impervious to the frosts.

2 december
Jerusalem
artichokes

When I first started growing Jerusalem artichokes I was confused about the difference between Jerusalem and globe artichokes and wondered if it was just different names for the same vegetable. They are in fact entirely different vegetables that bear little resemblance to each other. Jerusalem artichokes are actually part of the sunflower family, and when you grow them the family resemblance emerges. The plants grow to over 3m (10ft) tall, producing yellow sunflower-like flowers, and it's actually the knobbly root or tuber of the plant that we harvest to eat. The tubers resemble root ginger, are brown in colour and about 7–10cm (2½–4 inches) in length. The globe artichoke is unrelated – it is a more ornamental affair, grown for the flowering globe that grows at the top of its stems (from which are gleaned the much-coveted artichoke heart).

Interestingly, the Jerusalem artichoke has no relationship whatsoever to Jerusalem. The name is thought to have come from Italian settlers in the USA calling the plant *girasole*, the Italian word for sunflower. Over time, *girasole* morphed into 'Jerusalem'.

They were first cultivated in North America and brought to Europe in the 1600s. While they were originally celebrated for their taste, they suffered from being almost too prolific and were later relegated to peasant or animal food. Their reputation reached a nadir during the 1940s when they were particularly associated with the deprivations of the Second World War. But in more recent times their star has been on the rise again, particularly as a winter soup ingredient. Some research suggests they can improve insulin sensitivity in diabetics. In the kitchen they can even be used raw, since they have a nuttier and sweeter flavour than potatoes. The knobbly tubers of the Jerusalem artichoke are not to everyone's liking and they have an unfortunate association with flatulence (they're often nicknamed fartichokes, rather unimaginatively, it has to be said). The body can't digest the inulin that's in artichokes in the digestive system but breaks them down using bacteria in the colon – hence the flatulence, and the reason why you often see recipes that ferment them first.

There is much to recommend them to the grower. They tend to persist for years after being sown, which would lead you to believe that to grow them you can simply leave some behind in the soil to grow on the next year. You could do this, but the quality of the tubers will decline over time. They do better if you harvest them all and replant the next year in well-fertilised soil. They suffer no diseases and are exceptionally prolific (unlike their globe artichoke namesakes).

I leave the last and rather harsh word on artichokes to a 1621 book called *Gerard's Herbal*: 'Which way soever they be dressed and eaten, they stir and cause a filthy loathsome stinking wind within the body, thereby causing the belly to be pained and tormented, and are a meat more fit for swine than men.' Gerard wasn't sitting on the fence on the issue, clearly.

4 december
hiatus
month

Most GIYers are busy in their veggie patches right up to the end of November and of course come January we will be back to planning for spring. December, however, is a hiatus month in which we can take stock of this year's GIY achievements.

Many monthly to-do lists will have jobs that you *could* be doing outside in the veg patch, but in all honesty, they will probably be things that sensible people don't bother with, like cleaning your spade or mending fences and the like. Much nicer, I think, to be perusing seed catalogues by the fire at night and dreaming of next year's growing.

I also like the idea of December as a month to celebrate. Our ancestors have celebrated the passing of the shortest day of the year for over five millennia. In ancient Rome the winter holiday, called Saturnalia, honoured Saturn, the god of agriculture.

The pagans of northern Europe celebrated Yule (whence we get yuletide) in honour of the pagan sun god Mithras. So we have ancient licence to celebrate the turn of the year with gluttonous feasting of epic proportions.

The shortest day of the year is on the 21st of this month, so if you're a 'glass-half-full' kind of person you can take solace from the fact that from then on, the days are starting to get longer. Just as the harvest brings with it both joy and a measure of pathos at the impending winter, the arrival of winter brings, strangely, a sense of hope that it will soon be spring.

If ever there was a great starting point on the GIY journey, then it is surely growing your own herbs. They are relatively easy to grow, low maintenance and will save you lots of money from day one. Many a meal can feel homegrown if there are a few fresh herbs from your garden sprinkled on top. Here's a guide to growing the most popular herbs.

5 december
grow your
own herbs

Annuals and biennials:
- **Basil:** Sow in pots of compost in March and plant out in the polytunnel or greenhouse in June. Pinch growing tips regularly to produce bushy rather than leggy plants.
- **Parsley:** Sow seed in spring for a summer crop and again in autumn to have over the winter – but beware, germination is painfully slow, so you might want to buy a little plant instead. It will grow well indoors or out.
- **Dill:** Sow in April, about 20cm (8 inches) apart, direct into the soil. Harvest the leaves as soon as they start to appear.

Perennials:
- **Rosemary:** It likes a sunny spot in the garden and once it takes off you will have a serious crop – so much so that many people use it as a border or hedge. Prune in spring to keep it in check. Probably easiest to buy a small plant of rosemary to plant out in spring.

- **Thyme:** Once you get a crop going, you will never need to buy it again, so it's a good investment to buy a sturdy little plant to put out in spring. Every three years or so, divide the plants and replant.
- **Sage:** A beautiful shrub with grey-green leaves and blue flowers. A single plant will be enough for most people. Plant it in the spring in a well-drained spot and harvest regularly.
- **Mint:** It has really strong, invasive roots, so be careful where you put it or, better still, grow it in containers. It will thrive in all but the worst of soils.
- **Chives:** An attractive plant with lovely pink/purple flowers. You can grow it from seed in early spring and plant out in early summer. Divide the plants every four years or so to reinvigorate.

minestrone soup

Honestly, I don't know if minestrone is the right word for this soup, but it seems to fit. It is cobbled together using some vegetables that I brought in from the garden and some standard store-cupboard ingredients. The added pasta makes it a substantial feed and because it's not blitzed in a blender after cooking, it's chunky and delicious. You can play around with different vegetables if you don't have what I use here.

Serves 4
ingredients:
— 2 tbsp olive oil
— 1 onion, chopped
— 1 clove garlic, chopped
— 1 leek, cleaned and finely sliced
— 2 carrots, chopped small
— ½ butternut squash or small pumpkin, peeled and chopped small

- salt and pepper
- 500ml homemade chicken stock (or made with an organic stock cube)
- 400g tin of chopped tomatoes (or the same quantity of passata)
- 1 bunch of spinach leaves, stalks removed and chopped roughly
- 4 tagliatelle 'nests' (or any type of pasta), preferably organic
- crusty bread, to serve

directions:

Heat the oil in a large pot and cook the onion and garlic until softened. Add the leek, carrots and squash and toss well so they are coated in oil. Season well, then cover and cook on a low heat with the lid on the pot, stirring occasionally, for 5–10 minutes. Add the stock and tomatoes and cook with the lid off until the veg is soft (about 10 minutes) – don't overcook as you don't want the veg to go to mush. Stir in the spinach about 5 minutes before the end of cooking.

Meanwhile, cook the pasta as per the packet instructions in a pot of boiling salted water. When it's cooked, drain and stir it into the soup pot. Check the seasoning. Ladle into warm bowls and serve with some crusty bread.

6 december
spectacular
sprouts

That quintessential Christmas crop, the Brussels sprout, can be a little hard to grow, which is somewhat irksome if you are a fan of sprouts. They are a slow-growing crop, which means you must be on the ball for a long period of time to grow them successfully. My sprouts this year were sown at the end of April and planted out in the veg patch in June, which means that I have been tending to them on and off for almost eight months now. That's not ideal if, like me, you have the attention span of a gnat.

It doesn't help, of course, that Brussels sprouts are a member of the brassica family, the 'Pests and Diseases Love Us' family. In some years, the little seedlings have been munched by slugs shortly after being planted out in the garden. In other years I've managed to fend off the slugs long enough to get a decent plant going, only for the pesky cabbage white butterfly to lay its pesky eggs on the leaves, which turn into pesky caterpillars that end up eating the whole pesky thing. That's just pesky.

This year, through a combination of grim determination and sheer good luck, I managed to get the plants through to the autumn in fine fettle and have **finally** been rewarded with a decent crop of sprouts. Timing is everything – you want the plants to form nice firm sprouts by the time the first frosts hit, but not so early that they've become overly mature (and loose) by then. With the occasional frosts of the last month, their taste has continued to improve to a pleasingly sweet and nutty flavour. They are a handsome crop in the garden, particularly when the yellowing leaves are removed to expose the sprouts along the stalks, therefore providing an ever-present reminder of your awesomeness as a GIYer.

The big question is: with such an appetite for the lovely sprouts, will I have any left for Christmas dinner?

8 december
protecting your crop

If you haven't yet started, now is a good time to protect your plants, trees and soil from the more extreme temperatures, ensuring that you're guaranteed some crops come spring. Fleece will protect your crop or soil from frost and cold weather while admitting light, air and rain. Fleece is generally bought in large rolls or sheets and can be cut to the size of your plant/raised bed. It is also available in varying thicknesses, including a heavyweight version (30g) for arctic conditions. 'Fleece jackets' for larger plants/shrubs are available from some garden centres.

If you don't have a greenhouse or polytunnel, you may want to look at covering young or more delicate plants with cloches. These can range from glass bell jar cloches or ornate Victorian lantern cloches to homemade cloches made from glass jars, fizzy drink bottles or sneakily appropriated water cooler bottles from the office.

9 december a greener Christmas

I've been talking to various media outlets this week about the idea of having a greener Christmas. It's interesting to me that we move on from the splurge of Black Friday and Cyber Monday to an almost Lenten remorse that forces us to think about becoming more sustainable. The main sustainability problem about Christmas, of course, is our excessive consumption and the need to buy more stuff at a time when our planet desperately needs us to buy less. If we could address that, we wouldn't need tips for a greener Christmas. But admittedly, such sentiments wouldn't make for great radio.

A few times this week I've been asked whether we should buy a real or fake Christmas tree. I don't understand why that's even a debate. A growing Christmas tree produces oxygen and stores CO_2 while it grows, both of which are valuable traits in these times. Almost all Christmas tree growers plant a new tree when they harvest an old one. It's true that all that stored carbon in the tree will get released when it decomposes, but by chipping and mulching the tree you reduce the emissions by up to 80 per cent. Most local authorities take back trees after Christmas and will chip them too.

After Christmas we spend a bit of time stripping our tree down. The branches are snipped off and get chipped and used as mulch – pine needles are much loved by fruit bushes in particular. Then we chop up the trunk and stack it for a year to season it before using as firewood. The ultimate green Christmas tree would be a living one that's grown in a pot and moved in and out each year – but it would take someone with far more patience than me to manage such an endeavour.

Compare all that with a fake tree that's made from plastics and a nasty concoction of toxic chemicals that will take thousands of years to decompose. The cheaper ones will probably need to be discarded after five or six years. Oh, and it's probably made in China, using up more of our planet's scarce resources to be shipped here. The real tree, on the other hand, is supporting local jobs (at a time when our horticulture industry desperately needs that), but you should check that when buying it just to be sure.

Have a think too about what you're decorating the tree with. LED lights will reduce energy consumption by 80 per cent, and try to avoid adorning it with plastic tat (or at least continue to use the decorations you already have rather than buying new ones). It was pointed out to me by one interviewer that perhaps the greenest solution would be to not buy a tree at all. I don't agree. In the dark bleakness of winter, there's a magic to bringing a living plant into our homes, particularly when it's evergreen and comes with that evocative smell. In these days of just eight hours of daylight, the Christmas tree is a shining reminder that brighter times are ahead.

I'd like to coin a brand-new name for a psychological condition that can afflict GIYers – it's called Cage Envy, and it arises when one visits the veg patch of a fellow GIYer and discovers that they have erected a new fruit cage in their garden in which they are growing all manner of berries and currants – strawberry, tayberry, gooseberry, blueberry, raspberry, loganberry and the like. Cage Envy is a dangerous and debilitating condition, leading to feelings of inadequacy and jealousy. If afflicted, consult a professional.

I like to think I am pretty decent at growing veg at this stage, but I have an uneasy relationship with fruit growing. I have some apple, plum and pear trees down the end of the garden, and some years I get a decent harvest, other years I don't. I would certainly be nowhere near self-sufficient in those fruits (the way one might be self-sufficient in some veg, for example), which is a pity because we surely munch our way through about 700 apples each year in our house.

Things are even patchier with soft fruit. I grow blackcurrants extremely successfully, courtesy of two large bushes behind the polytunnel, which are basically running riot. I do autumn raspberries quite well, but they are a cinch to grow, with no messy pruning involved. I have tried to grow blueberries, with little success, and the same with gooseberries. I have a small raised bed that has about six strawberry plants in it, and they need changing this year because I think they are getting a little tired. A teacher would surely grade my soft fruit growing 'could do better'.

So my Cage Envy was indeed acute when I visited my mate Feargal's plot and saw his immaculately clean and well-ordered fruit cage. A Mypex and gravel groundcover creates an impeccably neat environment. It's clever because it keeps all his fruit growing in one spot, safe from birds, free of weeds and low maintenance. I feel an unexpected, expensive, hare-brained winter project coming on …

In the run-up to Christmas this year, perhaps spare a thought or two for the growers who will put the veg on your Christmas dinner table. There are only one or two vegetables that suffer from what you might call hyper-seasonality, where we only eat them at one, very specific time of the year. Pumpkins are one, with the vast majority of the crop consumed at Hallowe'en. Brussels sprouts are the other, with most people eating them only on Christmas Day (and the rest avoiding them like the plague). This intense seasonality puts these growers in a vulnerable situation since they must sell pretty much their entire crop at that time. The buyers of their crop have them over a barrel.

The sprout growers have been nurturing their crop since May of this year and the sprouts are on the shelves now. It's a tricky and labour-intensive crop to grow. One would expect to have to pay a premium for such a seasonal delicacy, but over the last number of years supermarkets have used Brussels sprouts (and other Christmassy veg like carrots and parsnips) in aggressive price promotions. In recent years the price of 500g of sprouts dropped as low as five cents as part of some dramatic supermarket price wars. Mainly these promotions are about getting you in the door so you will stack your trolley with luxury mince pies, Christmas-themed napkins, selection boxes and flavoured gins.

Supermarkets insist that they fund the cost of veg promotions rather than forcing price reductions on their suppliers. They tell the growers that these are short-term promotions designed to build the market for a particular vegetable. Consumer groups line up to say, 'Sure, don't people have a family to feed and isn't it great we have access to healthy food at rock-bottom prices?' All these arguments are short-sighted. In reality, promotions set a long-term price expectation that is never properly rectified. While that might seem like a good thing for consumers, in the long run it just means more growers leaving the industry and more imports replacing Irish produce on shelves all year round. As consumers, that gives us *less choice and less access* to local food that's at its freshest and most nutritious.

So, as you tuck in to your Christmas dinner, spare a thought for the Brussels sprout growers. Let's hope they have a bumper season and get a fair price for their hard-won produce.

Today I noticed that some of my bumper squash and pumpkin harvest, which I have been storing in the potting shed, was starting to get a little soft. I grew a lovely mix of squash and pumpkin – the beautiful and sweet blue-skinned Crown Prince, the giant red Rouge Vif d'Etampes, the slender yellow Delicata and the efficient Uchiki Kuri. The fruits have been happy in the potting shed up to now, but I think the constant change in temperatures in there (cold by night and warm by day if it's sunny) could take their toll if I left them there any longer. So it was time to take action.

I kept about 20 of them for ourselves and moved them into the house, where the more constant temperatures – on top of the dresser in the kitchen – should help them last until February or so. Any of the ones that were going soft will be used up first. The rest went to GROW HQ, where head chef JB can store them in the cold room. From there they will grace many a lunch menu and probably feature in jars of chutney and the like.

I planted out some chard, spinach and pea seedlings today that I sowed in November and that had germinated on a heating bench in the potting shed. I planted them out in the polytunnel – I know the peas will be fine, but I am little dubious about whether the chard and spinach will survive a cold snap. I covered them with fleece to give them the best chance of surviving. Whether they survive or not, it felt so good to be out planting things again. It struck me just how cold the soil felt on my hands – imagine how the poor little seedlings felt.

Anyway, the potting shed is now completely empty for the first time this year. I got my potting shed as a birthday present from Mrs Kelly back in 2011 and it's been a trusty companion in the years since. My brother-in-law Stephen (who has handiness embedded in his genes) built it for me as a lean-to on the end of the garage – it's timber-framed with Perspex sheeting for the windows and (slanted) roof and about 5m x 2m (16½ x 6½ ft) in size. On the wall side, there's a waist-height potting station made of marine plywood, where I do all my potting, and lots of little shelves and cubby holes for storage. I even DIYed a little rack on the wall for my secateurs and trowels, etc. – it's nerd heaven, basically, the kind of place your dad should spend his time.

On the window side, there's a slightly lower shelf where I put the rows of seed trays to soak up the sun. I also invested in a heating mat, which comes in very handy early and late in the year when seeds benefit from a little heat from beneath to get them going. Though it alarms me how sad this makes me sound, I must say that some of the happiest times of this (and every) year were spent in the potting shed. It's a place of hope, growth, solace and retreat and I can't wait to get potting again next year.

celeriac remoulade

A celeriac remoulade is delicious with a good homemade burger or slathered on some brown bread (and really great for the Christmas smoked salmon). The key here is to get the thinnest possible strips of celeriac that your knife skills will allow. It's not so nice if you have big hunks of celeriac! You can use the grating attachment on a food processor if you want to save time.

Serves 4
ingredients:
— 1 medium celeriac, julienned (chopped into very thin strips)
— juice of ½ lemon
— salt and pepper
— a few sprigs of parsley, chopped
— 3 tbsp mayonnaise
— 3 tbsp natural yoghurt
— 2–3 tbsp mustard (I like a yellow mustard, but Dijon will work too)

directions:
Place the celeriac strips in a bowl along with the lemon juice and toss to combine. Season with salt and pepper and add the parsley. Mix the mayonnaise, yoghurt and mustard together, then stir into the celeriac. Place in the fridge for a couple of hours for the flavours to develop before serving.

17 december
sustainable
christmas
dinner

I want to talk about food at Christmas, and in particular the greatest of all culinary set pieces, the Christmas dinner. Ironically the traditional Christmas dinner can be one of the more sustainable dinners of the year, in the sense that most of the ingredients are generally in season and produced in Ireland.

Depressingly, the aggressive price promoting on veg that we talked about earlier has made its way across the plate to the Christmas turkey and ham. This year I've noticed a supermarket promoting Bord Bia-approved Irish turkeys for €7.99. To put this in context, last year I paid €70 for a free-range, organic Bronze turkey and was happy to do so. Of course, the €7.99 turkey is a headline- and customer-grabbing figure and there can be huge variations in

quality, size and how they are reared. There can be differences in the weight of a fully grown turkey, from as small as 3kg (6½lb) up to a whopping 12kg (26½lb) or more. (The males, known as toms, are bigger than the females.) The age of the bird at slaughter is also a factor (the longer the farmer keeps it, the more it costs to rear) and this can range from as young as 11 weeks up to nearly six months. If they are free-range (as opposed to indoor-reared) this means they have more time to roam free, and they live a longer life – and of course this is good for the flavour of the meat. Then you also have to consider whether they are fed organic feed, which contains no GM ingredients and is about twice as expensive.

But regardless of all this, and regardless of whether the supermarkets are paying the farmer more than €7.99 for the bird, the net effect of these discounts (as we've seen with the discounts on veg) is to permanently lower the value of turkey in the minds of consumers. These discounting issues follow a by now pretty well-established trend – supermarkets tell the growers or farmers that the discounting is short term and about 'building the market' for their product, but they end up becoming permanent price points that result in an ever-decreasing downward spiral. Growers and farmers leave the industry, resulting in job losses and ultimately less choice for consumers and a bigger impact on the planet – more imports, more air miles, poorer quality.

So this Christmas we have a choice when buying the dinner ingredients. Yes, it's possible that everything on your plate could be Irish, but that doesn't necessarily mean it's more sustainable. How the food is grown and reared, and by whom, has an impact on how sustainable it is. If you can afford it, try to go local and organic across the plate. Best of all, try to buy it direct from a farmer or grower and pay them a fair price.

18 december
spud love
Today I gave a little love and attention to the potato harvest, which is doing Trojan work for us from its home in the shed. This year I managed to fill five large hessian sacks with spuds for

storage and we've been tucking in to them every other day. It's very handy to have them there, waiting patiently in the shed for their moment of destiny in the kitchen.

However, I must admit that we've lost more than the normal number of spuds to slug damage (particularly among the maincrop varieties), which is frustrating, particularly since you don't generally know that the spud is destroyed until you've gone to the bother of peeling it and then discover a little network of cavities inside it that render the potato inedible. It is these cavities that are the hallmark of slug damage – wireworms create the same small holes on the surface as slugs do, but they don't create cavities inside the potato. That issue aside, the spud is an incredible hardy foodstuff that in general stores very well and we've enough potatoes to take us right through to March or April.

It makes sense to check in every now and then on any stored food that you have squirrelled away to make sure that everything is in order. A rotting spud can quickly take out all the spuds around it, and before long the whole crop can turn to a squidgy mush. Removing the occasional rotting spud early on will prevent this from happening.

So today I checked all the spuds and removed any dodgy ones. In fact, they were holding up remarkably well, although I did find that a lot of them were starting to sprout. Sprouting in storage is normal and not a huge deal – in fact, the process of chitting them in spring before planting is encouraging them to do what some of my spuds have done quite naturally in storage. All the same, it's no harm to rub off the sprouts and make sure the spuds aren't soft or green before eating them.

Both the garden and nature in general offer us some ideal material to create beautiful homemade Christmas decorations. The most common are the holly wreaths that adorn front doors across the country, but there are many decorations that can be made from items foraged from local forests, fields and your own

20 december
decorations from the garden

back garden. You can make a wreath from the traditional holly or from willow, or any suitable material from hedgerows. For decorating your wreath you could use any of the following; or you could use them in their own right as individual decorations.

- Offcuts from the Christmas tree
- Pine cones
- Chestnuts
- Rosemary
- Dried fruit such as apricots/figs or banana pieces
- Nutmeg
- Cinnamon
- Star anise
- Clementines studded with cloves
- Brightly coloured chilli peppers (dried if preferred)

21 december
tunnel
decisions

I did a long-overdue clean-up in the small polytunnel today. Like most people who own a tunnel, I am borderline obsessed with mine – it's been such a good friend to me over the years, bringing table-loads of food, particularly at times of the year when there's little happening in the veg patch outside. So I contemplate it, consider it and generally fuss over it far more than I should.

As I worked to clear the detritus of this year's crops, I was debating yet another winter restructuring inside the tunnel. Some years ago, I changed the layout so that I have one wide bed up the centre, two paths on the outside of that bed, and then two narrow beds up the outside of the tunnel. That's brilliant to maximise the usable space in the tunnel, since you can plant right up to the edge of the plastic on each side (as you are able to reach in from the paths). It also means that I can grow tall plants (like tomatoes, cucumbers and runner beans) in the middle bed because they are growing in the centre where there is the maximum height in the tunnel.

The downside is that the paths are in a location where the roof of the tunnel is starting to slope down, so the headspace isn't great. I have to bend my head to one side when walking in the tunnel, which is not so bad if you're just popping in to grab a handful of tomatoes, but is downright uncomfortable if you're spending longer in there doing some work.

So I am contemplating going back to the original layout I had when I bought the tunnel first, with just one path up the centre and two wide beds on either side. That's a big job, but it will make working in the tunnel an awful lot easier. Obviously in the grand scheme of things this is not a major decision, but in the microcosm of my veg-growing world, it's something to be mulled over.

22 december
don't tread
on me

It's a happy coincidence that there's science to back up the fact that I don't feel inclined to be out working the veg patch at the moment. If you work on soil when it's wet, it will damage the soil structure. If the soil sticks to your boots when you walk on it, you shouldn't be walking on it. Turning soil at this time of the year, which was traditional, is now considered very damaging to the soil structure – it's easy to see why.

If you do have to walk across the soil to get at your veggies, put a plank of timber down and walk on that instead. The timber distributes your weight more evenly. If you haven't already done so, it's worth covering an area of your soil to warm it up – use cardboard or black polythene (the latter may not be very sustainable, but is more so if reused year on year). This will make the soil warm up far quicker than it otherwise would and will mean you can start sowing in it far earlier. In very wet weather it will also help to dry the soil out.

24 december
raised bed
mystery

We had our Christmas table quiz in my local GIY group this week, which was great fun, and with some GIY-related questions thrown in for good measure it was a fitting end to a great year for the group. The final round had a sheet with pictures of celebrities, all of whom had GIY or food-related names – who knew there were so many? Peaches Geldof, Sean Bean, Mr Bean, Jasper Carrott, Meat Loaf, Helmut Kohl – interestingly, although kohlrabi is not such a well-known vegetable, every group got this one right.

Over a Christmas drink I asked one of my fellow GIYers about her growing year. She has four raised beds in her garden, two on the left of the garden and two on the right. Her growing year was literally a game of two halves – the vegetables in the beds on the left did really well, but the ones on the right did really poorly. The seedlings she sowed in them did fine, but when they developed into plants, they didn't fare so well and growth seemed stunted. She couldn't understand it.

Someone suggested to her that it could be a result of roots from a nearby tree growing into the bed and depriving the vegetables of nutrients and water – but there was no tree near the beds and so the mystery continued. In the late autumn she decided to dig in the bed to investigate further and sure enough, there she found a huge quantity of roots, snaking their way this way and that in search of water. In a cunning act of thievery, all the lovely nutrients that she had worked so hard to put in the soil (manure and compost each year, etc.) were being snatched by these hungry roots. But where were they coming from?

As it turns out, she reckons they are coming from a neighbour's eucalyptus tree, which is likely since they have particularly aggressive and thirsty roots, growing up to 3m (10ft) in length. Other than moving her raised beds or asking the neighbour to cut the tree down (not likely to foster friendly relations), her options are rather limited. It's a timely lesson in being ultra-careful where you site your veg beds.

And why does Santa have three vegetable patches? So he can hoe-hoe-hoe, of course.

A bit of Christmas Day advice. If you are planning to GIY for the first time next year and are wondering what to grow, the key is to start small and stick to things that you like to eat. (There's no point in growing cauliflower if you hate to eat cauliflower!) Here are two tips to make sure you stick to this advice:

25 december
get
growing

- Pick five vegetables you like to eat, and grow them. It could be tomatoes, peas, carrots, broccoli and sweetcorn. Go out and buy the five packs of seeds, then do a little research in how to grow them (when to sow them, what type of soil they like, etc. – most of the information you need is on the back of the seed packet).
- Pick one vegetable you know nothing about and grow that too as an experiment. It could be Florence fennel or Swiss chard or anything else. The point is that you don't really care whether it grows or not, or whether you like the taste of it – it's an experiment!

Happy Christmas!

26 december
weather
round-up

I seem to spend a lot of time complaining about the weather (usually about the lack of sun and too much rain), but this year went against type, which was heartening. At least we can say that dreary, wet summers are not perhaps our default climate in Ireland after all.

We had a ridiculously slow start to the year, with the cold weather making life very difficult for the spring garden. In the traditionally busy month of May, it was too cold to plant some veg outside, and some were destined never to recover. The traditional burst of spring growth didn't happen in my veg patch until well into June, and little wonder – in early April, many counties in Ireland recorded night-time air temperatures of –7°C. Brrr.

But, wow, did the summer make up for it. July was glorious, with plenty of warm and sunny days. That made for very pleasant times in the veg patch, albeit with far more watering than normal and pressure from the family to abandon the garden and head for the beach. Most veg thrived as a result, with pumpkins and squashes faring particularly well. Some veg that like plenty of water (e.g. celery and celeriac) struggled a little. Thankfully, it was also a grim year for that most menacing of garden pests, the slug. The cold spring likely reduced the numbers that made it through to adulthood, and of course since slugs dislike dry weather (they need wet soil to slime around on) they didn't like the summer either.

However, on the downside there was a noticeable increase in the number of butterflies around, laying their eggs on the brassicas, which often led to caterpillar carnage. Into winter then, and November was mostly dry (until the end of the month) – I didn't even need wellies when traipsing down the garden to feed the poultry in the morning, and considering my winter garden normally resembles a paddy field, that's really saying something. So, all in all, I would say that us GIYers can't really complain when it comes to this year's weather.

brussels sprout and carrot fondue with smoked bacon

We sometimes forget that Brussels sprouts are essentially mini cabbages, and when you grate or finely chop them you basically have little slivers of cabbage. So from that perspective they are well suited to use in a slaw or hash. If you are a sprout hater who likes coleslaw, you are a complete mystery to me! Here's JB's recipe for a really simple one-pan cook-up – it could be a good way to use up leftover sprouts from Christmas.

Serves 4

ingredients:
— 500g Brussels sprouts
— 1 large carrot
— 50g diced smoked streaky bacon (lardons in French)
— a pinch of ground nutmeg
— 100ml fresh cream
— salt and pepper

directions:
Thinly slice the Brussels sprouts. Peel and coarsely grate the carrot. In a dry frying pan, fry off the lardons for a few minutes, until golden brown. Add the Brussels sprouts, the carrot and nutmeg. Stir for 3–4 minutes and add the cream. Cook for 3 more minutes. Season to taste. Serve straightaway.

28 december black-currant bushes

I have two blackcurrant bushes in the garden. They are prolific croppers and don't get a huge amount of love from me, if the truth be known. I always consider them a second-tier crop – not quite as tasty as, say, raspberries, strawberries or blueberries. At the same time, we always do our best to bring the crop in and get it in the freezer, because it's great for jams and ice creams. At this time of the year, we can grab handfuls from the freezer at night and let them thaw out so they can be thrown on porridge in the

morning. They are rich in numerous health-benefiting phytonutrients and antioxidants.

If there's a downside to them, it is that the bushes get enormous and if left unpruned they will quickly become overcrowded, which will lead to poor harvests. Naked stems at this time of the year make it easier to prune them, and of course the plant is dormant, so it's not knocked back by pruning. The basic idea is to create a light airy plant in a bowl shape, but keeping as much of last season's growth as possible since it is these stems that will bear most of next year's fruit. The new-season shoots should be relatively easy to identify – they are quite smooth, tea-coloured and clearly 'new' looking. The older shoots will be more gnarled and grey-looking. Start by removing congested and weak stems, any diseased branches or branches that are crossing each other.

Then take out some of the older growth that is clearly unproductive – that is, not carrying any new growth. I try to remove about a third of the plant, leaving about 10 strong, healthy shoots. You can also give the base a good dressing of compost. The result should be a healthy plant that will pay you back in spades.

29 december stocktake

As we start to think about next year's growing, I'm intrigued by the idea that this year's GIYing is still paying dividends. It's a good time of the year, therefore, for a bit of a stocktake. I use various locations to 'store' vegetables around the house and garden – our kitchen doubles up as a larder at this time of the year (you can barely get into the kitchen as there are veggies hanging out of every available space); then there's the garage, where I keep vegetables in sacks, boxes and the freezer. And finally, there are also vegetables still in the ground in the veg patch and polytunnel.

In the kitchen we have plenty of onions and about 30 garlic bulbs all hanging up in braids (looking very attractive, I might add) and about 20 squashes and pumpkins on top of the dresser. On a shelf in the utility room we have various chutneys, pickles, krauts, marmalades and piccalillis made from gluts of this year's produce – cucumbers, onions, cauliflowers, cabbage, beetroot, chillies, courgettes, pears and more. The pickled pears are particularly prized and were cracked open over Christmas for starters and desserts, while the pickled chilli peppers have been a godsend for adding to pizzas on Friday nights.

In the garage we have a chest freezer, the penultimate resting place for this year's tomatoes, broad beans, peas, runner beans, celery and whole chilli peppers. Every year I hope the tomato sauces in particular will last until the new-season tomatoes arrive in July (using roughly one tub of sauce a week) – it's this that has fed my alarming obsession with growing ever more tomato plants. In boxes and sacks in the garage I also have loads of beetroot, carrots and spuds.

The vegetables left in the ground outside now are parsnips, leeks, kale, purple sprouting broccoli, Brussels sprouts and celeriac. We work away on the celeriac, leeks and parsnips as we need them. The purple sprouting broccoli will start to come, hopefully, in February and March. The polytunnel is still churning out green leaves from the sowings in September – we've a marvellous supply of chard, spinach, mizuna, mibuna, red mustard, komatsuna, texel greens and tatsoi.

All in all, although there's a sense that the larder is depleting, it's not exactly empty yet. Will we make it through to April or May when we get our first crops from next year's sowing? Possibly not, but we will be damn close.

I always marvel at how suddenly the mood changes as the new year arrives at midnight on New Year's Eve. With the relentless march of the calendar it is no longer 'the end of the year' and instead is very suddenly 'the beginning of the new year'. That's an important emphasis shift for the GIYer, for even though it's only a few minutes later there is, all of a sudden, a whole lot to do.

So, as today is the last time I can really kick back and enjoy a break before next year's growing season begins in earnest, I'm going to enjoy it while I can. It's time for me to put my feet up, pour myself a glass of something, and before the madness begins all over again, contemplate my successes over the last 12 months.

Cheers!

31 december and breathe …

acknowledgements

A big shout-out to our content supremo, Tor McIntosh, for keeping this project on track and for her initial edits, and to JB Dubois for providing some utterly fabulous recipes from the GROW HQ playbook.

But, above all, to Eilish, Nicky and Vika – with love and thanks xxx

index

294, 296
D, 271
K, 294, 296

w

wallflowers, 148
warm bulgur wheat salad with
    squash, 287–9
wasps, 158
watering, 28, 33, 34, 35, 40, 53,
    62, 77–8, 79, 114, 118, 140,
    143, 145–6, 149, 150, 154, 155,
    173–4, 181, 258
watering systems, 77–8
weather, 326
weeds, 52, 79, 94–5, 97, 106,
    114, 123, 140, 146–7, 174, 181,
    184, 206, 208, 210, 256, 266,
    268
weed-suppressing membranes,
    26, 77, 181
Weldon brothers, 278, 279
white turnips, 68
whitefly, 147
wild garlic pesto, 115–17
windowsills, 14
winter frittata, 19–20
Winter Gem, 255
winter greens, 98–9, 196, 220,
    241, 243, 244
winter lettuce, 196, 255
winter purslane, 64, 243
    see also claytonia
wireworm, 125, 321
World Food Day, 268

worms, 125, 245, 280, 321
wreaths (Christmas), 321–2

y

yacon, 38, 69, 279–81
yield, 68–9, 135

z

zingy cucumber pickle,
    199–200